The Making of Israel's Army

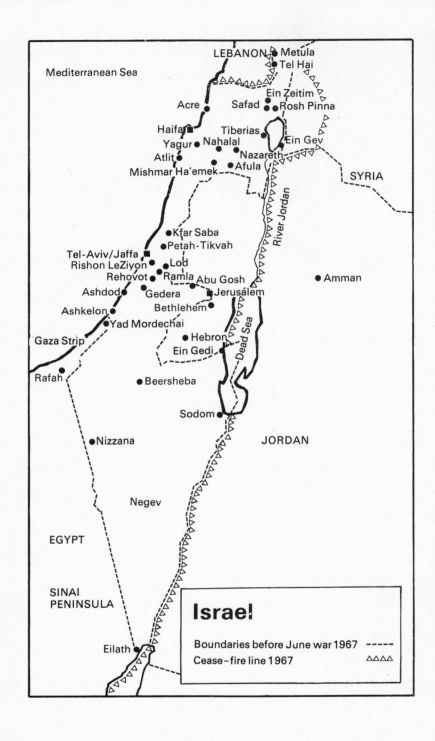

Mediterranean Sea

LEBANON
Metula
Tel Hai
Ein Zeitim
Acre
Safad
Rosh Pinna
Haifa
Tiberias
Yagur
Nahalal
Ein Gev
Atlit
Nazareth
Mishmar Ha'emek
Afula
SYRIA

River Jordan

Kfar Saba
Petah-Tikvah
Tel-Aviv/Jaffa
Rishon LeZiyon
Lod
Rehovot
Ramla
Abu Gosh
Amman
Ashdod
Gedera
Jerusalem
Ashkelon
Bethlehem
Yad Mordechai
Gaza Strip
Hebron
Ein Gedi
Dead Sea
Rafah
Beersheba
Sodom
Nizzana
JORDAN
Negev
EGYPT
SINAI
PENINSULA
Eilath

Israel

Boundaries before June war 1967 - - - - -
Cease-fire line 1967 △△△△

The Making of Israel's Army

Yigal Allon

Foreword by Michael Howard

UNIVERSE BOOKS
New York

To my parents Chaya and Reuven Paicovitch
pioneers in the revival of the Land of Israel

Published in the United States of America in 1970
by Universe Books
381 Park Avenue South, New York, N.Y. 10016

Library of Congress Catalog Card Number: 73-133424

ISBN 0-87663-137-5

Acknowledgements

Grateful acknowledgement is made for the use of the following illustrations:

"In training for the future" and "A forward attack from helicopters" by
kind permission of Camera Press Ltd. "Tank crews rush to take up position" by kind permission of Israel Sun Ltd. Other pictures are by courtesy
of the Haganah and Palmach Archives and the Zionist Federation, London.

Printed in the United States of America

CONTENTS

Illustrations follow page 150

FOREWORD

Modest self-effacement is not an invariable characteristic of generals who take to authorship. No one, however, would gather from reading Yigal Allon's own account what an outstanding part he played in the creation of the Israeli Army and Nation. In the work which follows his name figures hardly at all; and only his duty as a historian has compelled him to include, among its documents, letters and orders of his own which shed a unique light on the progress of Israel's earliest struggles. Allon is one of the greatest of Israel's founding fathers, but one of the least known abroad. It is typical of him that he has not used this book to make his own contribution to history more widely recognized.

Allon is a *sabra*, a native-born Israeli. He is unusual even among sabras in that not only his parents but his grandparents lived in Palestine. He was born in 1918 in a Galilean settlement founded by his parents. In boyhood, in the disturbed times of the 1930s, he gained his first military experience defending Jewish settlements against Arab attacks. He grew up in the *Haganah* whose history he writes here. In his early twenties he helped to found its striking force, the *Palmach*, in which he served throughout the latter years of the Second World War—becoming in 1945, at the age of 26, its Commander. In this capacity Allon was virtually the field commander of the Israeli armed forces. He was responsible not only for raids against the Arabs and the British occupation troops, but also for the illegal immigrations carried out in the face of British opposition, and the consequent illegal settlements, often deep inside Arab-populated areas, which had to be defended as they were built.

Once the British terminated their mandate, the survival of the Jews depended on nothing but the force of their own arms. From this first Arab-Israeli War of 1948–9 Allon emerged as the outstanding fighting leader. In the early stages of the war he organized the defence of the Eastern Galilee to meet the Arab invasions from Syria and Lebanon, and commanded the operation which saved that part of the country, including Safad, for the new state. Presently, on the Central Front, he commanded the forces which held back the armies of Transjordan from splitting

Israel in two and which kept open the road to Jerusalem. Finally on the Southern Front he conducted the operations against the Egyptians which secured for Israel the Negev and the vital outlet to the Red Sea at Eilat. It was his military campaigns that very largely ensured, not only that Israel survived, but that she did so as a viable state.

With peace precariously won, Allon turned to equipping himself as a statesman. After five years in universities in Israel and England he was elected in 1954 to Israel's Parliament, the *Knesset*, and ever since has been a major figure in Israel's political life, one of the most influential voices in Israeli councils both in peace and war. This book must be read, not simply as an academic study of Israel's military development, but for the insight it provides into the mind of a man who is likely, for a good while yet, to play a major role in the political events of the Middle East.

For the military analyst and historian the work is of course of absorbing interest. The Israeli Army was made in action. It was a regular and a conscript force at the same time. Conscripts, as Yigael Yadin had put it, were simply 'regular soldiers who happened to be on leave eleven months of the year'. It had—and has—a refreshing freedom from obsolete tradition. In its early days it effected a synthesis between the ideas of the British Army, in which so many Jews served, and the looser discipline of the Palmach; a synthesis which has been further refined under the severest of tests. It has taken not only foreign arms but foreign ideas—notably those of the late Sir Basil Liddell Hart—and adapted them to its own needs. It is now a uniquely successful military organization, commanding, especially since the Six Day War, a world-wide prestige.

A word of warning. Allon writes for his own people, not for foreigners and least of all for Englishmen. His account of British policy in operating the Mandate and of Jewish resistance to it is not dispassionate. Nor will it be only Arab readers who will be somewhat taken aback by his account of the 'liberation' of Arab towns and centres of population in 1948. Allon appears no more conscious than the majority of his compatriots of the irony of 'liberating' territory from a population which has lived there for centuries. But as Allon points out, the Jews in 1948 fought with the desperation of men and women for whom there was 'no alternative'. They still do so today.   *Michael Howard*

PREFACE

This book has grown out of an essay which I contributed to *The Theory and Practice of War: Essays presented to Captain B. H. Liddell Hart on his seventieth birthday.* It attempts to explain in a brief space the development of Israel's military doctrines of defence from the time the first Jewish settlements in Palestine undertook their own defence in the late 1870's to the Six Day War of 1967 and since. The book is not intended to be a history of the military events of this period. The events are referred to only in order to explain their effect upon the growth of the military doctrine, and its influence in turn—on the events.

There is a good deal of non-military, mainly political and social, material in the book. This was unavoidable because of the inseparable connection between the political, social and economic aspects of the growth of the Jewish community and the Jewish state and the developments in military strategy and strength. Again, I have referred to these extra-military matters only in so far as they affected, and were affected by, military developments.

In the second section of the book I have included a selection of authentic documents and contemporary accounts, covering the period from the foundation of the Haganah to the Six Day War. They are intended to give the reader an inside view as it were of the principles, the approach, and the spirit that directed and animated the growth of Israel's Defence Forces. They will also serve, I hope, to provide supporting evidence for my main account of the making of Israel's army.

In the writing of this book, my chief debt of gratitude is to Professor Dorothea Krook of the Department of English in the Hebrew University of Jerusalem, who edited the whole manuscript with admirable skill and made many valuable comments and suggestions. I also want to thank Mr. Gavriel Cohn, M.K., of the Department of History at Tel-Aviv University, for his interest and help, especially in connection with the documents which form the second section of the book.

My original essay in *The Theory and Practice of War* has been incorporated into the present book by kind permission of Messrs. Cassell, whom I thank accordingly.   Y.A.
Jerusalem, August 1969.

'*The Jewish State is in its essence neutral.
It needs an army only for defence
(though equipped with every modern weapon)
to keep order at home and resist attack
from outside.*'

Theodor Herzl

The Jewish State, *1896*

PART ONE

Defending the Land

CHAPTER I

Before the State
of Israel

The Israel Defence Army was officially created on 27th June, 1948. When this happened, the Jewish *Haganah*[1] had already for some six months been fighting a war of self-defence against local Arab guerillas reinforced by volunteers from the neighbouring Arab countries. Just six weeks before, on 15th May, 1948 (following the United Nations Resolution of 27th November, 1947), the British Mandate of Palestine had been terminated, the State of Israel proclaimed, and the newly formed Jewish state invaded by the regular armies of six Arab states, which had joined forces with local Arab units. The invading armies were those of Egypt, Transjordan, Iraq, Syria, Lebanon, and contingents of Saudi Arabia incorporated into the Egyptian army. To have proclaimed the State of Israel in the face of open threats of destruction by joint Arab forces of an overwhelming numerical superiority may appear to have been an act of extraordinary audacity, not to say foolhardiness. It can be properly understood only in the light of the previous history of the making of the Jewish military force—a force which had started some seventy years earlier as a collection of small groups of watchmen, and was to develop into the brilliant modern army which won the Six Day War.

Of capital importance throughout its history was the close interdependence of the growth of the Jewish defence organization (whether as an underground, semi-underground or legal, regular

---

[1] *Haganah* (the Hebrew word for 'defence') was the name of the underground organization for self-defence of the Jewish community in Palestine under the British Mandate. It was controlled by the elected national institutions of the Zionist movement.

army, whether under Ottoman, British or indpendent rule) and
the social, political and economic development of the Jewish
community in Palestine. Each phase of one had its parallel in
the other, and each was constantly affected by the other. There
was also a reciprocal relation between the civil and the military
functions of Jewish resettlement in Palestine. The people and
their elected national and local institutions supplied the Haganah
with manpower, capital, strategic bases, ideological motivation and
political authority for the establishment, maintenance and operation of its organization. The Haganah on its side provided the
Jewish community and the world Zionist movement with a means
of direct self-defence, individual and collective, becoming in
due course a military instrument of general value for the ever
more daring enterprises in the fields of settlement and politics
undertaken by the community.

As early as the 1880's, when the country was still under
Ottoman rule and the Jewish population numbered hardly more
than a few tens of thousands,[2] local 'cells' had begun to be formed
for self-defence against robbery, theft, marauding, murder and
rape. These were for the most part non-political in character, yet
indirectly they had political implications and consequences. The
Jews, recognizing that they could not safely depend on the
Ottoman authorities, became more and more accustomed to
depend upon themselves for the protection of their lives, the
honour of their women, their property, and indeed their very
right to live in the Holy Land. Thus by the beginning of the
present century various embryonic military organizations with
political leanings had made their appearance. Of these the most
important was *Hashomer* ('The Watchman'), which became the
forerunner of the Haganah. These began to think for the first
time in terms of nation-wide service: they were ready to
volunteer for any defence task in any Jewish settlement, however
remote—indeed the remoter the better; and jointly with local
farmers and youth groups they undertook to protect these isolated
villages, their fields and plantations.

During the First World War, especially after the Balfour
Declaration[3] and the entry of the United States into the war, the

---

[2] More than half of the estimated Jewish population of 24,000 lived in
Jerusalem, nearly all the rest in Hebron, Safad, Tiberias, Jaffa and Acre.
[3] The Balfour Declaration (1917) was the famous statement issued by the
Lloyd George War Cabinet, in which it proclaimed the British Government's

Palestinian Jews were (rightly) suspected by the Turks of dis-
loyalty to the Ottoman Empire and co-operation with the British.
When the Turks discovered that intelligence work was being
carried out behind the German-Ottoman lines by NILI, a
Jewish group of early settlers composed mainly of young people,[4]
they clamped down on all Jewish military or semi-military organizations, and expelled to the North (the Galilee) all the Jewish
communities settled close to Egypt in the South, from where the
British forces were approaching Palestine. During this period,
the first Jewish battalions were created within the framework of
the British army fighting in the Middle East theatre. These
battalions were composed of volunteers and conscripts from
Palestine, Britain and America, and provided young Jews with
their first opportunity to acquire better military training and
organization. They were also able to accumulate a certain amount
of light military equipment, which subsequently proved to be of
great value.

Immediately after the war the British Mandate over Palestine
was established on behalf of the then world community, the
League of Nations, and the undertakings of the Balfour Declaration concerning the right of Jewish immigration and settlement
in Palestine and the creation of a Jewish national home began
to be carried out in practice. It was from this time that the tension
between Arabs and Jews assumed a more political character. At
the start Arab hostility was confined to a very small section of
the Arab community; but it soon began to spread, as a consequence of certain events: principally, the expulsion from
Damascus of King Feisal I,[5] and the indecision and hesitant

---

'sympathy with Jewish Zionist aspirations,' and explicitly declared that 'His
Majesty's Government views with favour the establishment in Palestine of
a national home for the Jewish people, and will use their best endeavours
to facilitate the achievement of this object.' It was obtained principally
through the initiative of Dr Chaim Weizmann, the outcome of the prolonged
diplomatic effort he had directed to this end. The letter containing the declaration, dated 2nd November, 1917 and addressed to Lord Rothschild, was
written by Arthur Balfour, later the first Earl of Balfour, who as Foreign
Secretary had played a leading part in securing the commitment of the
Coalition Government to the support of a Jewish national home in Palestine.

[4] NILI are the initial letters of the Hebrew phrase *netzah Yisrael lo yeshaker*,
meaning 'the glory of Israel will not lie ' (I Samuel, xv: 29).

[5] Emir Feisal (later the first King of Iraq) led, together with Lawrence of
Arabia, the Arab revolt against the Turks. As the heir to the throne of his
father. Sherif Hussein, King of the Hedjaz, who was then the leader and

policy of certain circles of the Mandatory Government. It never, in fact, extended to the whole Arab population. Nevertheless political tension between the Jews and Arabs became from this time a permanent feature of life in Palestine, and the new situation significantly affected the development of the Jewish military organization.

The inter-war period (1920–1939) was marked by a series of Arab attacks on Jewish settlements and centres of population, known as the 'Arab Riots'. They came in cycles, each being on a larger scale, better equipped, and more properly military than its predecessor. There were three major conflicts: in 1921, in 1929 and in 1936–39. The British forces often intervened to establish peace and order; but sometimes they adopted a so-called 'neutral' attitude; and even when they wanted to help, hours and sometimes days elapsed before they could bring relief to the beleaguered areas.[6] The Jews, finding they could not rely on the Mandatory authorities alone, had no alternative but to develop their own embryonic military organizations. These were declared to be illegal by the authorities; but the Jews persisted undeterred, and thus the Haganah gradually came into being.

During this period, the Haganah was bolstered by the influx of Jewish immigrants from many countries, especially from Eastern Europe. These not only increased its manpower resources quantitatively but also reinforced them qualitatively, in that the majority of the newcomers were young, passionately idealistic, and had in many cases already experienced the taste of para-

---

spokesman of Arab nationalism, Feisal represented the Arabs at the Paris Peace Conference of 1919. He supported the Balfour Declaration, expressed sympathy for Zionism, and accepted the British Mandate in Palestine on the understanding that the Arabs would receive independence in the rest of the Middle East.

[6] After the 'Hebron Massacre' of 1929, in which 59 Jews were murdered, the London *Times* carried the following eye-witness report: (Friday, 30th August, 1929): 'The first house attacked was a large Jewish house on the main road, and the occupants locked themselves in. For some unknown reason the gates were opened to allow two young boys to leave, and they were immediately killed. This inflamed the crowd, who entered the house and beat or stabbed the inmates to death. The local police force, which consisted of only a British Officer, two Arab Officers and 30 Arabs, made every effort to control the situation, but the crowd was out of hand, and attacked other Jewish houses, beating and stabbing the inhabitants—men, women and children. The police fired, but the situation was not definitely in hand until the arrival of 12 British police and 12 Royal Air Force personnel from Jerusalem.'

military underground activities when defending the ghettos of Eastern Europe against anti-Semitic pogroms.

The planning and development of pioneering Zionist settlement were from the start at least partly determined by politico-strategic needs. The choice of the location of the settlements, for instance, was influenced not only by considerations of economic viability but also and even chiefly by the needs of local defence, overall settlement strategy (which aimed at ensuring a Jewish political presence in all parts of the country), and by the role such blocks of settlements might play in some future, perhaps decisive all-out struggle. Accordingly, land was purchased, or more often reclaimed, in remote parts of the country deep in Arab-populated areas and when possible close to the political borders of the country. The settlements—ordinary villages, *kibbutzim*[7] and *moshavim*[8]—thus came to be isolated from one another by geographic distances, topographic barriers, and demographic differences, not to speak of political obstacles created by the Mandatory regime. Consequently, every Jewish settlement had to be also a Haganah fortress. Economic and agricultural planning were accompanied by military planning and arrangements, and the Immigration budget had to take care of both swords and ploughshares.

These needs introduced into the military thinking and execution of the Haganah various new elements—including a more coherent nation-wide strategy, which took into account local conditions; comprehensive planning; greater mobility; a more extensive use of automatic light machine-guns. Above all, they hastened the establishment of an underground civil High Command (fully authorized by the Jewish community's legal political institutions), and of an underground military General Staff, composed of all the usual branches and with a Chief-of-Staff at the head.

The riots of 1936 and 1939, initiated by the Grand Mufti of Jerusalem Haj Amin El Husseini (who later found refuge in Nazi

[7] *Kibbutz* (plural, *kibbutzim*): form of pioneering collective settlement, based on collective ownership of property and a communal mode of life. It observes the principles of complete social equality, mutual responsibility and direct democracy.

[8] *Moshav* (plural, *moshavim*): another form of pioneering co-operative settlement. While retaining some private ownership, it practises—like the kibbutz—a high degree of mutual aid on collective principles.

Berlin), inflicted heavy casualties and damage on the Jewish community. At the same time, and indeed for this reason, they stimulated and accelerated the further expansion of the Haganah. During the riots, the Arab guerillas grew in size and strength; and generally the British forces (there were honourable exceptions) either showed themselves unwilling to suppress this wave of violence—as it was their duty to do in accordance with their Government's undertakings—or, when they did attempt to do something, proved their inefficiency by over-reacting. The Haganah authorities recognized the new situation and its dangers. It was clear that if the riots were not brought to an end immediately, they might grow more serious; and in that case they would inevitably provoke a full-scale confrontation at a time when the Arabs enjoyed the advantages of superiority in numbers, territorial continuity with neighbouring Arab countries, and the neutrality of the British—if not their indirect support. A confrontation in these circumstances was bound to result either in an undermining of the Jewish hold on certain areas of the country, or in the enforcement in London of a policy contrary to the Balfour Declaration and the Mandatory undertaking. The need for effective Jewish defence accordingly became more than a need for the protection of lives and property; it was now reinforced by the need for political survival.

Two encouraging initiatives on the part of the British contributed a great deal to the development of the Haganah at this time. The first, which was official, was the establishment of a legal Jewish Settlement Police (JSP). This was composed of three main elements: (a) a small number of fully mobilized units, paid and equipped with small arms by the Mandatory Government to carry out all local guard duties; (b) a larger number of special police, who were allowed to use the weapons of the mobilized units for training and emergencies; (c) mobile units, confined to specific areas, also maintained by the Government, and responsible in their areas for patrolling roads and crops, reinforcing settlements under attack, and ambushing Arab guerillas on their approach to or retreat from Jewish zones.

The other 'initiative' was unofficial, but at least as important. This was the appearance on the Palestine scene of Captain (later General) Orde Wingate. It was the interests of the Iraqi Petroleum Company that brought Wingate into the picture. The Arab guerillas had inflicted heavy damage on the Company's oil pipeline to the Haifa refineries, and as a consequence a mixed Jewish-English unit, known as Special Night Squads (SNS), was formed under Wingate's command to protect this vital pipeline. The unit, however, was too small and its weapons too poor to accomplish its appointed task. Wingate therefore co-operated illegally with similar Haganah units already in operation, often borrowing weapons from the Haganah arsenal to carry out raids and ambushes, mostly at night, over wide areas in the Galilee on both sides of the pipeline. In the morning the illegal units generally disappeared, while the legal unit returned to its base.

These two police forces, one legal, the other semi-legal, were manned by the Haganah and used as a cover for training and operation. The appearance of Wingate, with his extraordinary Zionist ardour inspired by the Bible, his unconventional military gifts and his outstanding courage, was an event of historic importance for the Haganah. When Wingate appeared, the Jewish fighters saw before them the Englishman of their ideals, who had absorbed the tales of the Bible with his mother's milk, who regarded the message of Prophecy not as the mummified stuff of books, but as the plain and simple truth. In his mind, the People of the Bible and the Land of the Bible were one. He fell in love with the Land of Israel, and, in his absolute and uncompromising integrity, he dedicated himself without reserve to the task of co-operating with the Jewish underground army.

Wingate's Jewish counterpart and comrade in the illegal branch of the Haganah was Yitzhak Sadeh, a military genius of world calibre, one of the greatest commanders in Jewish history, the father of modern warfare, the teacher of most young Israeli commanders, including myself. He and Wingate together significantly modified the tactics of the Haganah. By teaching the Haganah units to patrol remote fields, plantations and roads, to ambush enemy paths, and to carry out raids against enemy bases which helped to check the enemy's initiative, they effectively pulled the Haganah out of its trenches and barbed wire into the open field, making it adopt a more active kind of defence.

Like Wingate, Sadeh was a born leader, but despite the resemblances between them, there were also polar differences. Wingate was proud and self-contained; Sadeh, also proud, was open and warm. Wingate was lean and ascetic, Sadeh, burly, a professional wrestler, a lover of life, full of vitality. Wingate was born into the tradition of the English Dissenters and Puritans, more religious than emotional. Sadeh was a product of the winds of change that blew through the Jewish world, and of the great Russian Revolution in particular. Both of them were far-sighted men, fashioning their revolutionary military doctrines in obedience to the imperatives of the present with the distant past—the heroic tales of the Scriptures—as their primary model. Despite all the differences, their destinies, too, were characteristically similar, perhaps because of the boldness of their thinking and the tempestuous drive of their spirit: always in the van, misunderstood at the beginning of the road, and solitary.

The meeting of these two men was extraordinarily fertile. 'For some time,' the late Yitzhak Sadeh wrote, 'we did the same things as Wingate, but on a smaller scale and with less skill. We followed parallel paths, until he came to us, and in him we found our leader.' Without undervaluing in the slightest Wingate's contribution to the moulding of Jewish military thought, I would say that, by the very fact of his appearance, as a professional soldier and a non-Jew to boot, he confirmed the validity of those 'parallel paths' which Yitzhak Sadeh and his colleagues had had to struggle so hard to mark out.

The characteristic features of Wingate's approach, which left their mark on the military doctrines and tactics of the Haganah, may be summarized as follows:

First and foremost, there was the personal example of the commander, whether in bold and original action or in the endurance of long and exhausting marches. Wingate's men often spoke of the encouragement they drew from his personal example. His word was law. Second, he insisted on the most meticulous, purposeful discipline, with the emphasis on the practical aspect, and he was relentless in punishing even the most minor offences. Third, he was thorough and careful in drawing up preliminary plans prior to operations. Before every operation he would make sure his men understood the basis and purpose of his plan. He regarded them as partners in thinking and action, whose readiness and comprehension had to be won before the start of the operation. However, though he was meticulous in preparing plans, he was also unusually gifted in improvisation, in accordance with the changing conditions of battle. He therefore gave authority to his subordinate officers and trained them to be leaders capable of assuming command, of making up their own minds and of taking their own independent decisions. Fourth, he perceived the importance of concentrating forces on the major objective under conditions of anti-guerilla fighting—which was the nature of the battles he waged in Palestine in 1938. Yet, at the same time, he was skilled in managing fragmented and scattered forces when the circumstances made in necessary. He also laid particular stress on the exploitation of surprise and mobility. Finally, he emphasized the ideological motivation in warfare. With the eye of the spirit he saw himself as a modern Gideon, operating in the very same terrain where Gideon fought the Midianites. He frequently quoted the Bible and believed in the uniqueness of the Jewish people and its right to return to its historic homeland.

But it was not only the Jewish past in the Land of Israel, but also the Jewish present that captured Wingate's heart. He was deeply impressed by the constructive enterprise of the Jewish population, especially in the kibbutzim and moshavim. He was fascinated by the settlements established in distant and isolated areas of strategic importance, and the erection of the Northern Fence along the Syrian-Lebanese border by Jewish labour under Jewish protection. And as a devotee of active defence (or, in the language of modern Israeli military doctrine, of 'carrying the war into enemy territory'), he was enthusiastic about the conceptions and operations of the commando companies which advanced beyond the protection of the stockade. By attaching Jewish fighters to his units, he also helped to provide facilities for practical training, under relatively convenient conditions. He regarded himself, in practice, as a member of the Haganah, and that was how we all saw him—as the comrade and, as we called him, 'the Friend'.

By the end of 1936 it had become evident that the guerilla war was not going to be brought to an end by an ultimate collapse of either side's concentration of forces. Since both sides were regarded as illegal by the British authorities, neither could for any length of time achieve such a concentration in the presence of the British forces. Thus, the British presence had the effect of putting a limit to the size of the units in combat, and the Haganah was therefore forced to concentrate on guerilla tactics, making the most of its few legal units and resorting to its more numerous illegal units when the need was most pressing. The Haganah, and especially its field unit FOSH (the initials of the Hebrew words for 'field companies'), learned to fight in the field, by night as well as by day, mostly in sections and platoons, sometimes as a company and very occasionally, in co-operation with Wingate, within the framework of a battalion subdivided into smaller units. These units learned how to search for an enemy in hilly country as well as in cultivated areas; to place an ambush; to carry out a raid; to outflank an enemy; and to disengage rapidly whenever necessary for military or political reasons.

The immediate aims of the Arabs were to annihilate as many existing settlements as possible (either by isolating them or by direct attack), to prevent the creation of new settlements, to break down Jewish resistance, to deter the Jews from claiming state-hood. Their ultimate aim was to force the British to repudiate their commitments to the Zionist movement, and establish a state with an Arab majority. The aims of the Zionist movement were exactly the opposite. It sought to protect all Jewish settlements, rural and urban, however remote or difficult to defend; to maintain normal life as far as possible, in production, business, transport; to prevent economic breakdown, and thereby refute the Arabs' claim to be in control; and to expand Jewish rural settlement in still remoter areas of strategic importance.

The years 1937–39 accordingly became a peak period, both of pioneering settlement and of military penetration into vulnerable areas based on the newly formed kibbutzim. The combat units of the Haganah, supplemented by engineering units, undertook (along with all their other tasks) to establish prefabricated 'stockade and watchtower' settlements equipped for defence. The method employed was as original and unmilitary as it was effective. On the chosen site they would erect a whole settlement-outpost prefabricated out of wood, composed of a number of wooden huts, a communal dining-hall, kitchens, and so on. In the middle of the campus there would be a watchtower with a searchlight at the top; the whole was surrounded by a wooden double-wall filled with bullet-proof rubble and punctuated by firing-slits; and this in turn was encircled by barbed wire and mine strips. The erection of such a settlement, on nationally-owned Jewish land, was generally accomplished in the space of a single day, starting early in the morning and ending late at night. The settlers were usually young people, members of the Zionist pioneering move-ment and of the Haganah; they put themselves at the disposal of the national institutions, which decided—generally in consulta-tion with the candidates—where and when they were to settle for good. By day, the Jewish Settlement Police provided the immediate defence, while the illegal units undertook the ambushes and patrols further off, guarding the approaches to the new settlements. The settlers themselves, carrying light arms while at work, and taking it in turn to guard their settlement, were a modern version of the labourers in Nehemiah who with one hand 'wrought in the work, and with the other hand held a weapon.'[9] Under the protection of this settlement-fortress the surrounding land was cultivated, and in due course a new and better campus built nearby. The completion of the new campus was always a great event duly celebrated when the mothers and children could be brought from the original base to their new home. It was all indeed very unmilitary; but in the conditions prevailing in Palestine in the 1930's, it was a remarkably effective method of achieving political and military goals. New areas were successfully developed and new strategic bases created by means of these settlements, in which the settlers were simultaneously soldiers and farmers.

Under the pressure of militant Arab nationalism, the Haganah itself grew in size and strength. Its membership at this time included almost every Jew and Jewess working in an appropriate unit. It trained a large number of young N.C.O.s and officers. It acquired more and better weapons. Above all, it developed its nation-wide character and strengthened its command; it even made a successful beginning in establishing a permanently mobilized unit in reserve. All this was accomplished without minimizing the importance of regional and local commands, and never at the expense of the tactical initiative of lower commanders. There were, of course, setbacks and defeats; but from a military point of view this period as a whole may be said to have given the victory to the Jews. Not a single settlement was abandoned, and new settlements, forming new Jewish blocks in important areas, were added. As the Arabs found their attacks to be ever more costly, their initiative gradually diminished, until a relative peace (though an uneasy one) was achieved towards the spring of 1939. The greatest achievement, however, was the development of the Jewish military organization, based on geo-strategic areas (that is, geographic areas viewed from a strategic point of view). It advanced steadily during this period in quantity as well as in quality, in the standard of training and discipline, and in confidence drawn from its combat experience. The Haganah could not

[9] Nehemiah, iv: 17.

yet claim a battalion as a tactical unit; but it could claim a battalion as a logistic framework, with a company as the highest tactical unit. What this meant in effect was that the Haganah was emerging as a modern militia, an army in the making.

The Zionists may have won the Palestine war of the 'thirties; but the Arab Supreme Committee undoubtedly won the political struggle. It seems that the rising strength of the Axis powers and their propaganda in the Middle East increased the bargaining power of the Arabs in this crucial period. They successfully opposed the recommendations of Lord Peel's Commission (1937) to partition Palestine into two states, one Jewish, one Arab, and extracted from the British Government the infamous White Paper (1939). This undertook to stabilize the relative number of Arabs and Jews in Palestine to the permanent disadvantage of the Jewish community by drastically limiting Jewish immigration, even from Nazi Germany. It prohibited Jews from settling in extensive areas of tiny Palestine, even where the land was owned by Jews, thus creating a new ghetto in the Promised Land itself. It ordered the disbanding of the Haganah; and it promised self-government in the near future, which in the circumstances would simply have put the Jews at the mercy of the Arab majority. It was clear that this new policy, if carried out, would mean the end of the Jewish dream of statehood, and perhaps also the physical extinction of the Jewish community in Palestine. This was more than any Jewish leader—even the most moderate, such as Chaim Weizmann —could accept. It seemed that despite the long working relationship between the Jews and the British in Palestine (which though not wholly successful had not been a total failure), an open clash was after all unavoidable.

And indeed preparations began almost immediately to fight the White Paper policy by different ways and means—the White Paper policy exclusively, and not the United Kingdom as such. A number of ships carrying illegal immigrants from Europe— fugitives from the Nazis—reached the Palestinian coast (other ships, such as the *Struma*, were to sink on the open seas).[10] A

---

[10] The *Struma* left Rumania for Palestine in 1941 with 769 refugees on board. The ship reached Istanbul but was turned back when it was learned that they had been refused entry into Palestine; it foundered in the Black Sea (February 1942) and all but one on board were drowned.

number of new settlements were established in prohibited areas by the old familiar method: with this difference, that they were now to be used as a means of war against the British of the White Paper policy, not against the Arabs; and that they had to be erected between evening and morning, not between morning and evening as in the past, in order to avoid British patrols. The preparations had gone as far as the creation of a special group of volunteers, who were being trained in sabotage and commando operations with a view to extending the struggle to the military sphere, when the Second World War broke out. This put the Jews in a dilemma. The British were fighting gallantly, and at the start virtually alone, the deadliest enemies of the Jews in history. In the circumstances, could the Jews continue to fight the British in one of their vital bases in the Middle East, thus weakening their military effort against the common enemy? The answer was, of course they could not; and the main problem became that of finding a way of being accepted as allies, declared or otherwise, in the actual fighting against the Germans and Italians. On the other hand, could the Jews adopt a position which might be interpreted by London as implying reconciliation to the White Paper policy? Again the answer was, of course they could not: the idea of resistance to the White Paper had to be kept alive, and military preparation for the struggle actively maintained. David Ben-Gurion, the Chairman of the Zionist Executive, memorably defined this paradoxical position when he declared: 'We shall fight the war as if there were no White Paper and we shall fight the White Paper as if there were no war.' This was admirably said; but in practice the second part of Ben-Gurion's proposition proved to be less easy to carry out than the first. What in fact happened was that the Jewish community in Palestine devoted itself to the general war effort against the Axis powers but neglected its own independent illegal units. This was perhaps inevitable; and the more so since, along with the genuine anxiety to contribute to the defeat of Nazi Germany, there lurked in many Jewish minds the illusion that history might repeat itself, and that this war might produce a new Balfour Declaration with a clearer and firmer British commitment to Jewish statehood.

Events on the Western Front in the first years of the war created a new situation in the Middle East. France was overrun, and the French forces in Syria and Lebanon declared their loyalty to Vichy. Turkey was still uncommitted, but suspected of a readiness to join the Axis powers if their successes continued. Egypt was threatened from the Axis bases in the Western Desert, and Arab circles leaned towards Berlin and Rome; while in Baghdad, Rashid Ali's pro-German *coup* agitated the entire Middle East. It seemed that the whole area was threatened by a gigantic pincer movement. Observant leaders of the Jewish community in Palestine suddenly realized that Palestine could become a battleground of major campaigns, and that it might even (like other territories) be evacuated by the Allies. If this happened, the Jewish community would face two enemies, the Germans and the Arabs. It was this realization that marked a fresh turning-point in the history of the Jewish military organization in Palestine.

It operated as an immediate spur to action. In May 1941, the High Command of the Haganah, with the approval of the World Zionist Executive, responded to the suggestion that an independent, underground striking-force, consisting of nine companies regularly mobilized for action at any time and in any place, should be established as quickly as possible. This unit, known as the *Palmach* (the initials of the Hebrew words for 'striking companies'), was designed to act either independently or in co-operation with the Allies according to changing circumstances. The formation of the Palmach coincided with the Allies' decision to invade Syria and Lebanon in August 1941. The Allies, it appears, were pressed for time in preparing for this invasion; accordingly, the first two companies of the Palmach were invited, through the mediation of the Political Department of the Zionist Executive, to participate in the campaign in autonomous operations—as guides and saboteurs, as advanced units, and on intelligence assignments behind the enemy's lines. All these operations were successfully carried out, to the great satisfaction of the Allied Command in the area. From that time until the Allied victory at Alamein, this unofficial co-operation was continued, implying a *de facto*, though indeed provisional, recognition of the illegal Palmach by the British authorities. The members of the Palmach were never incorporated into the British army (in contrast to the tens of thousands of young Jews who had joined the British forces officially); and this was in accordance with the wishes of both parties. The Palmach insisted on remaining independent of the British, and the British stressed the strictly temporary character of their co-operation with the Palmach. It seems that both sides realized that they might before long find themselves on opposite sides of the barricades; accordingly (to adapt Aristotle's saying about old men), they felt bound to love as if they would one day hate.

The co-operation with the British, short-lived though it was, gave the Palmach a unique opportunity to acquire much better training, under legal and therefore easier conditions, by instructors (their own as well as British) specializing in sabotage, commando operations, intelligence and communications of the kind needed to fight the Germans in the event of their reaching Palestine. Under cover of the few hundred who were recognized and financed by the British, thousands received similar training and experience. Some members of the Palmach operated as individual paratroopers in German-occupied Balkan countries, to promote Jewish resistance to the Occupation forces. Some acted, together with British troops, in long-range raids behind the enemy lines in the Western Desert. Some, who knew German especially well, infiltrated the German P.O.W. camps for intelligence purposes; and many, for the same purpose, disguised themselves as Arabs and settled in Syria and Lebanon in preparation for a possible German invasion of these countries. The bulk of the Palmach men, however, prepared themselves to become the leading element in the resistance to the Germans and Italians should they succeed in invading Palestine.

The necessity to prepare for a campaign against a modern military machine such as the German gave the Palmach commanders an opportunity to think, to plan, and to train their men on the most modern lines. The inequality of strength was obvious. A general frontal engagement would mean the end of the Jewish forces. A plan therefore had to be drawn up which would take into account these grave limitations and at the same time suit the specific conditions of the country. The motive behind the plan was the determination to save as many lives as possible among the civil population; to hamper the advance of the German army, in order to help other fronts; and if death was the issue, to die fighting rather than in the crematorium. The scheme devised was a highly imaginative one. It was resolved to turn the area consisting of the whole of Mt. Carmel, the valley of Zebulun (between Haifa and Acre), the mountain chains of the Western Galilee based on Haifa Bay on the Mediterranean, and an airfield strip on the coast into a huge, well-fortified escape fortress for all the Jews of Palestine (numbering just over half a million): a kind of modern Massada, only stronger and therefore with better chances of survival than its historic prototype.[11] It was thought that the combination of a hilly country with some access to the sea and air, fully supported by the Allied forces in the matter of supplies, defended in depth and assisted by guerilla raids against enemy lines of communication, bases and installations, carried a fair chance of success. The subsequent experiences of the Allies at Tobruk, Leningrad and other surrounded bridgeheads were proof that the scheme was not unrealistic. It was even hoped that, if and when the tide turned, this Carmel fortress might become a bridgehead for invasion, making it possible to meet the advancing enemy armies halfway.

Fortunately it never became necessary to carry this plan into effect. But the very planning of such a grand strategy—the military training and organizational preparation, and the study of the enemy's structure, strategy and tactics it involved—gave the Haganah and its striking-force, the Palmach, a new dimension of military imagination and experience. It distinctly advanced Jewish military thinking to a more mature stage. Indeed, the Second World War as a whole substantially strengthened the Jewish community in Palestine. Tens of thousands of volunteers who had served in British uniform in various branches of the armed forces acquired valuable training and technical knowledge. They brought back their know-how to the Haganah, to its great benefit at later stages.

The development of the Palmach during the war years is a story in itself. When the period of its co-operation with the British had come to an end, it continued for some time to grow in numbers and constantly to improve its standards of training. The point was soon reached, however, when lack of funds threatened its existence: the difference between the British and the Zionist budgets made itself felt, and the Palmach was faced with a grave decision. It could disband itself and join the British army, or go home; in either case, this would mean the virtual disappearance of the backbone of the Haganah. Alternatively, it could

---

[11] Massada was the stronghold overlooking the Dead Sea where, three years after the destruction of the Temple of Jerusalem by Titus in 70 A.D., 960 Jewish rebels or 'Zealots' chose to take their own lives rather than submit to the besieging Roman armies.

attempt to become economically self-supporting, and thereby ensure its further existence as a permanent mobilized unit. The second alternative was not an easy one to adopt. What it meant was that people who were serving full-time in an army would be required also to earn their own living—an unusual demand, to say the least. Moreover, the improvement in the situation on the front after Alamein had had the effect of diminishing the sense of urgency which reconciles men to sacrifice. In the end, however, the knowledge that the Allied victory for all its historic importance was not yet the final victory of Zionism, and that the Zionist struggle for independence was likely to begin when the world war was over, gave a fresh impetus to the acceptance of hardship. The dilemma itself was, of course, crystal clear. If the White Paper remained in force, the Jews would fight the British. If it were abrogated, the Arabs might initiate large-scale riots. In either case, the Haganah men, and especially the Palmach fighters, had to prepare for the military clashes which seemed inevitable when the Allies celebrated V-Day and began demobilizing.

To save the Palmach from extinction, an original plan was finally adopted. All the Palmach platoons were to be stationed in kibbutzim throughout the country. Adjoining platoons would form companies, and adjoining companies would form battalions. All members of the force would spend half of each month working in the fields of their kibbutz and the other half in training. Their earnings from the half-month's work would be enough to maintain them for the whole month. The plan completely succeeded in solving the financial problem of the Palmach's continued military existence. But it was a success also in other, unexpected ways. Besides giving the young people of the Palmach the experience of working for a living, it proved also to be invaluable as a moral and social education, and as such helped to create the high morale and spirit which the unit sustained to the end.

The introduction of battalions as tactical units and the beginning of the formation of the brigade were not allowed to undermine the flexibility of the Palmach as a guerilla force. The individual soldier continued to be trained to think and act in the smallest possible units (it used to be said that the ultimate unit of the Palmach was the soldier and his weapon); consequently, he retained his individual quality even within the larger framework. Though greater importance was now attached to the stabilizing of well-defined units (from the section, through the platoon

and company, to the battalion and brigade) in actual operations
the use of the task-force—composed of various elements of warfare, sometimes drawn from different units—remained the
common practice according to the nature of the military objective.

The successful co-operation and co-ordination of junior commanders in smaller units require in a marked degree the qualities
of intelligence, insight and imagination; and in the Palmach the
intensive training in guerilla tactics helped to develop these
powers. Experience shows that it is easier and safer to turn
guerilla units into a regular force than the other way about. It
seems to me now that the multi-purpose training of the Palmach
was one of its greatest assets. Its members received a rigorous
physical training of a distinctly Spartan kind. They learned to
use different types of weapons, from a knife and a hand-grenade
to machine-guns and mortars as well as explosives. They received
very intensive courses in field-training, for fighting by day and
by night, in small and big groups. Their sense of orientation was
sharpened. They learned on foot the topography of the country
across its length and breadth. They became intimately acquainted
with specific terrains in which they might be expected to fight.
They even devoted a great part of their studies to learning the
national habits and military structure of possible future enemies
—mainly, the British and the Arabs. In addition to their infantry
training at commando level, they all received elementary amphib-
ious training, to prepare them for the landing of illegal immigrants. After a hot debate between the Palmach commanders and
the British-trained Jewish officers, the British conception of
battle-drill was rejected as an over-schematic and artificial way
of acquiring fighting habits in the field. Finally, in order to be
able to expand the force if and when general mobilization took
place, the Palmach put any promising member through a commander's course, even when there was no immediate prospect of
giving him a unit of his own and he had to go on serving as a
private for a while. In the event, this method did enable the
Palmach to expand rapidly when faced with an emergency.

Since the Palmach was the only permanently mobilized force,
it undertook to develop the beginnings of two new services—
namely, a navy and an air force. By the use of civil, maritime and
air sports-clubs, more than a score of soldiers learned to fly
simple aeroplanes (the only ones available), for reconnaissance
and supplies as well as for primitive bombing. Hundreds of

soldiers were trained as professional sailors, having in mind future illegal immigration from Europe as well as the need to create the beginnings of a fighting navy. A good number of the Palmach men received specialized training as reconnaissance scouts and saboteurs. Explosives became almost a personal weapon for a member of the Palmach—certainly for the boys, and to some extent also for the girls. The explosives were to be used in two main ways: for destroying chosen installations in order to create confusion; and for hitting fortified positions in order to 'soften' them before they were stormed, as an alternative to softening up by artillery (which did not exist in the Haganah arsenal).

When the first Palmach recruits had completed their third year of active service, it was decided to establish a Reserve system within the Palmach. Every private was released from active service after two years and placed in a reserve unit. For section commanders the period of active service was three years, for junior officers it was four years, and for company commanders and above the period was decided individually by the commander of the Palmach. The reservists were called up for training and exercises for a few weeks each year, and were required from time to time to participate in operations. This was the beginning of the Reserve system which has been a feature of Israel's armed forces ever since and has proved its unique value in all her subsequent wars, from the War of Liberation in 1948 to the Six Day War in 1967.

The Palmach became the laboratory of the Haganah, where new systems of training and organization could be tested. Its achievements, of course, belonged to the whole Haganah, and its high standards served as a model for other units. It was in fact the first fully mobilized Jewish army to act under a completely independent Jewish political authority since Bar-Kochbah's some eighteen centuries earlier. Accordingly, the Palmach was rather more than just one of the military units of the Haganah. It was an inspiring element within the Jewish community for resistance against foreign oppression, and a dependable instrument of the political leadership for achieving national goals. By the end of the Second World War, four well-organized, well-trained and well-disciplined Palmach battalions were ready for action; and around them were many more Haganah units ready to be mobilized whenever necessary.

B

There was now only one question in everyone's mind. What would the next British Government's policy be in regard to Palestine? The British Labour Party had committed itself wholly to the establishment of a Jewish State in Palestine; indeed, its commitment went further than any expected or asked for by the Zionist leaders.[12] Great hopes were accordingly pinned on a post-war Labour Government; and it is easy to understand the disappointment experienced when these hopes were proved false.

In 1945, however, the year of Labour's victory, hope ran high in the Jewish community in Palestine. It brought the danger of a relaxation of vigilance, among members of the Haganah and the general population alike. Every army is greatly influenced by the prevailing mood of its society at a given historical moment, and how much more so an army which is a voluntary underground militia. Add to this the desperate fatigue induced by a barely ended war, and the possibly disastrous effects of the post-war spirit on the fighting alertness of the Jews in Palestine are easily appreciated. Luckily, the Zionist leadership was fully aware of the danger. Some of the political leaders, and most of the commanders of the Haganah—particularly the Palmach commanders—warned repeatedly against any relaxation until the new British Government's policy was definitely known. Accordingly, when this Government showed all too soon that it was intent on pursuing the same anti-Zionist policy as its predecessor, the Haganah, with the full authority of the elected leadership of the Zionist Movement, embarked on its struggle against the British, with a view to forcing London either to reverse its policy, or to hand back its Mandate over Palestine to the United Nations, the successor of the League of Nations.

In any military undertaking, decisions about strategy, tactics, training and organization can only be taken in the light of all

[12] At the 1945 Labour Party Conference, Mr Dalton, on behalf of the Executive, formulated the Party's official policy as follows: 'This Party has laid it down and repeated it so recently as last April that this time, having regard to the unspeakable horrors that have been perpetrated upon the Jews in Germany and other occupied countries in Europe, it is morally wrong and politically indefensible to impose obstacles to the entry into Palestine now of any Jews who desire to go there. We consider that Jewish immigration should be permitted without the present limitations which obstruct it, and we also have stated very clearly that it is indispensable that there should be close agreement and co-operation among the British, American and Soviet Governments. In my view steps should be taken in consultation with those two Governments to see whether we cannot get that common support for a policy which will give us a happy, free and a prosperous Jewish State in Palestine.'

the relevant factors. To understand these aspects of the Haganah's military action against the British in Palestine, it is necessary to indicate the specific conditions which influenced, if not determined, its subsequent conduct of the struggle. The Jews were still a minority in Palestine: they numbered about half a million —that is, about one-third of the population. They were concentrated in cities and villages, mainly along the coastal plains but also in certain blocks in the Galilee, and scattered in isolated settlements—mainly kibbutzim—in the Arab interior, the Judaean hills and the northern Negev. Even the most thickly populated Jewish areas were interspersed with Arab settlements, and in some cities the population was mixed. British military bases and police stations, by contrast, were spread throughout the country, occupying strategic positions; the Mandatory administration was in full control; and the British navy was conspicuously present in the Mediterranean. The British troops were well trained and equipped, and seasoned by their participation in the recent World War. They, too, however, were suffering from postwar fatigue; and both the British economy and British public opinion were impatient for the speediest and most complete demobilization. As far as the Arab world was concerned, it was recognized that if a struggle took place between the Jews and the British in Palestine, the most that could be expected from them was an unfriendly neutrality towards the Jews; while in the country itself co-operation between the Arabs and the British was exceedingly likely.

What strategy was to be chosen? A full-scale, openly-declared war would have furnished the British with an excuse to take severe action against the Jewish community, with the best chances of success. The British forces suffered none of the disabilities of illegality; consequently they had the advantage in mobility, as well as an overwhelming superiority in the means of waging war. Since the country had no jungles or large forests, and since most of the hills and mountains were populated by the Arabs, the strategy of classical guerilla warfare was ruled out. The choice, in the end, reduced itself to one of three alternative strategies: (a) at one extreme, terrorist tactics, directed without discrimination against all British targets and personnel; (b) at the other extreme, a 'limited' struggle, which renounced military action, and confined itself exclusively to bringing in illegal immigrants, establishing new settlements in prohibited areas, and hold-

ing mass demonstrations; and (c) the 'middle way' in fact
adopted: this rejected personal terrorism, both on moral and
on practical grounds (it was considered immoral because it was
against the Jewish ethical code, with its respect for human life,
and impractical because it could provoke counter-terrorism), and
accepted the second alternative—illegal immigration, new settlements in prohibited areas, and mass demonstration—as the best
way of conducting the struggle, supplemented however by direct
military action based on guerilla tactics.[13]

The term 'struggle' has been used deliberately (and I believe
accurately) instead of 'war', even though the struggle included
military action. For, first, though the actions were based on
guerilla tactics, it was not an overall guerilla war; and, second, it
was a definite part of the Haganah's strategy and tactics to avoid
casualties or at least to reduce them to a minimum—on the
British side as well as the Jewish—in all attacks including those
on military objectives. Accordingly, a great deal of care was
exercised (and a great many risks taken) in the planning and
execution of the military operations to achieve this last aim.

The following outline of this strategy (which came to be known
as the strategy of 'constructive warfare') attempts to deal briefly
with each of the elements mentioned. Illegal immigration was
effected mainly by sea, but some of it also on foot across the
land borders, and some even by illegal air-flights. By the end of
the three-year period 1945–48, some sixty-five ships had crossed
the Mediterranean, and the number of immigrants, most of them
survivors of the Nazi holocaust, had reached a total of nearly a
hundred thousand. It had three main purposes: first, to save the
remnants of the Jewish communities of Europe; second, to increase
the actual number of Jews in Palestine; third, to expose the pitiful
inadequacy of the White Paper immigration quotas and to win
world sympathy, including British public opinion, for the Zionist
cause, thus forcing Whitehall into as tight a corner as possible
against a background of broken promises and the tragedy of the
Jewish people. The illegal settlements aimed at two objectives:
to achieve footholds in strategically vital areas against anticipated

---

[13] Concerning terrorism, it has to be added that although it was rejected
outright by the national authorities, it was adopted by two small, separatist
underground groups which dissociated themselves from and defied the
authority of the elected bodies. These were the *Irgun Zvai Leumi*
('National Military Organization') and its offshoot, *Lohamei Herut Yisrael*
('Fighters for the Freedom of Israel').

events; and (again) to expose the White Paper policy, which in effect declared the greater part of Palestine to be out of bounds to the Jews. The object of the military actions was not to destroy the British forces in Palestine: this would have been beyond the scope of the Jewish forces—though they were indeed capable of annihilating substantial units and bases. It was rather to undermine their position, their sense of security, their prestige, and above all to convince Whitehall once and for all that without the consent of the Jews Britain could not keep Palestine as a safe and workable base in this vital region. By the renunciation of killing, on the one hand, and on the other by the high military accomplishment of the Palmach raids and actions with the participation of the people as a whole, it was hoped simultaneously to arouse sympathy and even admiration of the Jews in Palestine, and to prove to the world—including the Jews themselves—that they were a force to be reckoned with.

The unusual combined operation sketched above—illegal immigration, illegal settlement, and illegal military action—was therefore aimed at forcing the problem on all parties concerned, and forcing them to seek a positive solution. It was hoped, in short, to prove to Britain and the rest of the world that an unjust and unworkable policy may cease to be a policy at all; and thereby to induce Britain to change it for a better one—or, alternatively, for a worse one, in which case the Jews would receive fresh impetus to continue the struggle for a solution. The struggle itself was, of course, a means, not an end; it was intended to prepare the ground for Zionist political activity in London, in other capitals, and in the United Nations, directed and coordinated by the Political Department of the World Zionist Executive in Jerusalem. It should perhaps be mentioned that there were differences—luckily, not radical—among the supporters of the general strategy outlined above. Some critics, myself among them, were doubtful about the feasibility of attempting to change the policy we were fighting while the British remained in control in Palestine; we preferred the aim of forcing Britain to hand over the Mandate to the United Nations. Again, though we completely endorsed the prohibition against avoidable killing, we also thought that the military side of the struggle should be intensified and more continuously sustained.

In the military struggle itself, the preparations made during the Second World War (to a great extent, with British help) to

resist a possible German-Italian invasion proved to be of great
value to the units which now had to direct their operations
against the British. These were carried out with much less
intensity and with greater restraint than (one may suppose)
would have been used against the Germans and Italians. The
immigration ships were for the most part manned by Jewish
sailors, radio operators and medical staff, often gallantly assisted
by non-Jewish volunteers, mainly Italian and Greek. Whenever
a ship succeeded in penetrating the naval blockade, and reached
its appointed destination on the Palestinian coast, generally at
night, the bridgehead was defended by ambushes composed of
infantry on land, and occasionally also by boats at sea. The immigrants were unloaded on to small boats, some of which had
been carried on the ship itself and some brought from the coast.
Those who could not help themselves were carried ashore on the
shoulders of their rescuers, and taken the same night, by guides
and armed escorts equipped with false Palestinian identity cards,
to selected towns and villages where they were safely deposited
among the civil population. This rescue-work had, of course,
been preceded by intensive preparations in Europe. These
included the organizing of an underground among the refugees in
the D.P. camps; the transportation of the refugees from East and
Central Europe to the Mediterranean coast of Europe; the pur-
chasing and equipping of the ships; and finally the loading and
despatching of the ships across the Mediterranean. All this was
arranged by the illegal Haganah command in Europe, consisting
mainly of Palmach men, Palestinian Jewish ex-servicemen of the
British forces (who stayed behind in Europe for this specific purpose), reinforced by fighting elements of the refugees themselves
—ghetto-fighters, partisans, and other combatants. It was a
gigantic enterprise, which cut across international borders, and
defied effective British intelligence (in Europe as well as in Palestine), British naval control of the Mediterranean, British air-
reconnaissance, and the strong mobile forces of the British in
Palestine itself. It compelled the Haganah to develop into a
military organization capable of planning, directing and executing
such a complex operation; and it provided the units engaged in
the actual landings with valuable experience in combined coastal
operations, including their logistic and other organizational and
administrative aspects.

The strengthening of the Haganah, moreover, was matched by

that of the people as a whole. The Jewish community in Palestine by its intimate participation in the whole enterprise learned by experience the price of nationhood. Whenever a ship was successfully brought in, the news was publicly announced on the following day, to make sure that none of its political meaning was lost on the community. When a landing had to be carried out by day, the fighters were instructed to hide their arms, and the people were summoned to the beaches to mingle with the refugees in order to prevent their arrest by the British. Some of them lost their lives while marching against machine-gun fire. This kind of episode had the effect of strengthening the solidarity of the population with the fighters, and did a great deal towards uniting the people into a nation.

The establishment of illegal settlements was a simpler undertaking than the illegal immigration, but it also greatly extended the military experience of the Haganah. As already explained, the necessary planning involved the choosing of the site, the engineering of a whole pre-fabricated settlement or village, the handling of transport, defence arrangements, and co-operation between soldiers and civilians. Though some of this was quasi-military, it helped to develop the Haganah as a military force conscious of a national responsibility.

The most valuable experience, however, was obviously provided by the strictly military operations, both the big and the small. The chosen targets were railways, bridges, armoured vehicles, police-stations, military bases, refugee and prison camps, radar stations, armed patrol boats, ships in Palestine and Cyprus. All these targets were defended by stationed guards or mobile patrols or both. Some were near the Jewish areas, and some in remoter parts along the borders of Palestine. Except for the Transjordan Frontier Force, which was manned by Arabs and commanded by British officers, the Arabs did not participate in the actual fighting against the Jews; but they willingly supplied British intelligence with information about the movements of Jewish units (though there were occasionally Arabs who co-operated with the intelligence service of the Haganah). Most of the Haganah's operations had therefore to be carried out at night. Because of the need to avoid Arab observers as well as British patrols, the approach to and retreat from a target sometimes took hours. When the target happened to be especially far from Jewish bases, these had to be extended over two days, the men marching by night and hiding by day. Such an operation required, besides great physical stamina, a high degree of tactical and executive skill. It involved the ability to act as small units, or as co-ordinated small units over wide areas—or even as a company or a battalion—against a single target or adjoining targets; and above all to employ big and small units in one operation under a brigade command. This experience was gained not only on the battlefield but also in exercises of movement and fire in the empty desert south of the Dead Sea. The fact that practically every man of the Palmach, along with a good number of people from other field-units of the Haganah, was deliberately given the opportunity to acquire combat experience at all levels served to temper the fighting ability and spirit of the Haganah for the greater engagements of the future.

Side by side with the development of the land forces, a naval nucleus of the Palmach gained important experience. Commanding ships and boats of the illegal immigrants on the one hand, and sinking British vessels on the other, contributed to the development of Israel's future navy by helping to create, besides a conventional surface navy, a special sabotage branch.

As most of the Haganah operations had the character of raids, the clashes between Jewish and British troops were seldom protracted. They tended to be short engagements, for the Jewish underground fighters had to disappear before they lost the cover of darkness, and also needed time to remove all tracks leading to their bases. The British counter-actions had the character of police actions rather than full-scale military operations. At a later stage of the conflict, the British were indeed obliged to intensify their counter-operations, extending them beyond the Haganah units to civil settlements and the arresting of national leaders. These more severe (and more successful) police actions, however, already marked the beginning of the end of British rule in Palestine. For they proved that the British were fighting not merely isolated small groups of militant extremists but a national liberation movement which embraced the entire community. They alienated world public opinion, and turned their para-military victory into a political defeat. The end came in February 1947 when Whitehall announced its decision to refer the whole problem of Palestine to the United Nations. In November of that year the United Nations voted for the partition of Palestine into two states, one Jewish and one Arab. Britain's Mandatory regime was terminated and 15th May, 1948 set as the date for the final withdrawal of all British troops and personnel from Palestine.

It remains to add that the two dissident Jewish underground units, which were mainly terrorist in character, contributed their share to the overall pressure that finally led to the withdrawal of the British. Their operations were often very daring, and their individual members for the most part brave men and women who proved themselves capable of acts of great self-sacrifice. They could not by themselves, however, have brought about the ultimate defeat of the British, chiefly because of their isolation within the Jewish community. By contrast, the operations of the Haganah had the best chance of victory not only because of the greater scale and variety of its operations but also because it enjoyed the active support of the population as a whole. Not least important to the development of the Jewish military force, at this stage as at all other stages, were the non-military phenomena already touched upon: the close relationship between the civil and military branches of the community, the full control of the military organization by the elected civil bodies, and the conscious loyalty of the troops to their undeclared and as yet unrecognized national Jewish Government. The maturity this indicated may count as perhaps one of the greatest achievements of the Haganah, as pre-eminently a national army of liberation and defence.

B*

CHAPTER II

The War of
Liberation

Tension between the Jews and Arabs had begun to mount throughout 1947 during the prolonged deliberations of the United Nations. Both sides began to speed up their military preparations by expanding their manpower, intensifying their training, and accumulating more arms. It soon became evident not only that the British would evacuate Palestine but that an all-out clash between Arabs and Jews was therefore inevitable. When, on 29th November, 1947, the General Assembly of the United Nations resolved by a two-thirds majority (which included the United States and the Soviet Union) to partition the country into two sovereign states, with a common economic framework and an international enclave in the Jerusalem area, the Arabs immediately rejected this decision. Arab riots began in Palestine, and Arab guerillas made their first appearance in the remoter areas of the country.

The war which came to be known as Israel's War of Liberation can be divided into four distinct periods or phases. Each left its mark on the development of the Israeli forces, and each extended Israel's hold on the country. The first phase lasted about six months, beginning on 30th November, 1947 and ending at different times in different areas—in March or April or the first half of May 1948, depending on the date of the British evacuation, which varied from area to area and was not completed until 14th May, 1948. So long as the British remained in the Jewish areas, the Haganah was forced to continue to act underground (though on a much more extensive scale than ever before), using legal units as far as possible as a cover for its operations. The Mediterranean and the coast were still controlled by the

British. Jewish immigration was still illegal; most of the vessels that tried to run the blockade were captured by the British navy,[1] and the immigrants imprisoned in internment camps in Cyprus. Arms which were vitally needed had to be smuggled into the country. The Arabs, on the other hand, had the advantage of British-free zones in the interior as well as along the borders of the country, and consequently enjoyed freedom of movement between Palestine and the neighbouring Arab states.

The Mandatory Government proclaimed its neutrality, and the British forces in Palestine were ordered to guard only the remaining provisional bases and the remaining routes to Haifa harbour, the gate for evacuation. A United Nations proposal to set up an international 'caretaker' agency for Palestine, to supervise the carrying out of the United Nations resolution, was rejected by London.

The strategy of the Haganah in this first period of the war may be summarized as follows:

1. Remote settlements were on no account to be abandoned.[2] It was recognized that this would impose a considerable military burden on the High Command by forcing it to maintain long lines of communication and supplies. On the other hand, the settlements could be expected to divert to themselves part at least of the Arab pressure on the Jewish centres in the plains; they could be used as bases for guerilla operations behind the enemy's lines; and they would serve as ultimate objectives to be reached when the time came for a liberatory offensive in the whole area.

2. Direct clashes with the British were as far as possible to be avoided, so as not to impede their plans for evacuation. Major offensives against the Arabs were likewise to be postponed, in case these should lead to British intervention, and thus again delay their departure.

3. Jewish territorial continuity was to be established in each predominantly Jewish zone, and as far as possible also between the zones themselves. Territorial continuity meant

[1] Fifty-eight of the sixty-three immigrant ships that sailed clandestinely for Palestine between April 1945 and January 1948 were intercepted.

[2] The single exception was Beit Ha'arava, on the northern shore of the Dead Sea. But even in this instance the inhabitants were only moved to Sodom, further south on the Dead Sea, which though isolated was less close to the major route between Amman and Jericho than the original settlement.

greater safety for internal roads of communication, the saving of manpower, and the possibility of establishing a reasonable military posture to meet the openly threatened official invasion by the armies of the several neighbouring states.

These aims were for the most part achieved, and helped to prepare the ground for the larger aims of the immediate future. This preliminary phase also helped to shape further the military organization itself, in the following ways:

1. The Palmach, the striking force of the Haganah, entered the war with four fully mobilized battalions organized within a brigade, and expanded rapidly into ten battalions divided into three brigades; these were under a central command, quartered close to the High Command of the Haganah to facilitate hour-by-hour communications about its special tasks within the country or across the borders. It was assigned special operations of its own within the framework of the overall strategy, or was used as the spearhead of major operations on difficult fronts under the front commander. In the latter operations, the Palmach acted in conjunction with other units.

2. In this phase of the war, the embryonic navy and air force were separated from the Palmach, and gradually developed into distinct forces with their own commands; however, to the end they remained subordinated to the General Staff of the army.

3. A substantial number of battalions, drawn from the field corps of the Haganah, and gradually formed into brigades, were permanently mobilized. At the start they were confined to given territories, but soon abandoned their quasi-territorial character and became mobile on a nation-wide scale, thus enabling the High Command to concentrate forces in any theatre.

4. A Home Guard, composed of older men, women and young people under the age of eighteen in the villages and towns, was partly mobilized within the framework of the Haganah's National Guard. They generally undertook the passive defence of Jewish quarters in mixed cities, on farms, and in settlements; but sometimes they were mobilized and sent from the cities to rural areas as reinforcements, acting as

watchmen and workers. In addition to the importance of the direct service which the Home Guard gave, it helped to relieve field-units of defensive duties, thus freeing them for active combat.

5. Various services, such as transport, medical aid, civil defence, and engineering, were established without undue difficulty. As most of the civilian population was in one way or another organized by or connected with the Haganah, it was relatively easy to find the manpower and civil equipment required for these services.

The advances outlined above were all accomplished by voluntary methods; for there was as yet no Jewish State with the power to enforce service. It seems that the combination of idealism and a common danger was able to effect the mobilization of an army in the making for the defence of a state in the making.

The second phase of the war was very brief but decisive. It covered the interval—sometimes only a matter of days, never more than a few weeks—between the British evacuation of particular areas and its final evacuation of the country as a whole on 14th May, 1948, the date of the expiry of the Mandate. In this brief period, the Jews and Arabs confronted each other in the physical absence but political presence, so to speak, of the British.

This curious situation gave the Haganah the opportunity to initiate main efforts in crucial areas, directed towards establishing territorial continuity within and between Jewish areas, extending Jewish control over areas previously held by Arab forces, and consolidating defence arrangements in preparation for the threatened invasion of the Arab regular armies from across the borders. During this period, not only were most of the Arab attacks on the settlements repulsed but the Jewish forces liberated such vital areas as Upper and Lower Galilee, including Arab centres like Samach and Beisan, and mixed Jewish-Arab towns like Safad and Tiberias; Western Galilee, including the mixed city of Haifa;[3] the large Arab centre of Jaffa; important parts of New Jerusalem; and many strategically important villages in many

[3] The Arab town of Acre was liberated two days after the expiry of the Mandate; and the clearing of Western Galilee was completed a few days later, on 22nd May, 1948.

parts of the country from North to South. Hardly less important were a number of successful field campaigns undertaken to relieve besieged places in the Jerusalem Corridor and at the entrance to the northern Negev. Although the Haganah suffered some painful setbacks during this period—heavy casualties, the destruction of Jewish convoys and transport vehicles on their way to isolated areas, and the loss of a number of Jewish settlements around Jerusalem—the balance sheet on the whole was extremely favourable to the Haganah. These achievements proved to be crucial in establishing a sounder geo-strategic posture for defence against the imminent invasion of forces of superior strength.

The third phase of the war, which lasted from 15th May to 10th June, 1948, brought at last the long-threatened simultaneous offensive of all the neighbouring Arab armies on all fronts. It was a very difficult period. The Arabs' superiority in numbers and equipment was all too obvious; and the psychological effect of the invasion was potentially as disabling as the enemy's military strength. In these circumstances it was fortunate indeed that the Haganah, though not ready to embark at once on a full-scale counter-offensive, still rejected a purely defensive strategy. If it had concentrated solely on defence, the war would have been lost; for in that case the initiative would have remained with the enemy, which was in a position to choose almost freely its time and place for attack, and to concentrate forces sufficient to break the Jewish lines of defence almost everywhere. The Haganah accordingly adopted a combination of defensive methods and offensive action which came to be known as 'active defence'. There was, of course, no continuous line of defence. Every settlement or group of adjoining settlements was defended for the most part by the settlers themselves. In some places, strategic hills and strong-holds were held by regular troops; and a series of night raids, carried out by the Israelis on the enemy's soil, sometimes deep into his territory, forced the enemy to exercise great vigilance in the defence of bases, bridges and other military objects. During this period the first pieces of artillery—very few in number and very old-fashioned—were used by the Israelis. A small number of light aeroplanes, such as Piper Cubs and Austers, which had been bravely used for reconnaissance, light transport and even primitive bombing and strafing, were now supplemented by a few better aeroplanes, mainly Messerschmitts. The psychological value of the artillery and the aeroplanes was as great as (if not greater than) their military value.

The number of Israeli raids and local counter-attacks, most of them made by night, gradually increased. Most of the enemy's direct attacks on the fortified settlements failed, and the very few (some two or three) that succeeded proved to be extremely costly. Yet the enemy did achieve, at least on two fronts, substantial gains. The Egyptians managed to advance to within twelve kilometres of Rehovot; the Syrians established a bridgehead across the Jordan in the Upper Galilee; the Transjordanians were stationed in the two Arab towns of Ramla and Lydda—the latter including the international airport, half an hour's drive from Tel-Aviv—and also succeeded in repulsing Israeli attacks around Jenin and Latrun.

Gradually a stalemate was reached. The Arab armies lost their offensive momentum, and the Israelis, though becoming increasingly more active in defence, were not yet prepared for large-scale offensives. It seemed that both sides were seeking a breathing-space; accordingly, both agreed to respond to a United Nations call for a one-month cease-fire, beginning on 11th June.

Having in mind the inequality of strength, it was understandable that this phase of the war should have been regarded as an Israeli victory, though not a decisive one. Not only had the enemy been held back in most areas, but considerable territorial gains had been made. On the debit side, however, there had again been some severe setbacks: the loss of several settlements, and (most painful of all) that of the Jewish Quarter in the Old City of Jerusalem.

The Israelis, encouraged by their successes and drawing lessons from their defeats, used the month of the cease-fire to consolidate as far as possible every aspect of their military organization. During this period the first legal ceremonies were held. The Haganah was formally declared the official army of the new state, to be known as *Zahal*, a word composed of the initial letters of the Hebrew words for 'Israel Defence Army' (*Zavah Haganah LeYisrael*).[4] All the troops took an oath of allegiance to the State. An official uniform was introduced. Ranks were created for officers and N.C.O.'s, the highest of which was that of *rav-aluf* (major-general), held by only one person, Ya'acov Dori, the new Chief

---

[4] This in fact happened eleven days before the cease-fire, on 31st May, 1948.

of Staff, formerly Chief of Staff of the Haganah. The commanding officers of the various fronts and of the Palmach, the air force,
the navy and the armoured brigade, and a few key officers of the
General Staff, held the rank of *aluf* (brigadier-general).[5] The
remaining small, semi-autonomous, underground organizations
were ordered by the Government to disband, and their members
were absorbed as individuals by the army. This transformation of
the Haganah into the regular army of an independent state was,
in one sense, nominal rather than substantial. The overall organization, the chain of command, the personalities, the loyalties
remained as before. But in another sense the change was real
indeed. For it symbolized the historic transformation of Palestine
into a sovereign Jewish state and of its Jewish community into a
nation, and as such it had great spiritual significance.

The entire field army now consisted of seven regular brigades,
three Palmach brigades, and one armoured brigade. The last was
still very poorly equipped, but the rest were now better equipped
with Czechoslovak and French arms, including better (though
still insufficient) artillery. The air force acquired a number of
Czech-made Messerschmitts and English-made Spitfires bought
on the Continent, and a number of Dakotas for transport and
bombing. The navy improved its equipment and training, for
naval guerilla warfare and small landings as well as coastal patrolling. Each of the various units now had its own direct command,
but these were all part of a single army subordinated to the
supreme command of the Chief of the General Staff, who in his
turn was responsible to the Prime Minister and Minister of
Defence, David Ben-Gurion, and to his Deputy, Yisrael Galili.[6]
A War Cabinet was formed, which was authorized by the whole
Cabinet to make certain decisions on behalf of the Government;
and another important new body, the Defence and Foreign Policy
Committee of the *Knesset* (Parliament), was authorized by the
House to act on its behalf. As a whole, the Israeli forces were
still inferior to those of the enemy in numbers, equipment and
geo-strategic conditions, but superior in organization, discipline,
fighting spirit, unity, and the sense of *no alternative*. 'Either you

---

[5] In 1969, a new rank was created, that of *tat-aluf*, equivalent to brigadier
general. An *aluf* has thus become a major-general and a *rav-aluf* a lieutenant-
general. The latter is still the highest rank, held only by the Chief of Staff.

[6] Mr Galili had been the last Commander-in-Chief of the Haganah, an office
corresponding in the underground army to that of Minister of Defence.

win the war, or you will be driven into the Mediterranean—you individually along with the whole nation': this was the meaning of no alternative, a phrase widely used at this time by troops and civilians alike to express the nation's consciousness that it was fighting for its survival. It was obvious that once the cease-fire was over both sides would try to take the initiative in a resumption of hostilities.

The fourth and final stage of Israel's War of Liberation, which started on 11th June, 1948, saw a radical change both in the fighting ability and the logistics of Israel's Defence Army. Because the enemy was so strong and so close to the most heavily populated Jewish areas, the Israelis dared not adopt a purely defensive strategy. It was clear that if the invading armies were allowed to enjoy the advantage of offensive action, they might break through Israel's sparse line, crush its forces and gain possession of all Jewish-held territory, which because it lacked the dimension of depth was all too easy to subdue. The strategy decided upon was therefore the only correct one: to take the initiative as soon as the United Nations' imposed cease-fire had ended. Not wishing to violate the U.N.'s decision by anticipating the enemy's offensive even by one day, and knowing that the enemy was accustomed to attack in daylight, the Israelis decided to anticipate the enemy by just a few hours and launch their own offensive at the exact moment the truce officially ended, namely, at midnight.

The war could not have been won without crushing the enemy's forces. The accomplishment of this ultimate goal required a concentration of Israel's forces on specific fronts greater than any previously attempted, with the object of achieving a local superiority to offset the overall inferiority of its forces. This, of course, could not be done on all fronts simultaneously, and an order of priorities had to be set up. The first, most urgent tasks seemed to be the following: to eliminate the danger to Tel-Aviv and its immediate surroundings by liberating Lydda and Ramla and penetrating the hilly country east of the coastal plain; to lift the siege of Jerusalem; to outflank the Transjordanian-held Old City from the north. The second task was to secure the Haifa region by liberating Nazareth and the remaining parts of Lower Galilee. At the same time, the Egyptians in the south, the Iraqis in the east, and the Syrians in the north had to be checked by tactics of active defence, based on settlements and mobile forces, until offensive action could be undertaken against them.

These operations—which included, in the liberation of Lydda and Ramla, a daring raid of a mechanized battalion into Lydda itself—were wholly successful. Engaging four brigades under a single command (the Palmach command) on the Central Front, and two brigades under a single command (the Northern command) on the Northern front, they gave the Israeli army new experience, new scope and greatly increased confidence. Although much larger forces were now engaged against a single target, guerilla tactics were not abandoned. Fighting by day and night in large bodies supported by artillery was combined with guerilla actions, which were fused into the general planning in a way that proved to be highly successful throughout the War of Liberation and its aftermath. Generally speaking, all the goals were achieved; and had a second cease-fire not been imposed by the United Nations on 19th July, 1948, the Israeli offensive might have continued more or less unabated, shifting the main effort from one front to another until a complete destruction of the enemy, or at least his withdrawal from the entire territory of Mandatory Palestine, had been achieved.

The second cease-fire lasted until 10th October, 1948. From this time the Israeli command was obliged to take into account in its planning not only the usual factors but also the possibility of further United Nations intervention in the form of cease-fires. These were again likely to be imposed when the Israelis had the upper hand and the exploitation of their success could yield substantial gains in territory, as well as further destruction of the enemy's units. The immediate military consequence of this situation was that every operation, besides being part of an overall plan, had also to be complete in itself.

During this period, another important symbolic event took place. The first legal parade held by a Jewish army under a Jewish government since the destruction of the Second Temple was held in Tel-Aviv in July 1948.

The period of the second cease-fire, 19th July to 10th October, 1948, was successfully used by the Israelis to rest their forces, to reinforce their units with fresh manpower (drawn from the growing local youth and from the new immigrants flocking in—now legally—from the camps in Cyprus as well as from Europe), to issue more and better equipment (supplied by Czechoslovakia and

France), and to reorganize the army's chain of command. The reorganization took the following form. The entire country was divided into four territorial commands, always referred to at this time as 'fronts'. These were the Northern Front, which included the entire Galilee, and thus confronted the Central Galilee Forces of Lebanon, Syria and Iraq, as well as the so-called Army of Liberation led by Fawzi al Kaukji; the Eastern Front, covering the Samaria and Sharon areas, and confronting Iraqi and Trans-jordanian forces in the Triangle;[7] the Central Front covering the Tel-Aviv–Jerusalem axis, and confronting the main body of the Transjordanian forces flanked by Iraqis in the north and Egyptians in the south; and the Southern Front, which covered the southern half of Palestine from Rehovot in the north down to the Red Sea, most of this area being held by Egyptian forces reinforced by a Saudi Arabian contingent. A further act of reorganization during this period was one directly affecting the Palmach. Although its three brigades remained intact to the end of the war, the headquarters of the Palmach were disbanded. A new unit called NAHAL (the initials of the Hebrew words for 'pioneer fighting youth'), designed in part to replace the Palmach, was created, which organized both collectively and on an individual basis all the embryonic youth movements, each platoon comprising simultaneously a military unit and a group of prospective settlers.

My own view of the reorganization was that it was generally correct, subject to two reservations. First, I felt that the head-quarters of the Palmach should have been retained, as the command of a special unit for special operations directly responsible to the Chief of the General Staff. This error was later at least partly corrected by the creation of a special corps of paratroopers, trained for special operations against difficult targets or behind the enemy's lines, which they would reach either by parachuting or by long-distance marching. My second reservation con-cerned the number of frontal commands. I thought four too many, and that no more than two, or at most three, were needed. This seemed to me both better suited to the small size of the country and its geo-strategic character, and better adapted to what I saw as the immediate strategy of the war. Our first task, as I saw it, was to crush the enemy in the South and in the North, and only

[7] The Triangle covers the hilly part of East-Central Palestine, and is so called because it includes the three main Arab towns of Tul-Kerem, Nablus and Jenin.

afterwards, when both flanks were secure, to attack the hilly Centre, including Jerusalem. (The attack could then be carried out by outflanking the Transjordanians and the Iraqis in the centre and approaching them from the rear, leaving a corridor or bridge for enemy withdrawal). In point of fact, the number of commands was reduced to three immediately after the war by the abolition of the Eastern command, and has remained three to the present day.

During the war the Israeli army avoided the divisional level, and instead (as explained) was divided into frontal commands. While the commands themselves were confined to specific areas, the brigades did not belong permanently to given fronts, but could be placed at the disposal of any frontal commander according to the changing needs of the war, and thus concentrated for major efforts on different fronts. This best suited the prevailing conditions of the Palestinian theatre, when the Israeli forces were small in size and inferior in strength, and therefore could only achieve superiority in particular battles by mobility, concentration, manoeuvrability, and the use of surprise. A reinforced Home Guard was relied on to fill the gaps in the depleted fronts. The Commanding Officer of each front was entirely responsible for all aspects of the defence of his area, including the operational planning and execution of the offensives. He also had special liaison with the civil organization, local and regional.

The Israeli offensives that followed the end of the cease-fire on 10th October, 1948, especially those in the Negev and the Central Galilee, not only helped to achieve and consolidate territorial gains and to weaken the enemy but also further improved the shape of Israel's strategy and military organization. The troops became more accustomed to operate in larger units, with better and smoother co-ordination yet without losing their guerilla flexibility and power of improvisation. They learned to make better use of their limited air and artillery support, acquired greater skill in field engineering, and above all developed greater mobility and manoeuvrability. During this period, too, the tactics of 'indirect approach' (so admirably expounded in Sir Basil Liddell Hart's teachings) were most extensively and successfully used, especially in the campaigns in the Negev and the northern Sinai Peninsula in January, 1949.

As a result of these campaigns, the entire Galilee was cleared and restored to Israel; Israeli troops reached the Litani River on

Lebanese territory; and the Egyptian siege of the Negev was lifted. This Negev front had stretched from Ashdod and Ashkelon on the Mediterranean through Faluja and Beit Jubrin to Hebron in the hills in the East, based on long lines of communication between El-Arish, Rafah and Gaza along the coast and between Ismailia on the Suez Canal and Abu Ageila, Auja El Hafir, Bir-Asluj and Beersheba in the Central Negev. The Egyptian forces were crushed, and the entire northern Negev, including Beersheba, liberated. Only one gallant Egyptian brigade, surrounded and isolated in the Faluja pocket, remained there until the armistice: its intelligence officer was a young major named Gamal Abdel Nasser.

Besides these decisive victories, an attempt was also made to liberate the Hebron-Bethlehem hills, formerly controlled by the now defeated Egyptians and not yet taken over by the Trans-jordanians. Two Israeli columns had almost reached their targets when the Government—misguidedly, in my view—ordered them to stop their advance. The vacuum thus created was filled, without battle, by the Arab Legion of Transjordan.

The final clearing of the Gaza Strip and of the Southern Negev down to the Red Sea had been left for separate operations. These were undertaken towards the end of December 1948. On 22nd December, a large-scale operation, spread over a wide area and highly mobile, was begun, with two objects in view: first, to clear finally the main road south of Beersheba down to the Sinai border, in order to eliminate the immediate danger to Beersheba and open the way to the final destruction of the Egyptian army in the Gaza Strip; second, to prepare the ground for liberating the entire southern half of the Negev held by Transjordan. Omitting details, it is enough to say that a combination of guerilla actions and rapid advances by large bodies completely broke the Egyptian hold south of Beersheba, and that in a very fast move the border of Sinai was crossed on 28th December. The main cross-road of Sinai, Abu Ageila, was taken after a brief and sharp battle, followed by other important places such as Kusseima, Kunteila, Bir-Hassne, and the airfields of Bir-Gafgafa and El-Arish, which all fell to the fast-moving forces. One small mobile task-force penetrated as deep as forty miles from the Suez Canal (then still in British hands); and the main body moved rapidly north-west-wards, with the object of taking El-Arish, the capital of Sinai, and approaching the Gaza Strip from the rear—that is, from the most unexpected and therefore least defended direction.[8] The entire Egyptian army had in fact been cut off from Egypt, and it seemed that it was about to be finally defeated. The main Israeli task-force was standing at the gates of El-Arish ready for the last blow when the Government, acting under American political pressure, ordered the advance to be stopped and all troops to be withdrawn from Sinai. The order was deeply resented by the troops; but their discipline was such that they nevertheless complied with it, and by 5th January the last Israeli soldier had left Sinai.

Another chance was given, however, to attack the Gaza Strip, this time from within Israeli territory. A fresh task force succeeded in crossing the dunes and putting a strong wedge south of Rafah near the Israel-Egyptian border, thereby cutting the entire Strip from its rear, blocking the main road, and leaving the railroad intact but controlled from a nearby position—in the hope that this would reduce the enemy's stubbornness and encourage him to withdraw back into Egypt. At this point, the Egyptian Government agreed to enter upon armistice negotiations, provided the Israeli wedge was lifted. This was done: mistakenly, because it greatly weakened Israel's bargaining position in the subsequent negotiations. The armistice agreement was signed on the island of Rhodes on 24th February, 1949, leaving the Gaza Strip in Egyptian hands.

Once the Egyptians were out of the war, the Israelis could concentrate greater forces for the final liberation of Palestine. In a long-range movement of three brigades, the entire southern Negev was conquered, including part of the gulf of Akaba (on 16th March, 1949). At the same time, the Western part of the Dead Sea, including Massada and Ein Gedi, and a part of the Judaean Desert were liberated.

These successes, however, were offset by failures elsewhere. Owing to mistaken political considerations, certain well-planned operations to liberate the rest of the country (the Hebron hills, Old Jerusalem and the Triangle) which had been on the point of liberation in several earlier phases and especially after the Egyptian defeat, were abandoned; and these territories remained

[8] According to conventional military doctrine, this plan would seem to have been quite illogical, involving as it did extended lines of communication without the support of adequate armour and artillery. But in a mobile war the illogical may sometimes turn out to be the most logical precisely because the illogical or irrational is, by definition, the unexpected, and being least expected by the enemy is least prepared for.

in Jordanian hands. Though the Israelis had been defeated in earlier small operations (against Jenin in the north, against Bethlehem and the High Commissioner's Palace south of Jerusalem), and in spite of the lack of initiative shown in the Jerusalem area, the liberation of the rest of the country could at this stage of the war have been attained with less effort and greater assurance of success than were the victories in the big campaigns in the Negev and Sinai. But this chance was missed; and soon afterwards armistice agreements were signed with the remaining neighbouring countries: with Lebanon on 23rd March, 1949, with Transjordan on 3rd April, and with Syria on 20th July. Iraq withdrew its forces from territory held by Transjordan without signing an agreement.

By these armistice agreements, the Israeli forces evacuated Lebanese territory south of the Litani; the Syrians evacuated their bridgehead in Upper Galilee; the surrounded Egyptian brigade was allowed to withdraw from the Faluja pocket; and Transjordan arrogated to herself the Samaria and Hebron areas, including the Old City of Jerusalem, and became the Kingdom of Jordan. As already indicated, Egypt continued her occupation of the Gaza Strip. All this of course prevented the establishment of an Arab State in Palestine as envisaged by the partition plan of the United Nations. The State of Israel on its side emerged from the war holding more extensive and strategically more advantageous territory than that originally allocated to her by the Partition Plan. This, however, was much less than it was within her military capacity to achieve, and much less than was necessary for her defence against further threats from the same enemies.

The Israeli army was made in action. This was as true of it at this stage of its history as it was to be subsequently. Certain aspects of its development from a small group of watchmen at the turn of the century to the modern army of today were undoubtedly the result of imaginative leadership. But its main development, especially in size and equipment, was imposed upon it by the enemy; and at least some of its successes were due to the enemy's mistakes and weakness. However, to know how to exploit—that is, use constructively—an opponent's weakness is itself a gift. In the case of the Israel army, the exercise of this gift required, besides a highly developed intelligence service, commanders and troops not only well trained and organized by the usual military standards but trained also physically and morally for the special demands of warfare directed towards national liberation and defence.

Israel's army in its present form stems directly from the army that emerged as a victorious force from the War of Liberation, which in turn sprang from the parent military organization, the Haganah. The distinctive features of the army in 1949 were permanently integrated into the character of Israel's Defence Forces. It emerged as a legal, regular army, but owing to certain sociological aspects of its history and composition, it remained basically a citizens' army, both in its relation to the nation and in its own traditions and habits.

The heritage of the Haganah was multifold. To begin with, the army owed to the Haganah its very physical existence—that is, its manpower and arms, both on a relatively large scale. It inherited a sovereign territory as a geo-strategic base for its operations; a highly trained and dedicated cadre of commanders, from the section commander to the Chief of Staff; and a close-knit framework of units, with an *esprit* and a code of conduct as excellent as their military record. From the Haganah it received also the example and habit of a deeply-rooted purposefulness, idealism, and belief in voluntary service; a spirit of comradeship and mutual responsibility, among units and ranks as well as individuals; and a peculiarly warm relationship with the nation.[9] The freedom from obsolete army tradition that had been so conspicuous a feature of the Haganah passed, virtually unchanged, into the new army. As far as military forms and conventions were concerned, it adopted only the minimum necessary for securing discipline and efficiency; its attitude to these matters, was (and remains) strictly functional.[10] Finally, if one remembers that the Haganah from its illegal underground birth had been the creation of a popular move-

---

[9] The vital sense of purpose was expressed in the last of the nine principles of war adopted by Israel. These principles of war are: (i) maintenance of aim; (ii) initiative; (iii) surprise; (iv) concentration; (v) economy of force; (vi) protection; (vii) co-operation; (viii) flexibility; and (ix) consciousness of purpose or cause.

[10] A vivid comment on this point is to be found in Robert Henriques' book, *A Hundred Hours to Suez* (London, 1957). The late Colonel Henriques writes (*op. cit.* p. 12): 'Although Israeli units can be extremely smart on a ceremonial parade, there is very little discipline in the normal sense. Officers are often called by their first names amongst their men, as amongst their colleagues; there is very little saluting; there are a lot of unshaven chins; there are no

ment for national liberation directed by democratically elected civil institutions, it is perhaps not surprising that the new army should have inherited from the Haganah its democratic values and absolute loyalty to the new forms of parliamentary and social democracy. It accordingly became, and remains to the present day, one of the principal safeguards of democracy in Israel.

---

outward signs of respect for superiors; there is no word in Hebrew for "sir". A soldier genuinely feels himself to be the equal of his officer—indeed of any officer—yet in battle he accepts military authority without question. I cannot explain, I cannot begin to understand, how or why it works. All my own military experience in the British and American Armies has taught me that first-class discipline in battle depends on good discipline in barracks. Israel's Army seems to refute that lesson.'

CHAPTER III

Towards the
Sinai Campaign

Once the armistice agreements had been signed and large-scale
hostilities were over, a further re-organization of the army took
place. It had to be adapted to Israel's specific defence needs and
conditions in this new phase of her national existence. First, it
was soon realized that the expectation, indeed the assumption,
that the period of the armistice agreements would be a short,
intermediate period quickly terminated by peace agreements was
(as some Israelis, including myself, had feared from the start) an
illusion. The Arab governments made it clear, publicly and
repeatedly, that they would not sign peace agreements, would
retain a state of belligerency, would undertake a war of revenge—
the much publicised 'second round'—as soon as possible. Accordingly, they embarked on huge schemes of rearmament; and while
honouring those clauses of the armistice agreements which suited
them, they violated the rest, with the object of maintaining a mood
of belligerency without risking a large-scale war until they were
prepared. Consequently, the Israeli authorities were forced to
take appropriate measures in counter-preparation. The aim of
these preparations was to avert the threatened war; the means
was to build up a powerful military instrument which would deter
the enemy from attacking, or if a war should nevertheless take
place, would win it.

The new State undertook at the same time huge schemes for
the absorption of immigrants, economic development, and the
provision of advanced social services. Economic resources were
limited; manpower was needed for settlement and labour. Military
service was universally regarded not as an end in itself but as an
inescapable condition of survival. It was therefore wisely decided

to maintain as small a standing army as possible, consisting mainly of conscripts and a permanent skeleton of command with the requisite experts and technicians. The bulk of the armed services was to be composed of trained reservists, who were to be called up for training and exercises for a few weeks each year and in any emergency—thus becoming (according to General Yigael Yadin's apt definition) regular soldiers who happened to be on leave eleven months of the year.[1] Special arrangements were introduced to secure rapid and efficient mobilization. For further economy, a large number of the services, such as transport, engineering, medical aid and communications, were based on appropriate civil organizations ready to be mobilized whenever necessary; salaries, allowances and general expenses were kept as low as possible. As far as means of warfare were concerned, the Israeli forces were equipped with the best weapons that could be acquired abroad or produced at home, even though this imposed great economic hardships on the nation.

The conscription of women was an important step. With the exception of girls from orthodox religious families, almost every Israeli girl was required to serve in the army for a fixed period. Although some women entered combat units, the majority were assigned to office work and services, and to territorial and civil defence, thus helping to release more men for the combat units— a saving very important for a small nation chronically short of manpower. It also had a considerable social and moral value, in that it emphasized (among other things) that national service and sacrifice were the privilege of both sexes equally.

It was obvious that even if the Jewish population of Israel increased many times, it would always remain inferior in numbers to the huge and ever-multiplying Arab population in the sur-rounding countries. Thus the Israelis did not dare subscribe to the aphorism that God is on the side which has the largest number of battalions; rather, they adopted the view that, miracles aside, the stronger wins the war, and accordingly took the measures necessary to compensate for their numerical inferiority by steady improvements in quality, designed to yield in the end actual military superiority.

The first task was the qualitative improvement of the human

---

[1] To avoid placing an unfair burden on any individual employer, it was decided to pay employee reservists during their period of military service out of a central fund raised by a small levy on all employers.

material. Since a high proportion of the new immigrants came from Oriental countries in which most of the population was illiterate, it was obviously necessary to start by giving them the elements of a European education. The Army undertook to supplement the normal education they received in the schools by supplying a basic general and technical education, laying special stress on ideological education with a view to helping them understand the national and social aims of the State and the cause they were called upon to defend. Besides the needs of the new immigrants, there were also those of the veterans to provide for. Thus commanders who had had little time for study during previous long periods of service were encouraged to undertake courses of higher study, general and military, at home and abroad, at the expense of the Defence budget. On the purely military side, training both of the individual and of the unit was intensified with the particular object of developing high standards of technical knowledge as well as physical stamina and mental readiness for daring actions.

In a young army with a tradition of voluntary service, it was natural that the individual soldier should be treated from the beginning not as an anonymous number but as a distinct personality with his own individual gifts and weaknesses. Therefore, besides the common training and necessary drill he received, particular care was also taken to develop his personality and special gifts. This in fact amounted to a reversal of the old-fashioned sergeant-major's principle, that it was necessary to 'break the civilian' in order to make the soldier. The view held in the Israeli army was rather that to break the civilian recruit was to break the frame of the good soldier.

As new equipment was introduced, greater expertise and know-how became necessary. It was felt that while with luck the Israelis could acquire weapons and equipment equal in quality to those of the enemy, they could never equal the enemy's means of war in quantity; nor could they hope to acquire any weapons positively superior in quality. The gap therefore had to be closed by conspicuously higher standards of scientific, technological and technical know-how; by improved organization and logistics; by human courage, and by the kind of skill in strategy and tactics which sometimes reaches the point of virtuosity.

As to the equipment itself: once it was recognized that there was no hope of reaching a quantitative balance, it became obvious that to fill this part of the gap it was necessary to equip the troops with the best weapons (if their purchase was politically possible), or to modify older weapons by new, more efficient components—for instance, better guns on old tanks, and so on. A higher standard of maintenance services also contributed its share to the closing of the gap.

Israel's geo-strategic position was now, of course, much better than in the pre-statehood period. But compared with that of its Arab neighbours, it was still very poor. Although an integral part of the Asian continent on her western shore, Israel was in effect an island—without the strategic advantage of being surrounded by sea. On her land borders, she was completely surrounded by hostile countries. Her Mediterranean and Red Sea ports were highly vulnerable to sea-blockades and landings. With the exception of the northern Galilee and the southern Negev, which enjoyed a reasonable dimension of depth, the centre of the country, the coastal strip on the Mediterranean, and the Jerusalem Corridor were conspicuously lacking in strategic depth. At one crucial point the distance between the Kingdom of Jordan and the Mediterranean coast of Israel was no more than 10 miles. The coastal plain, where most of Israel's population and industry were concentrated, lacked hilly barriers; Jerusalem the capital was partitioned; and two hostile armies were stationed in the Gaza Strip and on the west bank of the River Jordan, both of which could be used as bridgeheads for raids and invasions in an overall plan of war. Eilat and its harbour, Israel's only gate to the Red Sea, to the Indian and Pacific Oceans, and to the countries beyond their shores, was perilously exposed. It was squeezed inside a narrow strip between Jordan and Egypt, and threatened with blockade from the Tiran Straits at the entrance to the Gulf of Akaba. The plain fact was that most of Israel's territory was within easy reach of the enemy's long-range field artillery, not to speak of air force bombardment or land-to-land and seaborne missiles.

Along the Syrian border in the north-east—the source of Israel's main supply of water—the Syrians enjoyed a marked topographic advantage by controlling the hills overlooking Israeli valleys and its principal fishing ground in the Sea of Galilee—one of the most important basins of food-production in the country. This geo-strategic situation might invite Arab strategists (like any other strategists) to think as they did in 1948, in terms of a simultaneous invasion from different directions designed to make the Israelis split their forces and lose the initiative. Modern military technology, moreover, might enable them not only to launch a simultaneous offensive but also to use the element of surprise to the furthest limit. Envisaging possible intervention by the United Nations or others, they might plan to decide the battle and establish a *fait accompli* in the first few days of fighting. The main military strength of the Arabs lay in Egypt; Israel's main geo-strategic weakness was in the coastal plain facing Jordan, which was the 'soft under-belly' of her posture. The greatest danger Israel faced was a co-ordinated, simultaneous surprise attack—a kind of Pearl Harbour: beginning with an attempt to annihilate her air force, and followed by a main effort to split the country into several parts by a combination of land attacks and landings on the coast; these actions being supplemented by guerilla attacks by paratroopers and irregulars, and accompanied by mass bombardments and air raids against the civilian population and industries as well as military targets.

These were the theoretical possibilities. Israel had to be prepared for the worst, and her expectation of the worst had to determine her counter-strategy. To begin with, her territorial defence had to be further developed. By establishing a planned network of fortified and well-equipped settlements along the borders and in the interior, along expected axes and passages, the country would be provided with strategic depth to compensate for its lack of natural depth. The participation of the settlers in the defence of their settlements and regions would help, now as before, not only to hamper a possible enemy invasion but to improve the general day-to-day security situation, safeguarding Israeli control of the remotest areas to the very borders of the country, and relieving the regular army of passive defence—thus leaving it free to move and concentrate wherever necessary.

This, however, was only part of the answer to Israel's geo-strategic shortcomings. One could not hope to deter an enemy or to win a war by defensive means only; and though the moral and political aim of Israel's strategy was self-defence, to achieve this her armed forces had to be prepared to take the initiative in carrying out decisive offensives in the event of any attack, but in particular surprise attacks from different directions.

This preparedness was to be achieved principally by a proper structure of the armed services and a suitable strategy for using them. Without ignoring Israel's long Mediterranean coast and the gulf and straits of the Red Sea she shared with Arab countries, and without overlooking the growing importance of her strategic air force and missiles, it could yet be claimed that the Israeli-Arab theatre of war was basically continental—that is to say, its decisive battles would be fought on land. This had been clearly recognized since the end of the War of Liberation. Thus when economic limitations compelled the Israeli forces to observe a strict order of priorities in the matter of expenditure, the land forces with their air support were given the first priority. It was for this reason, too—along with the desire to avoid inter-services rivalry and waste, and to achieve the maximum of co-operation, efficiency and coherence—that all the armed services with their particular commands were placed under a single Central Staff headed by an army general.

In the period following the War of Liberation, the arsenals of Egypt, Syria and Iraq, already stocked from Western sources, were heavily augmented as a result of arms deals with the Soviet Union and Czechoslovakia, and those of Jordan, Lebanon and Saudi Arabia by Western supplies of arms. The main beneficiary was Egypt; and within a relatively short period, she acquired large quantities of tanks, artillery, tactical aeroplanes, bombers and submarines, along with other important items. These supplies were followed by the arrival of Soviet instructors in Egypt and the dispatch of Egyptian and other Arab trainees to Eastern Europe, which introduced into the Egyptian armed forces Russian doctrines and methods of warfare: the mass concentration of long-range artillery and tanks closely supported by tactical air force, and the reliance on main efforts—backed by weight as well as big reserves—to break through the opponent's lines of defence and to destroy his armour.

This development forced the Israelis to go a step further in developing their own land and air forces. Greater stress was now put on armoured units, accompanied by good maintenance services (which could if necessary rapidly traverse long distances) and well-trained mechanized infantry closely supported by aircraft of the same quality as the enemy's (though less in quantity). A special armoured corps was accordingly formed, equipped with transport which would enable it to move rapidly from one end of the country to the other according to need. The paratroop unit was expanded, and received improved training and equipment. The need for effective anti-tank weapons, for the territorial defence of the country as well as the regular units, was given serious attention. The infantry brigade remained the biggest basic tactical unit; but there was a new development in the creation of a number of operational commands, each incorporating several brigades. This new type of command is perhaps best described as a very large task force (in Hebrew *ugda*) similar to a division in size but as flexible as a corps in composition. The regional (formerly the frontal) commanders remained the general commanding officers of the principal theatres.

It was considered on the whole desirable not to concentrate on a strategic air force and a large navy. To spend too much on these branches, important as they might be, would reduce Israel's resources for developing her land forces, which were considered the more vital. It was rightly thought that to try and have a little of everything would add up to nothing in the event of an all-out war. It was hoped that mass bombardment of the enemies' cities could be avoided on grounds equally of humanity and self-interest: in order to reduce civilian suffering to a minimum and to confine the battles to their proper place, the battlefield. An efficient tactical air force, on the other hand, would serve not only for air battles but also to support the ground forces, attack naval units, and carry out necessary bombardments of vital military targets. The navy was not to be used principally for control of the open sea or to protect convoys, but was to be confined to protecting the coast, launching small landings on the enemy's beaches, and carrying out special operations against maritime targets by light but powerful detachments with a great destructive capacity.

Israel's government had deliberately and explicitly renounced any aim of territorial expansion. It was consistent with this position, and also in her economic and military interests, that she should wish to spend as little as possible on armaments, especially in view of the need to invest a huge portion of her economic and social resources in the absorption of the flood of new immigrants and the development of a basically under-developed country. But though Israel never initiated the arms race of the 1950's, she had no alternative but to ensure that she did not lag behind whenever the other side acquired new weapons. In this period again, as in the past, the enemy forced the Jews to develop their armed forces in order to survive; and being forced to do it, they saw that it was well done. Yet the disparity, quantitatively speaking, remained; and the enemy's oft-declared desire to resume a large-scale war remained. Understandably, the horror of a surprise attack dominated Israel's attitude. Such an attack might not necessarily be successful, but the risk of its being so was great; and though it would have made things politically and diplomatically easier for Israel to let the enemy attack first, militarily she could not afford to do so, whatever the political cost, since the nation's very existence was at stake.

The danger of such a surprise attack hangs over Israel to the present day. During this period it was first recognized that one of the principal ways of meeting it was by a 'pre-emptive counter-offensive', or 'anticipatory counter-attack' as it was also called. This was not to be confused with a preventive war. A pre-emptive offensive was justified when it was known for certain that an actual invasion was about to take place, and when the proof of its imminence was a visible concentration of aggressive enemy forces. Just as every nation possessed the inherent right to use arms when attacked, so it had the right to intercept the attacker on his way to the chosen target. If the enemy did not intend war, it was his business not to make movements which would justify a pre-emptive counter-attack. If he did intend war, he could not justifiably protest if his intentions were thwarted. It could be argued, moreover, that the recognition of the right of pre-emptive counter-attack increased the persuasive power of the defender's deterrent and thereby diminished the possibility of hostile action. For the mere possession of armaments did not necessarily deter the enemy; it was the knowledge that the defender was ready to use them, promptly and effectively—that is, his 'credibility'— that might prevent their having to be used at all.

This was the doctrine that was soon to be put into practice in the Sinai Campaign of October 1956.[2] Meanwhile, it was fully recognized that pre-emptive measures were to be used with the utmost caution, indeed only if and when the enemy's aggressive intentions had been sufficiently attested. Thus, both to avoid falling victim to a surprise attack and to prevent over-hasty pre-emptive action, a first-class intelligence service had to be developed and linked to the various elements of Israel's defence forces already mentioned—its well-knit system of territorial defence, its highly mobile armoured corps, its tactical air force,

[2] I shall discuss the question of pre-emptive or anticipatory counter-attack again and more fully later in this book (see p. 73).

C

mechanized infantry, paratroopers, artillery corps, small but bold navy, efficient engineering, transport, ordnance, maintenance and supply services. And supplementing the intelligence service, a network of technical early-warning systems had to be established. The combination of all these resources, reinforced by the fullest unity of purpose between the armed forces and the nation, seemed to give Israel a reasonable hope of averting an all-out war, or if such a war should nevertheless take place, the necessary military superiority to win it against any single Arab army or all the Arab armies together.

All this while, a disturbing development had been taking place along all Israel's borders (with the exception of the Lebanese) which further affected her military outlook. It had become customary for Arab irregulars, semi-regulars and sometimes regulars, either under official direction or official toleration, to cross Israel's borders by night or sometimes even in daylight for such purposes as personal terrorism against civilians and soldiers, sabotage, robbery, theft and intelligence. The period between 1951 and 1956 witnessed a mounting number of infiltrations, assuming an increasingly serious character.[3]

No modern country can surround itself with a wall; nor were patrols and ambushes enough to put an end to such infiltrations. Israel's borders, as explained, were very long—unmanageably long for the size of the country. Settlements were scattered all over the country, some of them almost isolated; farmers and shepherds regularly worked in the fields edging the borders; fishermen, using strong lights, worked close to the Syrian positions on the Sea of Galilee. These conditions made it all too easy for the enemy to disturb life in Israel by the methods of terrorism. These actions were, of course, a direct consequence of the state of belligerency stubbornly maintained by the Arab governments. In many cases official announcements admitted that they were authorized operations. The Egyptian Government even went so far as to establish a special unit bearing the medieval name of *fedayeen*, which specialized in crossing Israel's borders for terrorist actions. At the same time the Egyptians, in violation of the Constantinople Convention of

[3] In 1951, 137 Israeli citizens were wounded or killed by these infiltrators; in 1952, 147; in 1953, 162; in 1954, 180; in 1955, 258.

1888,[4] the Armistice Agreements and the Security Council's decisions, closed the Suez Canal to Israeli navigation and to shipments on foreign vessels going to and from Israel. A blockade was also enforced on Eilat-bound vessels in the Gulf of Akaba.

These developments created severe problems of security and sovereignty for Israel. The number of casualties, civilian and military, was steadily growing; the destruction of property was likewise increasing; and a sense of helplessness and frustration was beginning to infect the people. Israel's inability to put an end to the infiltrations by passive means was interpreted by Arab commentators as a sign of military weakness; and this served to whet the enemy's appetite for more. It became irresistibly tempting to expand this small war, which was inflicting so much damage on Israel with so little risk to themselves.

The situation had become intolerable, and led in the end to the dynamic strategy of reprisals. A series of well-planned operations was carried out—usually at night, mainly by paratroopers moving on land—against enemy military bases and outposts, as well as police stations close to the borders. The targets chosen were generally in or around the areas where the worst effects of the infiltrations had been experienced. With the exception of one regrettable incident, in which Arab civilians were killed (at Kibya in Jordan), all the targets were strictly military.

The Israeli operations were for the most part completely successful. Once again, high standards of military performance were achieved; indeed thanks to better weapons they surpassed those attained in the past. The fact that most of them were carried out by the special force of paratroopers caused some bitterness of feeling among the regular troops; but these actions nevertheless became a model for all troops in the future. They gave a fresh opportunity to planners and commanders to put to the test the training, tactics and weapons of Israel's constantly developing army, restored confidence in the rank and file of the nation and in the army, and proved to the enemy Israel's ability to defend herself. In general, these raids helped to subdue most

---

[4] *Article* 1 states: 'The Suez Maritime Canal shall always be free and open, in time of war or in time of peace, to every vessel of commerce or of war, without distinction of flag. Consequently, the High Contracting Parties agree not in any way to interfere with the free use of the Canal, in time of war or in time of peace. The Canal shall never be subjected to the exercise of the right of the blockade.'

parts of the border, with the exception of the Egyptian. The fact that in most cases the Security Council condemned Israel's actions, even though they were undertaken in response to the enemy's provocations, encouraged the Arab governments to persist in this method of harassing Israel. It was resumed at repeated intervals; tension mounted again; the arms race on both sides gathered momentum, and this in turn further increased tension to the point of explosion.

Since my concern here is with the development of the Israel defence force and its doctrines, I do not propose to describe in any detail the Sinai Campaign of October 1956. Israel's reasons for embarking on this pre-emptive war may still be matter for dispute in some circles; what has to be recognized is that the decision was made in the light of an evaluation of the situation reached by responsible Israeli strategists on the basis of reliable intelligence reports. The blockade of Israeli navigation in the Suez Canal and the Red Sea, besides being a violation of international law, was in fact part of an all-out economic war against Israel—in particular the blockade of the port of Eilat on the Red Sea, without which the southern half of Israel (the Negev), where the natural mineral resources of the country are concentrated, could not be economically developed. The Egyptian-controlled *fedayeen* raids from Sinai and the Gaza Strip had reached alarming proportions and become a security problem of the first magnitude; and the Israeli counter-raids, though costly to the enemy, no longer had the power to deter them. The concentration of Egyptian forces in northern Sinai, very close to the Israeli borders, and their operational disposition appeared highly threatening, and an Egyptian all-out offensive seemed imminent. Above all, the conclusion of a military pact between Egypt, Jordan and Syria on 25th October, 1956 and the formation of a single united command under an Egyptian general, threatened Israel with a simultaneous invasion from three directions, which if carried out would have forced her to fight on three fronts.

The fact that Britain and France were at odds with Egypt created a favourable situation, politically and militarily, for Israel. I am certain, however, that the Israelis would have taken the initiative even in the absence of this favourable situation. I believe also that the outcome would have been the same, or

even better, without the British and French, though probably
at the cost of more casualties: a view now amply supported by
the outcome of the Six Day War.

The security situation sketched above had left the Israelis
with no alternative but to embark on a pre-emptive war as an
evil necessity. For the best chance of victory, a local military
superiority on the Egyptian front had to be ensured. This
entailed a concentration of sufficient striking forces on this
front—of armour, mechanized infantry, light reconnaissance
detachments, tactical air force, paratroopers, field artillery, and
the necessary maintenance, engineering, supply and medical
services—even at the expense of weakening other potential
fronts. This risk could be taken, however, thanks to the total
mobilization of the reserves, the strengthening of the territorial
defence system, and the retention of substantial mobile units in
the rear for use wherever necessary.

The element of surprise had to be exploited to the utmost, in
regard to the preparations, the front itself, and the timing and
method of attack. The Reserve was swiftly and silently mobilized:
rumours were put about that Jordan was about to be attacked,
while the major forces were in fact being assembled very near
zero hour at their starting-points on the Sinai border. A daring
landing of paratroopers deep into the interior of Sinai was
followed by a rapid crossing of land forces composed of armour
and mechanized infantry, aimed at out-flanking and as far as
possible crushing enemy formations, capturing vital ammunition
and armaments, and compelling the remaining enemy forces to
retreat with a view to achieving full control of the Sinai Peninsula
and the Gaza Strip as far as the Suez Canal. The primary object
was, of course, to eliminate the immediate danger of a large-
scale Egyptian offensive against Israel; a further object was
to have Sinai as a bargaining counter in peace negotiations with
Egypt if and when these should take place. The movement of
the land forces was accompanied by tactical bombing and
strafing of enemy air fields, lines of communications and military
bases, and was closely followed by a column riding southwards
to the entrance of the Gulf of Akaba—its object being to capture
the islands of Tiran and Samfier. This multiplex operation not
only took the enemy by surprise but helped to achieve decisive
gains even in this initial stage of the campaign. After this, the
excellence of the mobile maintenance services enabled the

armour and mechanized columns to move rapidly ahead, bringing the Israeli advance units to the eastern bank of the Suez
Canal within a hundred hours. But for the Anglo-French ultimatum[5] to keep off the Suez Canal, the Israeli forces could have
crossed it, and brought about the downfall of the Egyptian
regime.

It is doubtless true that the Anglo-French ultimatum, followed
by the bombarding of military installations on Egypt's mainland
and by landings in Port Said, helped to confuse both the Egyptian
High Command and its regional command, and made an
Egyptian retreat from Sinai to the Suez Canal the only rational
move. But the Egyptian forces in the Sinai Peninsula had in
fact lost the battle before the Anglo-French intervention; and
when they did the rational thing, it was already too late. The
Israelis' decisive victory in Sinai was successfully exploited,
leading (though not without local battles) to the capture of the
Gaza Strip and an Israeli hold on the entrance to the Gulf of
Akaba.

Although the war was conducted mainly on land, the maritime theatre did not remain idle. The small Israeli navy kept
off the Egyptian navy, and even succeeded in capturing, intact,
the destroyer *Ibrahim El Awal* in the northern waters of Israel's
Mediterranean coast.

Although the greater part of Israel's force was engaged on
the Egyptian front, it was within the military capacity of the
Israelis to hold back the Jordanians and the Syrians, not to
speak of the Lebanese, and to penetrate deep into their territories. This was fully realized by the enemy, and no move was
made by Egypt's allies on the other fronts in spite of the
Egyptian call for help. Indeed, it is reliably reported that when
the Egyptian Commander-in-Chief of the tripartite military
alliance realized that his allies would not move, he went so far
as to order them not to attack in the interests of self-preserva-
tion. This order was obeyed to the letter.

Reviewing the Sinai victory as a whole, I think it attributable
to those features of the Israeli armed forces which by 1956 had
become a military tradition: their unconventional approach to

[5] On the second day of the fighting an ultimatum from the British and
French governments was received by both Israel and Egypt, demanding the
withdrawal of their forces to a distance of ten miles from the Suez Canal. It
was rejected by Egypt.

war, their adaptability, their strictly functional attitude, their
conscious discipline and calculated courage—combined on the
one hand with an intelligent understanding of the principles of
war and on the other with the precious practical skill of being
able to fight by night as well as by day. This composition, reinforced by modern means of warfare and highly developed
logistics, could not indeed prevent mistakes and local confusions;
but as a whole it proved its battleworthiness in active combat.

The Israelis subsequently had to withdraw from all the areas
beyond the 1949 Armistice demarcation lines. This much-
debated withdrawal was carried out not because of military
weakness but under the political pressure of the United Nations
and the joint effort of the United States and the Soviet Union,
in particular the former. As in 1949, the Sinai Peninsula was
handed back to the defeated Egyptians without Israel's insisting
on a lasting peace in return: a peace which, in my view, was at
both times feasible. There were indeed overall gains to compensate up to a point for the losses. The Egyptian High Command
was forced to recognize that small guerilla raids might accelerate
into a big war, and a threatening disposition of forces provoke a
pre-emptive counter-attack; consequently they became more
careful. The *fedayeen* raids grew much less frequent, and
though a tremendous rearmament scheme was undertaken by the
Egyptians, for nearly eleven years they did not risk concentrating
their forces in a threatening manner. During the same eleven years
Israeli navigation in the Red Sea and the Gulf of Akaba continued to be free (though the Suez Canal, of course, remained
closed to Israeli ships); and even the completion of the National
Water Carrier from the Sea of Galilee to the Negev in 1965 did
not provoke a war, despite loud threats.

CHAPTER IV

Between Sinai and
the Six Day War

As in 1949 so again in 1956 the opportunity to reach a permanent peace settlement between Israel and her neighbours was lost. The victorious Israeli forces were withdrawn not only from the entire Sinai Peninsula but also from the Gaza Strip—even though in modern times the Strip has never been a part of either Egypt or Sinai. In return, Israel was granted three arrangements which were supposed to ensure her security and rights. These were: (1) a promise by Egypt to refrain from any hostile action against Israel, infiltration not excepted; (2) Egypt's consent to the presence of small units of the United Nations Emergency Force (UNEF) at strategic points along her long border with Israel, including Sharm-al-Sheikh at the entrance to the Gulf of Akaba; (3) a promise by the maritime nations to secure free navigation for all shipping, regardless of flag or cargo, through the Tiran Straits. No explicit, effective guarantees were given either by the United Nations or by the Great Powers that these arrangements would be observed by Egypt indefinitely. The only guarantee, so to speak, was the unilateral declaration by the Government of Israel that a blockade of the Tiran Straits would be considered by her as a *casus belli*, and that in case of a blockade she would consider herself free to react, by military force if necessary.

Soon afterwards Egypt made it clear that she would insist on retaining a state of belligerency, but stated, with commendable frankness, that she would refrain from attacking Israel until and unless she was assured of victory. This showed a two-fold realism on the part of the Egyptian Government. On the one hand, it observed the letter of the law: for nearly eleven years the Straits remained open, and no terrorist actions occurred along the Egyptian-Israeli border, even when other borders were subject to incursions. On the other hand, behind the thin UNEF line, Egypt energetically embarked on a huge rearmaments scheme based on Soviet supplies. This included an expensive effort to develop land-to-land missiles as well as less conventional weapons, such as chemical and radiological (as distinct from nuclear) warheads. It was clear that Egypt, as soon as she felt herself ready to strike, would either ask to have the UNEF removed, or would circumvent it. Meanwhile, the Egyptian Government was able to use the presence of UNEF in Sharm-al-Sheikh as an excuse to her own nationalist elements for keeping the Straits of Tiran open.

Along with a great economic and technical effort to build a superior army, including a large navy and a strategic air force, the Egyptian junta did its utmost to strengthen its influence in the Arab world by diplomatic means, subversion, and even direct military intervention (as in Yemen). It tirelessly argued the necessity for Arab unity under Egyptian domination, or at least the establishment of a unified Arab command over all the Arab armies in order to secure victory in a war of annihilation against the common enemy, Israel.

The other Arab countries, too, were not sitting idle. While Egypt and Syria enjoyed generous military supplies from the Soviet Union, Lebanon, Jordan and Saudi Arabia were supplied from Western sources. Iraq contrived to have it from both. For the first time, other Arab countries, particularly Algeria, showed an interest in the Middle Eastern conflict, supporting the Arab position in general and Egypt's in particular. The establishment of the unified Arab Command in 1961 headed by an Egyptian general was, in spite of its uncertain authority and frequent setbacks, a clear indication that in the next war (in contrast to 1956) Israel might be forced to fight on more than one front simultaneously.

These political and military developments in the Arab countries left Israel with no alternative but to continue, indefatigably, to build up her own military strength. During the decade 1956–66, and in particular in the second half of it, she made remarkable advances in the scientific, technological, economic, social and demographic spheres of her national life. Her military strength increased substantially, and her military doctrine and organization grew correspondingly more mature and more sophisticated. The doctrine rested upon the following crucial points: first, that

-C*

the long-threatened Arab war should if possible be averted; second, that if it did nevertheless take place, it must at all costs be won by Israel; third, that only an army capable of winning would have the power to deter; fourth, that the hope to deter depended not on military strength alone but on the credibility of using it at the proper time and in a decisive way; fifth, that Israel had to be prepared to face all her enemies on all her borders simultaneously; and, finally, that she had to be ready to do the job herself without any military help from outside.[1]

A war is composed of a series of battles. A battle is the clash of opposing military forces. A military force in battle is the sum total of its manpower, means of warfare, logistics, terrain and climate, leadership qualities and fighting morale. The outcome of war is usually a victory for the stronger side; and military strength is a function of a nation's military potential. This potential may be said to depend on five main elements. These are its demographic strength; its geo-strategic position; its economic resources; its political position and status in the international arena; and its social and political regime. A review of the relevant facts and figures at this time plainly showed that under the first four of these five headings the Arab countries enjoyed a definite advantage over Israel, whereas Israel could claim superiority on only one count—in the kind and quality of her social structure, system of government and moral values.

From the demographic point of view, Israel's two and a half million Jews had to contend with more than a hundred million Arabs in countries extending from the Atlantic to the Persian Gulf[2]. Geo-strategically speaking, Israel was a narrow strip of

---

[1] The rest of this chapter is based on my various writings and addresses on defence matters during this period, and in particular on an address entitled 'Active Defence for Survival' (subsequently published in the Hebrew quarterly *Molad*), which I delivered on 22nd February, 1967. I have deliberately preserved the original sequence and emphasis of my arguments, in order to bring out the close correspondence between the military doctrine developed during this period and the actual course of the Six Day War, which was soon —less than four months later—to supply brilliant and conclusive proof of the practical validity of the doctrine.

[2] The population figures at the time of writing (February 1967) were as follows : Egypt, 30.907 million; Syria, 5.600m.; Jordan, 2.145m.; Iraq, 8.440m.; Lebanon, 2.520 m.; Saudi Arabia, 6.990m.; Yemen, 5m.; Kuwait, 520,000; Algeria, 12.540m.; Libya, 1.738m.; Morocco, 14.140m.; Tunis, 4.560m.; Sudan, 14.355m. : Total, 109.455m. Israel's Jewish population was 2.350m.; and her non-Jewish population (Israeli Arabs, Druze, non-Arab Christians, etc.) was 314,700.

land, had its back to the sea, and was surrounded; the lands of the enemy, by contrast, formed a sub-continent.[3] Israel was a country desperately poor in natural resources pitting itself against countries possessing almost inexhaustible natural wealth: oil, big rivers, vast areas of arable land, about half of the world's hydro-carbon reserves. Both in its own region and in the larger world Israel was uniquely isolated. Apart from its bonds with world Jewry, it had no ethnic or religious links with any other nation (ironically, its only ethnic link is with the Arabs); and it had just one vote in the United Nations with which to meet the monolithic bloc-vote of its enemies.

The single element of military potential in which Israel indisputably had the advantage over her enemies was in her social system. To be a political and social democracy in the midst of backward patriarchial, autocratic or dictatorial regimes was by itself an advantage; and in its effects it counterbalanced, and in some aspects even outweighed, all the other elements put together. The political history of the Middle East had shown that a genuine democracy such as Israel's could command the loyalty of its citizens as the regimes of the Arab countries had never been able to do. It guaranteed (to begin with) their fullest mobilization, both physical and moral, in times of national crisis; it enabled Israel to give arms to each and every one of her citizens; and it ensured the qualitative superiority of her fighting forces, expressed in their fighting morale, in the qualities of leadership at all levels, and in the efficient use of military equipment. It was conducive to more stable government, and to a greater sense of unity and common purpose. It ensured a conspicuously higher level of general culture and education, of scientific and technological know-how, of basic physical health. Added to these (and also stemming from the democratic system, which involved every individual citizen in the common destiny) was the phenomenon already mentioned as a powerful binding force and motive for self-sacrifice—the sense

[3] The following are some of the relevant figures (again in February 1967):

Country	Land	Water per annum		
Egypt	1,000,000 sq. kms.	84,000 million cu. metres		
Iraq	438,000 sq. kms.	40,000	,,	,, ,,
Jordan	96,600 sq. kms.	689	,,	,, ,,
Lebanon	10,400 sq. kms.	3,000	,,	,, ,,
Syria	185,000 sq. kms.	29,600*	,,	,, ,,
Israel	20,000 sq. kms.	1,350	,,	,, ,,

* (Excluding the Euphrates, which yields several billion more.)

of 'no alternative' of a people fighting for its very existence, in
the clear knowledge that a defeat in war would mean its end as a
nation.

Israel's superiority in these vital respects enabled her at least
to narrow the huge gap between herself and her enemies in the
other military potentials. Israel's population was small, and its
standing army was minute compared with the great armies of
other nations. To compensate for this, it was able to keep a considerable number of reservists at a high pitch of preparedness by
regular and excellent military training; and it could count on
practically the whole population to bear the burden of various
aspects of any war effort. It lacked the dimension of depth in its
geography, so it had created strategic depth instead: it had a
highly developed territorial defence system, relying heavily on
civilian settlements (civilian but armed), and had developed a
strategy of initiative the aim of which was to carry the battle into
enemy territory. It tried to offset the deficiency of its economic
resources by cutting down on unnecessary spending, and by
laying down stringent priorities in military expenditure. It
attempted to reduce its isolation in the world of international
relations by endeavouring to win friends wherever possible.
Without neglecting its relations with the major powers, it laid
stress on establishing relations with smaller countries, and in
particular with developing countries in Asia, Africa and South
America. It had refused to impose on itself any rigid orientation
towards any given major power or block of countries, and had
avoided a state of dependence on any single ally.

Nevertheless, the initial superiority of Israel's enemies in four
of the five military potentials enumerated remained. Accordingly,
Israel had to be especially strict about three things: her order of
priorities, the quality of her army, her defence doctrine.

Taking the last first: in spite of striking improvements in the
territorial defence of the country, it was more than ever recognized
that to assume a purely defensive strategy that allowed the
enemy to choose freely his time, place and method of attack was
to expose Israel to the gravest of risks. The only answer to a
threatened attack was an overall initiative on the part of Israel,
if necessary a pre-emptive counter-attack, having as its object
the destruction of the enemy's forces. For reasons military and
political, any future war would have to be short and decisive. It
was assumed that the major battles would take place on enemy

soil, and that the Israeli armies should therefore advance as far as was needed to ensure the defeat of the enemy's armed forces, to establish a new strategic posture to meet further possible attacks, and to hold enemy territory until peace was achieved and permanent strategic boundaries fixed.

This, in bare outline, was the defence doctrine that emerged in the years following the Sinai Campaign. It invited a corresponding adjustment of various facets of the military organization: the order of priorities in the development of the several arms of the defence forces, the standard of military training and moral education, the emphasis on the courage and daring of the troops, both individually and collectively. All these were extended or intensified, in compliance with the revised doctrine. Furthermore, and in accordance with this doctrine, special stress was put on the development of the offensive and striking power of the Israel Defence Army; this affected every section of the armed forces.

Although the main theatre of war envisaged was to be on land, a swift military victory was unthinkable without air superiority. Accordingly, the tactical air force was expanded (at the cost of great economic sacrifices on the part of the nation), attaining new dimensions of size, firing power, flying height, flying distance and manoeuvrability. It developed into a multi-purpose force, capable of engaging in air combat, of attacking targets on land and sea, of giving close support to rapidly advancing land forces; it also performed various additional tasks, such as reconnaissance, transport, landing of troops (including paratroops), communications, ambulance work and rescue operations. The introduction of helicopters, in great numbers and of different sizes, was a valuable development; for they could be used to carry out many of these services, in particular the landing of troops and equipment behind the enemy's lines.

The armoured corps became the decisive branch of the land forces. It was expanded and improved accordingly: in the number of its tanks, their firing-power, their ability to cross unaccustomed terrain by day and by night, their manoeuvrability, and their staying-power. They became capable of breaking through solid defence lines, of outflanking, surrounding and crushing the enemy armour. Hardly less important was the development of the corps' maintenance services, which were brilliantly adapted to the needs of fast-moving tanks covering great distances without pause.

The infantry likewise grew in size and equipment. It became
highly mechanized, and trained to fight separately or in co-operation with the armour and air force. The same was true of the
field-artillery, which acquired better guns and became increasingly
mobile to match the speed of advancing ground forces. The
paratroop corps ceased to be a relatively small, select unit of daring volunteers carrying out commando-like operations. Although
it was still (like the air force) composed of volunteers, it grew
significantly in numbers and equipment, and became a first-class,
multi-purpose ground-force. It could still carry out commando
operations in small or big units; but now it could also fulfil the
tasks of an infantry in difficult sections of the fronts: parachutists
could be dropped behind enemy lines in large-scale operations, or
thrown into the heat of battle.

Similar advances were achieved in the navy. Heavy and expensive ships being ruled out for economic reasons, it continued to
develop its light, speedy craft, consisting of torpedo, artillery and
missile carriers, capable of intense as well as long-range fire. A
special naval commando unit was created, and a small number of
destroyers and submarines added. It relied mainly on speed, firing
power and daring: these together would enable it to attack enemy
vessels on the open sea, to defend Israel's coastline, to pin the
enemy navy down to its home harbours or to raid its bases.

The auxiliary units—armoury, engineers, signals, medical and
transport corps—were likewise developed, continuing to be based
as far as possible on the appropriate civilian services. They were
so organized as to be capable of rapid integration into the war-
machine. And in view of the new danger of mass bombardment
of population centres and military bases (including airfields) by
bombers and missiles, much serious attention was given to the
improvement of the anti-aircraft system and the civil defence of
the country. The anti-aircraft network acquired guns of different
calibres and land-to-air missiles, thereby contributing greatly to
the over-all strengthening of the military posture. Bomb-proof
shelters were built, especially in the exposed border settlements,
but also in the cities and towns: for it was recognized that in the
event of an air attack the whole country was equally vulnerable.
There were plans to have land-to-air missiles, and in due course
also anti-missile missiles; to acquire vertical take-off aircraft whose
bases are less vulnerable than long air-strips; and to develop the
capacity for rapidly repairing damaged military and air-field

installations. The principal defence, however, of the air fields and the civilian population alike, was to be in the over-all strategic plan: to put the enemy bomber units out of action at the very beginning of the war, and to keep enemy warships and rocket launchers at a safe distance from the coastal cities.

The decade under review and especially again the crucial last five to six years of it, produced a number of para-military or politico-military doctrines each of which played its part in the military thought of the period. The chief of these concerned: (1) interim arrangements with the Arabs, in particular non-aggression treaties; (2) preventive war; (3) the nuclear deterrent; and (4) the whole burning question (again) of 'anticipatory counter-attack', or pre-emptive war.[4]

There were people, including myself, who urged the view that there might be a third alternative between the stark 'either—or' of full peace treaties on the one hand and a shooting war on the other. There might be possible interim arrangements to be pursued in the absence of the peace we yearned for. The Arab governments (we argued) might be induced to enter into non-aggression treaties with us, which would provide for effective mutual inspection and control by mixed Jewish-Arab supervisory units equipped with the best means of communication to safeguard both sides from a surprise attack. Such treaties might be used either to reinforce the Armistice Agreements, or to replace them; and though they would not of course give us peace, they could help to prevent, or at least delay, another full-scale war; for once both sides had voluntarily relinquished the means of launching a major surprise attack, from the air or by land, they had in fact relinquished the possibility of launching any major attack at all. This idea, however, had to be abandoned as a wishful dream. As the decade advanced, it became clear that the tremendous stock-piling of arms by the Arab states, and by Egypt in particular, could mean only one thing: that they wanted non-aggression no more than they wanted peace; that what they did want was military superiority for another all-out war against Israel, under conditions ensuring an Arab victory.

We had at this time to contend also with a pessimistic view of our situation, which if allowed to prevail might have led us into

⁴ See p. 73.

fatal errors. It expressed itself in the cry, voiced both by experts
and by laymen, that time was against us. The population in the
Arab countries (it was argued) was increasing at a terrifying rate;
their standard of living was constantly rising; more and more of
their young people were receiving a secondary and higher education. In other words, a significant improvement in quality was
taking place in Arab society; before long, the Arab states would
catch up with us; and once quality was added to their numerical
superiority, their military power would be such as to enable them
to overcome and destroy Israel.

This was the pessimistic approach that might have led us into
error in one (or all) of three ways. We might have felt impelled
to start a preventive war; we might have been led to put our trust
in a major power guaranteeing our position; we might have been
tempted, out of fear and despair, to create a 'balance of terror'
on the model of the nuclear powers by the mutual deterrent of
nuclear weapons available to both sides.

My own view was that time was not necessarily against us.
Time by itself was by its nature neutral; what mattered was how
one made use of it. The enemy had indeed become stronger and
made impressive advances. But I was also convinced that we were
stronger than the enemy—relatively speaking, much stronger than
we had been in the two previous tests, in 1948 and 1956. Thus
up to now at least time had not been against us, and in the
immediate future it would not necessarily be against us for at
least two more generations. There was a close connection (I con-
tended) between social progress and development on the one hand,
and the power to apply rapidly developing scientific and
technological know-how on the other. The Arab social structure
might be advancing, but military technology was advancing much
faster. Therefore, to put ultra-modern, complicated weapons of
war into the hands of a backward society did not necessarily
signify an increase in military might. On the contrary, it might
prove to be an encumbrance rather than a help. And the rapid
increase of population in the Arab countries was obviously a curse
rather than a blessing, since the appalling conditions of poverty
into which the new generation of fighters against Israel was being
born precluded any conspicuous improvement in their quality.

I rejected the idea of a preventive war on both moral and
political grounds. It would be morally wrong (I argued) to precipitate a war as long as war could be put off without endangering

the State of Israel: there was always the hope, after all, that conditions might change and that a war could be avoided for many years if not for ever. A general Arab attack was a possibility, perhaps even a probability, but it was not a certainty; one should therefore do nothing to change this uneasy *status quo*. On purely political or prudential grounds, it would be an historic mistake for Israel to become involved in a war of aggression. She would lose friends throughout the world; and she might even find embargoes imposed on her, which would make it difficult to renew and replace her arsenal of war.

As for dependence on a foreign power for her security: Israel (I urged) must absolutely eschew such a policy. It was, of course, a good thing to have friends throughout the whole world, and especially among the major powers which wield influence and produce armaments. But while appreciating the friendship and goodwill of certain countries, Israel must in no circumstances let her existence be militarily dependent on any guarantees from outside—for several very cogent reasons. First, this would involve a dependence inviting political dictation as to ways and means of solving the Arab-Israel conflict, which might well rebound in our enemies' favour. Second, the guarantor power might not necessarily always be in agreement with us in evaluating the actual state of affairs. Third, in our day and age the outcome of a war was decided during the first few days, sometimes even in the first few hours; consequently our allies' help might come just too late to be of use. Finally, we lived in a do-it-yourself world, and the continued existence of our State depended on our own ability to defend ourselves unaided. I believed firmly that we were well able to defend ourselves without having recourse to outside military help, except for the supply of war materials.

Indeed, even in regard to war materials it seemed desirable to become less and less dependent on others. The achievements of our military industries showed plainly that the local production of war materials of high quality could be extended and intensified. In addition to its political importance and its value for national defence, such an effort would also promote our metal and science-based industries.

Concerning the nuclear balance of terror: the most widely held view, which I shared, was that given the choice between both sides having nuclear weapons to act as a mutual deterrent and both being prevented from laying hands on them, we should definitely prefer a balance of power kept by conventional armaments. Leaving aside the international and political implications of a situation in which nuclear arms were being developed by countries at present outside the 'nuclear club', it was felt that Israel would be exposed to a fresh danger of the utmost gravity if any Arab country got hold of nuclear bombs, irrespective of whether or not Israel herself possessed similar bombs for retaliatory purposes. The regimes of the Arab countries were militant, unstable and irresponsible enough to be capable of dropping the first bomb on almost any pretext. And there would be little consolation for the surviving remnant, huddled together in anti-radiation shelters, in the knowledge that they could engage in nuclear retaliation.

There was, however, always the danger that the enemy might eventually develop unconventional weapons, or be supplied with them by some nuclear power. It was therefore essential for Israel to follow closely developments in all the Arab countries, and in Egypt in particular, and at the same time to maintain a high standard of research and technology in the nuclear field on the lines pursued by the developed countries of the world. This was necessary in the first instance for the economic, scientific and political development of the country itself. But it is well known that nowadays the scientific and technological know-how of a country constitutes its potential for the production of nuclear weapons; and if Israel was not to be caught napping she had no alternative but to keep up her potential.

In this connection it had indeed to be recognized that it was precisely Israel's progress in the field of physics and nuclear science that might spur on the enemy to launch an air attack against her scientific institutes and nuclear reactors. This might be done under the pretext (addressed to world public opinion) that the object was only to prevent the introduction of nuclear weapons into the Middle East. And this was another reason why up-to-date conventional armaments were of the utmost importance to Israel: to enable her to defend herself against every kind of attack launched under any pretext.

The following, it was widely recognized, were the contingencies under which Israel would be entitled and even obliged to go to war:

1. when such offensive forces were being concentrated as to constitute a danger to Israel;

2. when it was clear that the enemy was preparing a surprise air-attack on Israel's air-bases;

3. in case of an air-attack, even localized, directed against our atomic installations and scientific institutions;

4. when guerilla warfare—the planting of land-mines and harassment shellings—reached such a point that passive defence and reprisals were unable to cope with it;

5. if Jordan should enter into a military pact with another Arab country and permit the concentration of alien military forces on her territory, and especially on the West Bank of the River Jordan;

6. if Egypt should close the Straits of Tiran.

Any one of these contingencies would constitute a *casus belli*, giving Israel the right to engage in a defensive war by methods, in theatres and at a time to be determined by herself.

The concentration of offensive forces had one aim only: aggression. The mustering of forces for an offensive was the first phase of the offensive itself, and was to be treated as such.

Air supremacy ensured the maximum chance of victory. The enemy air force would not be allowed to hit our air force on the ground. When the imminence of an air attack became apparent, either through intelligence sources or on the radar screens, it was to be forestalled, and the enemy air force was to be destroyed, if possible even before take-off.

Cairo, it was known, was acutely aware of our nuclear installations. The President of Egypt had fulminated against them on several occasions. One could not rule out the possibility of a daring sortie flown against them, accompanied by a declaration that Egypt aimed at destroying these installations and no more. It had therefore to be made clear that such a 'localized attack' would call forth an immediate general counter-attack. If this were understood, Egypt might think twice before attempting an adventure of this kind.

Guerilla warfare, sabotage, the shelling of border settlements, were all aspects of active belligerence. Israel was not obliged to toe the enemy line or play the game according to the enemy's rules of strategy and tactics. She reserved the right to act according to her own guidelines; and this included the occupation of territories if this were necessary to drive out the enemy from bases of aggression. If they knew that Israel might react in this way, they might stop. If they did not stop, it was up to Israel to make them: to put an end to acts of terror and sabotage.

As for Jordan, a glance at the map was sufficient to show Israel's grave vulnerability from that side. The territories occupied by Jordan on the West Bank of the River Jordan faced the 'soft under-belly' of the Israel defence lines. An offensive military force worthy of the name would try to cut Israel into two or three parts, as the opening gambit in a general offensive on a number of fronts. Jerusalem was a city divided, and its western part lived under constant threat. So did Eilat, at a stone's throw from Akaba, Jordan's Red Sea port. What all this implied was clear. As long as Jordan respected the Armistice Agreement, no harm would befall her. If, however, she joined a warlike coalition against Israel and permitted other Arab armies to enter her territory, Israel would have no alternative but to turn the West Bank from a potential wedge against herself into a grand trap for the enemy forces.

The Straits of Tiran had repeatedly been the subject of declarations by the government of Israel, which had said clearly and emphatically that blocking the Straits of Tiran would be considered tantamount to an act of war calling for an Israel reaction. In my book *Curtain of Sand* I had explained that the closing of the Straits of Tiran to Israel shipping was to be regarded as 'an act of open warfare,' and that 'from the point of view of vital strategy Israel must not undertake to engage in defensive warfare "linked" to a given theatre of war (such as the area of the Straits of Tiran) or to any given date (such as the actual date of the blockade) chosen by the Egyptian ruler. For he would obviously attempt to lay down the time and place most convenient to himself and unfavourable to Israel. There is no greater mistake to be made than to permit the enemy to dictate the emplacement of the action, its timing and therefore its method.'[5] Closing the Straits of Tiran was not a local action inviting a merely localized reaction. It amounted to a declaration of war, which permitted Israel to lay down the place, the scale and the zero hour for her action.

The third chapter of *Curtain of Sand* is called 'A Country with its Back to the Sea Wall.' In this chapter I describe in some detail the methods (already touched on earlier in this book) by

---

[5] *Curtain of Sand* (Hebrew title: *Masach shel Chol*), Israel: Kibbutz Hameuchad (1960), p. 348. This and subsequent references are to this edition of the book.

which an enemy might carry out a sudden surprise attack. To recapitulate, it would consist of the following stages:

1. an air attack on the Israel air force while still on the ground;

2. a simultaneous offensive on several fronts, carried out by land forces enjoying superior air support;

3. landings of marines, either to harass and pin down forces or else as part of a grand invasion; putting guerilla bands into action, dropping parachutists and landing marines behind the lines, with a view to causing maximum disruption and chaos and cutting off communication lines;

4. air raids and shelling from the sea, directed against civilian centres and industrial areas.[6]

This or a similar way of opening hostilities would aim at establishing a number of *faits accomplis* before Israel had had time for a general mobilization, and 'before a ceasefire is called for—if it is called for at all—by international intervention.'[7]

Israel's only way of saving herself from such a surprise attack was to maintain her military readiness and her moral title to carry out an anticipatory counter-attack. This is how I defined the term 'anticipatory counter-attack': 'Israeli operational initiative taken against concentrations of enemy forces, and the occupation on enemy territory of targets having a vital security significance, at a time when the enemy is mustering his forces for an attack but before he has had time actually to start his offensive.'[8]

It had been argued that there was some sort of *contradictio in adjecto* between the words 'anticipatory' and 'counter-attack'. Could one speak of a counter-attack in respect of an action initiated at a time when the attack itself had not yet taken place? The contradiction (I maintained) was a purely verbal one, and as such apparent, not real. The realities of the situation were that the enemy was concentrating his forces with an attack in view, that such preparations for an offensive were an integral part of the offensive itself, and that the enemy was bent on securing mastery of the air by an attack on Israel's air force while it was still on the ground which, if successful, would at one stroke paralyze Israel's whole defence structure and expose her to total defeat. Given this situation, it could surely not be doubted that

[6] *Curtain of Sand*, pp. 61–62.

[7] *Ibid*, p. 60.

[8] *Ibid*, p. 73.

both from the moral and from the political point of view Israel
was entitled, indeed called upon, to wrest the initiative from
the enemy.

As all the world knew, it was Israel that desired peace and the
Arab countries who stubbornly insisted on maintaining a state of
belligerency. Israel could not allow them to have their cake and
eat it: to build up and concentrate offensive forces against her in
the name of their state of belligerency, and at the same time to
expect her to behave towards them as if there were peace. As it
was Israel's very existence that was at stake, it was her duty to be
prepared, both militarily and morally, to take an anticipatory
initative whenever the need should arise, even in the face of
United Nations condemnation. Every effort should indeed be
made to convince the world body and world public opinion of the
vital necessity of such an initiative, if and when it should arise.
But there could be no question of Israel's waiting for the consent
of the world before it acted. While she waited, she might be destroyed; and the world's approval would then be tragically
gratuitous.

In an anticipatory counter-attack, one would aim first and
foremost at air superiority. This was to be achieved by destroying
the enemy air force and its installations on the ground. One would
then aim at breaking the concentrations of land forces, and taking
up suitable positions on enemy territory to prevent a resumption
of the aggression. These would also serve as bargaining points in
any future peace negotiations and frontier demarcations.

It was impossible to lay down hard-and-fast rules as to how
much in advance of an anticipated attack the Israeli action should
be deployed. In general, the enemy should be left to concentrate
his forces for as long as possible so as to give Israel the best chance
of destroying the major part of his army. I venture to quote again
from the more detailed account in my book: 'An anticipatory
counter-attack is to be launched sometimes months ahead, sometimes weeks ahead, and sometimes even just a few days before the
expected enemy attack, in order to ensure a turning of the tables.
When there is no other way out, it may be necessary for the
Israel forces to forestall the invaders even by a few hours: the
vital thing is to forestall.'[9]

This was the case for a pre-emptive or anticipatory counter-
attack. Its obverse side was the avowed duty never to resort to an

[9] *Curtain of Sand*, p. 76.

action of this kind unless and until the absolute necessity for it had been established beyond reasonable doubt, and having been established, had also been subjected to the most serious political scrutiny. To recapitulate: the difference between an anticipatory counter-attack, which on the operational level is an offensive action but morally speaking a defensive action, and a preventive war, which is an act of aggression not only operationally but also morally, is that the anticipatory counter-attack is determined by either (a) an actual, visible, tangible mustering of enemy forces for an offensive operation, or (b) a radical deterioration in the whole security situation as a consequence of the enemy's violations of his obligations. It was obviously imperative not to interpret every movement of military forces as a mustering of forces for a real attack, nor to treat every bragging, sabre-rattling impudence uttered by a demagogue in power as a declaration of war. It might be difficult, but it was not impossible, with the help of efficient intelligence services such as Israel possessed, to distinguish between the massing of forces for an attack and, say, divisional man-oeuvres, or one further move in a war of nerves. These were the discriminations that Israel was required to make, with a constant, tireless vigilance, if she was to sustain her right to engage in anticipatory counter-attack when there was no other way of ensuring her survival.

CHAPTER V

The Six Day War

The policy of the Israel Government had been to prevent war, either by means of interim agreements or by the deterrent power inherent in the military strength of the Israel Defence Forces. In the event, this policy proved futile and abortive. The enemy apparently did underestimate the military power of Israel, her state of preparedness, and her readiness to *use* that power in an offensive strategy. He therefore proceeded with a series of provocations which forced Israel's hand and made it imperative for her to deploy her full military might.

It seems that as from mid-May 1967 every possible Rubicon was crossed by the Governments of Egypt, Jordan, Syria and Iraq. And having crossed, they had no way out: a military confrontation had to take place. Impressive Egyptian forces were massed in the Sinai peninsula. The Straits of Tiran were closed to Israeli shipping. Jordan entered into an aggressive military alliance with Egypt, throwing her borders open to Egyptian and Iraqi troops and putting her own military forces under Egyptian command, as well as concentrating armour on her West Bank. The Egyptian President admitted, with astonishing frankness, that all these preparations were directed towards a war of extermination against Israel.

The successive phases of the May crisis constitute a remarkable object lesson. They show how easy it is to slide down the slippery slope to war. It all began when the Syrians claimed that Israel was massing military forces in Galilee and preparing to invade Syria. The Soviet Union took up this totally unfounded claim. Not only did the Russians hurl groundless accusations at Israel; they actually counselled the President of Egypt (according to his own testimony) to concentrate armour in the Sinai peninsula, so as to deter Israel from her alleged nefarious intentions in the North by the menace of a second front in the South.[1]

The Soviet Union knew of course that Israel had not the slightest intention or plan to invade Syria. When the Soviet Ambassador in Israel was invited by the then Prime Minister and Minister of Defence, Mr. Eshkol, to join him in a tour of Galilee and the border areas to see with his own eyes that there were no concentrations of military forces in those areas, he declined the invitation. He needed no proof of something he already knew perfectly well. What the Russians feared, it seems, was massive Israeli reprisals against Syria, in retaliation for Syrian provocations—their countless acts of sabotage and shelling of border settlements. They were afraid that such reprisals might topple the Baath regime in Damascus, which was especially favoured by the U.S.S.R. That apparently is why the Soviet Union spurred on the ruler of Egypt, urging him to concentrate military forces in the Sinai peninsula as a deterrent, even though they knew this was to risk a confrontation between Israel and Egypt.

Much publicity and ostentation accompanied the Egyptian military moves. The Egyptian leaders found themselves greatly encouraged by the strong impression these made on the home front and throughout the Arab world. They were swept forward to make one further move. They demanded that the commander of the United Nations Emergency Force (UNEF) drew back his troops, thus removing the barrier between the concentrations of Egyptian forces and the borders of Israel. The U.N. Secretary-General's reply was to ask Egypt to choose: the UNEF were either to stay at their posts as heretofore, or else to be completely withdrawn. To a man like Nasser, consumed with the passion for prestige, this was an irresistible challenge. He had to take it up. His bluff having been called, he bridled at the implied taunt, and plunged head-long into an unpremeditated move. On 18th May he demanded the total withdrawal of the UNEF. Secretary-General U Thant responded with an immediate order for the withdrawal of the body. The precipitate action taken by the Secretary-General wiped out in one stroke all the elaborate arrangements made in 1957. At that time it had been made a condition of the Israel

[1] By 9th May the Secretary-General of the United Nations had ascertained from his own forces on the ground that no Israeli troop concentrations existed, and this fact had been directly communicated to the Syrian and Egyptian governments.

withdrawal from the Sinai peninsula that the thin blue UNEF line should stand between Israel and Egypt. Unbridled ambition then further overcame the clever politician in Nasser. It goaded him into announcing (on 21st May) the closure of the Straits of Tiran to Israeli shipping, although he knew very well that Israel regarded a blockade of Eilat as an act of war entitling her to engage in counter-action.

Apprehensive about possible Israeli reactions, Nasser bolstered his forces in Sinai with further motorized infantry and armour divisions, and alerted his air force and navy. The concentration of Egyptian forces became a menace *per se*. Israel's anxiety increased. She was evidently facing more than an attempt on her freedom of navigation; there was a real danger of an imminent invasion of her territory. The Arab rulers, with Nasser first and foremost among them, had been promising this for a long time. The tension in Israel mounted with the growing flood of violently threatening speeches and broadcasts—heard and seen by millions outside Israel on the television screens of the world—by official Egyptian spokesmen and leaders.[2] The Government of Israel found itself compelled to proceed to a general mobilization of the Reserves.

The King of Jordan saw that Israel preferred, at this stage, to resort to diplomatic means and to consider all possible solutions before resorting to armed force. He also saw the tidal wave of the soaring prestige of the Egyptian President threatening to engulf the thrones of the hesitant. So he flew to Egypt and on 30th May signed a military pact with Nasser. He subordinated his army to the Egyptian High Command. He put his country at the disposal of Iraqi, Egyptian and Palestinian units preparing to invade Israel.

In point of fact, the Arab armies as a whole and the armies of Egypt in particular were far from ready with their programme of reorganization, and were thus actually unprepared for a confrontation with their enemy. A substantial part of the Egyptian army was bogged down in the Yemen. It appears, then, that there was a considerable element of gamble and wishful thinking in the Egyptian moves, supplanting cool strategical thinking. The crisis that led to the brink of war, and finally to war itself, was thus a fortuitous process of slipping down a slippery slope, rather than a series of soberly thought out steps planned by the Government of Egypt. In the light of subsequent events, it is almost appalling to

[2] On 25th May Cairo Radio announced: 'The Arab people is finally resolved to wipe Israel off the map. . . .'

recall how far wrong the Egyptian ruling junta went in assessing the situation. They made light of Israel's strength, notwithstanding her victories in the past. They overestimated their own power in spite of the ignominious defeats they had experienced, not only in their wars against Israel but even in their clash with tribal warriors of the Yemen.

Each and every one of the steps taken by the enemy would on its own have constituted a sufficient cause and justification for Israeli military counter-measures. All of them together certainly did. Blockading the port of Eilat was a warlike act. It not only gave Israel the freedom to act, but made it incumbent on her—in order to counter Egyptian aggression and to preserve her very existence—to lay down where, when and how the main action was to take place. No sovereign state capable of defending itself (and certainly none of those who counselled moderation and exhorted Israel to hold her hand) would have tolerated an arbitrary blockade of any of its ports, or would have hesitated to resort to arms to break such a blockade.

The enemy's openly declared intention of launching an attack from the Sinai peninsula and the concentration of offensive forces therein was tantamount to the first phase of an attack. Once those forces had been marshalled, air, land and up to a point also naval initiative by Egypt and her allies became an imminent possibility. In view of her own geo-strategic position, her limited resources, the smallness of her numbers, and the terrifying vulnerability of her towns and cities, Israel dared not let the enemy have the advantage of operational initiative on top of all his other advantages. Not to have wrested the initiative would have been, in the strict, literal sense of the word, suicidal. The gravity of the situation increased when it became evident that Arab air and land offensives might be launched simultaneously on three fronts: the Egyptian, Jordanian and Syrian, and at a later stage also the Lebanese. When Egyptian and Iraqi troops were integrated into the Jordanian geo-strategical set-up on the West Bank, the die was virtually cast. Those who brought about this confrontation must have known that they were issuing a challenge to war.

Even at this late stage, however, war might still have been averted had there come forward some competent international authority capable of persuading Egypt to agree to a gradual de-escalation of the build-up of military forces, to the re-opening of the Straits of Tiran, and to an undertaking that acts of infiltra-

tion and terrorism would cease. But no such initiative was forthcoming, and war became inevitable.

There were no doubts as to the respective priorities of the
various operational theatres and as to the main efforts to be
deployed. The doctrines and plans of warfare had been thoroughly
hammered out, and were complete to the last detail. Up-to-date
information about the military set-up of the Arab states, about
their positions and intentions, was available to Israeli intelligence.
The Israeli military forces could therefore adapt their plans in
accordance with those of the enemy.

On the recommendation of the Prime Minister and Minister of
Defence, the Government of Israel instructed the Chief of Staff,
General Rabin, to proceed with a virtually total mobilization of
the Reserves. The two armies faced each other on all the fronts,
with priority rightly going to the Egyptian front, where the
largest of the Arab armies, entrusted with the leadership of the
Arab hosts, was concentrated.

Of great importance was the swift and practically complete
mobilization of the Defence Force of Israel, for the dual purpose
of discouraging the enemy attack and of repulsing it, should he
move forward. The Israeli forces were thus ready to take over
the initiative in any one of three ways: by an anticipatory counter-
attack (the way obviously preferred); by a concurrent counter-
attack; or even (if there were no other way) by a repulsing counter-
attack.

Militarily speaking, the situation was both extremely serious
and completely clear—that is, free of obscurity. It was quite certain that the Arab armies had mustered to attack Israel, even
though they were not yet quite ready. The Arab air forces were
on the alert, planning to fly grand surprise attacks against the Israel
air-force bases. They intended to catch the Israeli planes on the
ground, having never been over-keen on meeting them in mid-air.
Then there was to be invasion on land and shelling from the sea,
with Arab air cover from a position of superior strength.

In my opinion, the Israel Defence Force should have attacked
when the enemy concentrated the major part of his forces in Sinai,
but had not yet time to deploy or organize them properly. That
was the right moment for smashing the enemy forces with a
minimum of losses on our side.

But at this stage political consideration blurred the picture. In 1957 Israel withdrew from Sinai and Gaza on the understanding and universal expectation that the maritime powers would guarantee freedom of passage for shipping through the Straits of Tiran[3]. In the circumstances that arose in May 1967, the Government of Israel decided to postpone military reaction to the Tiran blockade until a special diplomatic effort had been made to ascertain whether the maritime powers were ready to stand by their obligations and open the Red Sea Straits. To my mind, this was a mistake, both politically and militarily. Freedom of navigation had become a secondary consideration. The concentration of offensive forces in Sinai and the subsequent entry of Jordan into the military pact had become the crucial challenge. It is very doubtful whether the maritime powers would actually have attempted to force Egypt to lift the blockade of Eilat. But it is quite certain that they would not have sent any military force whatever to help Israel in the Sinai desert. In the light of subsequent events, it can truthfully be said that the Israel Defence Force was in no need of any help, except for the shipment of armaments and spare parts. It was also perhaps natural and understandable that none of the maritime powers should wish to be involved in an action that might cast on them the suspicion of having acted in collusion with Israel; they could not therefore be expected to give a clear, unambiguous endorsement to any Israeli initiative. The diplomatic feelers put out to the leaders of the Atlantic powers did, however, invite them to exert pressure on Israel—to refrain from any military move, to display patience, and so forth. All this made for unnecessary and dangerous delays. It was, of course, quite right that Israel's position should be explained in the Western capitals: but the proper time to do this was immediately after the war had started.

Even supposing that an international fleet had reached the Red Sea, this in itself would have had no effect on the land and air fronts. On the contrary, it is not unreasonable to assume that, in anticipation of the arrival of such an international expeditionary fleet, the Arab High Command might have put forward the date of its attack on Israel in order to establish a *fait accompli* before the arrival of the fleet—which would thus have found itself overtaken by events.

[3] See p. 60.

The Soviet Union took a wildly anti-Israel line, ignoring completely and in bad faith all the facts of the case. The three friendly Western powers, each in its own way, gave out counsels and pleas for moderation. Each one in its own manner and style entreated Israel to wait for 'the first Egyptian shell.' Certain friends, in undoubted good faith, even suggested that Israel should dispatch a trial ship through the Straits of Tiran—then, if Egypt really blocked its way by firing on it, this would 'constitute an excellent *casus belli* and open the way for Israel to launch a general attack on Egypt.'

Israel could not afford to listen to any of these proposals. She could not wait for something to turn up—not even an illusory international fleet. She could not wait for a major Egyptian attack before launching her counter-attack: since wars nowadays do not start with a 'first shell' but with a major air attack, this might have proved fatal. And Israel could certainly not wait for a ship stopped at Tiran to constitute the *casus belli* or zero hour. The declaration of a blockade is as good a *casus belli* as a ship actually stopped. Besides, it is quite probable that the Egyptian high command, seeing through such a stratagem, would have refrained from attacking this isolated ship and instead launched its full-scale offensive against Israel as outlined above. Thus to wait for an Israeli ship to be stopped in Tiran would have been tantamount to instructing the Israel Chief of Staff to send a cable to his Egyptian counterpart informing him of the exact date and time of the beginning of operations.

Once more, as in the past, the enemy helped us out of our quandary. He provided Israel with more than a first shell by embarking on murderous shellings of settlements bordering on the Gaza Strip: these began on 2nd June. He also moved heavy armour in the direction of the Negev, probably with the intention of cutting it off as a preparatory step to the conquest of Eilat in a pincer movement from Sinai and Akaba (thus confirming the futility of any attempt to open the Straits for shipping), and in order to effect at last the much sought-for territorial link-up of Egypt and Jordan. And as if all this were not enough, the Egyptian air force engaged in suspicious activities, quite clearly visible on Israeli radar screens. Coming on top of all the other warlike manifestations and activities, they added up to an indication of imminent attack.

The Defence Forces of Israel were drawn up and ready. The general mobilization was complete except for a few reserve units. Training and logistics, fighting morale and the mettle of the officer corps were superb.

For over five years, in my capacity as a member of the Cabinet Defence Committee, I had been taking part in regular consultations attended by the Chief of Staff, in which military theory and doctrine, as well as the order of priorities and the set-up and equipment of the forces, had been discussed and laid down. From the period leading up to the war, during the war and thereafter I served as a member of the Prime Minister's inner advisory defence committee. I was privileged to watch at close quarters the smooth and total dovetailing of defence doctrine, strategic planning, and the field operations that executed them. A few changes and modifications here and there were introduced on the eve of battle, some for better and some for worse. But apart from these, the whole campaign unfolded according to the moves laid down by the doctrine.

The first phase of the war was marked by an understandable desire to avoid another front. Diplomatic efforts were made through General Odd Bull, the head of the United Nations Truce Supervision Organization, to dissuade King Hussein from joining issue. But the genius presiding over the destinies of the Jewish people must have willed otherwise, ordaining the liberation of the Cis-Jordan Land of Israel and the creation of an undivided Jerusalem. The Jordanian king jumped onto the Cairo bandwagon, lured by the mendacious 'Voice of the Arabs' communiques recounting fictitious Egyptian victories. It therefore became apparent, practically from the start, that there was to be war on three fronts (Egypt, Jordan and Syria), with a reasonable chance of Lebanon's keeping out unless things went against us.

Sinai presented the main danger in point of military force; Jordan's threat was geo-strategic; Syria's that of her harassing power. The principal effort was therefore rightly directed against Egypt, which had the largest forces in the air, on land and on sea, and claimed to be the Arab overlord in war. The possibility of a strategic surprise had been sacrificed, for the opposing armies were already fully on the alert. The only form of surprise still possible was on the operational and tactical levels—in the field, in the theatre of war.

Egyptian forces were drawn up, at the ready. Their grand

offensive could be launched at a moment's notice. The Egyptian war-machine had been put into gear. Israel could no longer afford to leave the initiative in Arab hands: she had to 'counter-attack' in anticipation. From the legalistic point of view, this was a counter-attack because the Egyptians had already opened hostilities on a local scale. However, since they had not yet managed to cross the border and develop their large-scale offensive, the Israeli operation could be properly described as an offensive in anticipation of an imminent invasion.

Supremacy in the air was obviously the key to victory, although it would not by itself ensure victory. Our air force was able to surprise the Egyptian air force, even though we had long since lost the advantage of strategic surprise.

The surprise was complete, both operationally and tactically, thanks to the initiative, resourcefulness, daring and technical skill displayed by all ranks. The first blow put enemy bombing squadrons and fighter groups, air strips and all essential equipment out of action. In less than three hours, at the very beginning of the campaign, the Egyptian air force ceased to exist as an effective instrument of war. In its wake followed the Jordanian air force, after which the Syrian and Iraqi air forces were heavily hit at bases relatively close to Israel. It is worth mentioning that the Israel air force managed to surprise not only the Egyptian air force (the first victim of the Israeli operational initiative), but also the air forces of Jordan, Syria and Iraq, which were attacked only several hours after zero hour.[4]

Israel gained superiority also in the very few air battles that occurred. Except for a few light and ineffective sorties, Egyptian bombers did not appear in Israeli skies. The civilian population was several times hurried into shelters, but was in fact practically sealed off from all real danger by an air umbrella, and thus preserved from the horrors of bombing and strafing from the air. Further reservists were called up—without any interference from the skies. Israel industry came through unscathed, and production lines remained undisturbed. Transport in the civilian rear, to the front and at the front itself, continued without a hitch. The land forces engaged in battle without the fear of deadly air attacks, and could even count on effective air support against their

---

[4] Since the bulk of the enemy air force was hit on the ground, most of his fliers were unhurt. Restoring it to pre-June 1967 strength has therefore been only a matter of supply (replacement of the aircraft lost) and not of training.

objectives. Transport, supply, intelligence, rescue-behind-the-lines and ambulance shuttle-service operations were fully carried out. The Israel Air Force established new international records in its operational achievements both as a force and in its individual performances. This war also marked the first large-scale appearance of helicopters in the field.

The Sinai peninsula can serve as a buffer zone between Egypt and Israel, as a spring-board for an Egyptian attack on Israel, but also as a trap for the forces massed in it for such an attack. It all depends on the strategy of the opposing forces. Since 1957, when the Israeli forces withdrew from Sinai and the Gaza Strip, returning them to Egyptian rule, there had indeed been some rebuilding of Palestinian-Egyptian forces in the Strip and of fortifications of land and air bases in Sinai. Except in the Gaza Strip, however, no considerable military force had been concentrated in Sinai, which thus served as a buffer zone that might one day be put to use as a spring-board for a renewed Egyptian invasion of Israel. Now that the larger part of Egypt's armour and infantry mustered for the attack was concentrated in Sinai, it had become a convenient base for an invasionary army of a size never before witnessed by that desert. It was therefore up to the Israel Defence Forces to turn the Sinai spring-board into a major trap for the Egyptian army.

The task was admirably accomplished by the three armoured divisions of Southern Command. The whole Egyptian army concentrated in Sinai was put out of action by those three divisions, a combination of armour, motorized infantry, and paratroopers acting mainly as a crack infantry force, ably assisted and supported by mobile artillery, air-force units, a resourceful engineering corps, armaments personnel trained for acting in the closest co-ordination with the advancing forces, medical officers and orderlies in the very line of fire, and even cultural and entertainment units moving along with the army.

The Israel land forces, and especially the armour and the infantry, also contrived to make up for the loss of the element of strategic surprise by pulling off a series of operational and tactical surprises. The classical strategy of the indirect approach was carried out in exact accordance with the rules, except in so far as initial break-through actions on a grand scale—on three

D

different axes, in the north, the centre and the south of the Sinai peninsula—preceded the outflankings, the surroundings and the barrings of mountain passes in the rear on all the battle fronts.

The axes constituting parallel roads from the Negev to the Suez Canal are separated by some very difficult terrain, practically impassable for armour and motor vehicles except at a few spots. This geographical factor enabled the fast-moving columns of the Israel Defence Forces to concentrate on the main targets since it saved them from having to dissipate their forces by detailing large units to guard their flanks. They had the advantage of operational initiative, and geography was on their side too, not only freeing them from anxieties about their flank but also disrupting any possible communication lines of the enemy, whose units were cut off from one another along those three axes.

Their powerful thrust, their intensive and effective fire and the swiftness of their advance through difficult terrain (some of it hitherto considered impassable) enabled the land forces, with their air support, to break all records in reaching the mountain passes to the enemy's rear, thus cutting off his retreat to the Suez Canal and to Egypt, making the destruction or capture of most of his war material inevitable, and completely routing his army.

The Gaza Strip had no hope of holding out in view of the rapid process of destruction overtaking the choice Egyptian army formations. The fact, however, that the planned assault on the northern part of the Strip and especially on the town of Gaza had to be delayed robbed the Israel Defence Forces of the surprise element even on the tactical level and certainly on the operational level. For this reason the battle there raged more fiercely than had been expected.

The victory itself—its scale and the speed with which it was achieved—had been anticipated almost to the last detail in the plans of the general staff, the air force, the Southern Command and divisional commands. This perhaps is the most striking proof of the excellence of the overall planning and leadership which made the victory possible.

When the Israel Defence Forces reached the eastern bank of the Suez Canal and took possession of it, Cairo was shaken with the fear that they would cross the Canal and reach the capital itself. It was this fear that induced the Egyptian government to assent, on 8th June, to a cease-fire.

The Jordanian and Syrian fronts had been considered of secondary importance when the war began. But once the Egyptian air force had been reduced to impotence and Jordan and Syria had opened hostilities against Israel, the Israel Defence Forces were bound to turn their attention to these two fronts. One may wonder how the Israeli army was capable of launching an attack against Jordan when it was still fighting hard in Sinai. Were not the Israel forces stationed on the Jordanian and Syrian fronts much too small to attempt an offensive with any reasonable chance of success?

Our forces on these two fronts were indeed small—too small to be able to afford defensive action and tactics. They had to attack. They had to force the enemy into defensive positions. The very smallness of their numbers dictated an offensive strategy, in order to turn the tables: to put the enemy on the defensive, to rob him of his initiative, to break his lines of defence and his military set-up, to undermine and if possible destroy his military power, and to force him back to a line (the River Jordan) that would make geographical sense and diminish his ardour for the fight. And all the time, of course, there was the victorious air force available for action on any front, as a kind of grand reserve unit.

The Jordanians rushed armour reinforcements to the West Bank. Their artillery engaged in indiscriminate shelling of West Jerusalem. On 5th June Government House, serving as U.N. Headquarters, was seized by Jordanian forces, who also closed in on Mount Scopus. From positions in Kalkilya long-range artillery started shelling the Israeli coastal towns. There was reason to fear that similar batteries in Jenin would open fire on our Ramat David air-base. Egyptian commandos came to Latrun to make sorties against the coastal plain.

It was clear that the Kingdom of Jordan had joined wholeheartedly in the war against Israel. The Israel army thereupon took the initiative on the Jordanian front, locally at first and then in general, starting with a series of limited counter-attacks, which presently developed into a grand parallel counter-offensive. Joint operations were conducted by armour, infantry and paratroopers acting as infantry shock-troops wherever the battle raged most fiercely—for instance, in East Jerusalem. A grand pincer movement along the mountain ridge gave Israel (by 7th June) command of all the territories that had been occupied by Jordan on the

West Bank of the River Jordan. The head and crown was Jerusalem: Jerusalem re-united; the Old City within the walls, with all the precious, imponderable values those walls enclose, restored to the Jewish people.

On the Syrian front no Israel initiative seemed to be forthcoming. It nearly did not come at all. The Syrians were deploying heavy artillery and continuously shelling the settlements in the Huleh and Jordan valleys, and had even attempted an armoured breakthrough and invasion in Upper Galilee. Nevertheless, Israel maintained a strategy of defence on that front for the first few days, even though its military forces there were quite capable—as they were soon to prove—of ejecting the Syrians from the Golan Heights.

This dangerous delay was caused by political hesitations. The staying-power of the Syrians was exaggerated; the Egyptians were not expected to agree to a cease-fire as quickly as they did; and it was feared that a clash in Syria, whose regime was so particularly favoured by Moscow, might drag the Soviet Union into the war, or at least some heavier form of pressure. In my judgement, Israel should have launched an offensive on the Syrian front immediately after its air force had put out of action the Arab air forces, including the Syrian. An effort should have been made there and then to dislodge the Syrians from the ridge, to smash their armed forces, to compel the remaining rump to re-deploy itself in the defence of Damascus, and to conquer the whole of Southern Syria.

If this had been done at the right time, in addition to the obvious gains a further political end of great value might have been achieved. The Israel forces could have established a direct link with the Druze people, long oppressed by Damascus, and helped to set up a Druze body politic—an independent Druzia. Judging by Israel's experience with her own Druze citizens, who have willingly accepted military conscription, voluntarily and in substantial numbers joined the gallant Border Police, and maintained the most cordial relations with their Jewish fellow-citizens, it may be reasonably supposed that similar relations could have been established with the Druze communities outside of Israel. A Druze state could thus have acted as a friendly buffer state between Israel and both Syria and Jordan, thus contributing a great deal to the stability of the area.

This opportunity, among others, was lost as a consequence of

the unnecessary, avoidable hesitations mentioned just now. The
Israel offensive was delayed until it was almost too late—when
Damascus had already apparently responded to the Security
Council call for a cease-fire. But Syria's agreement to the cease-
fire did not in fact stop its artillery fire directed against Israeli
settlements, which continued unabated. Israel was thus given a
further and probably last chance, politically speaking, to remove
the Syrian scourge from its strongholds on the Heights, from
which the Huleh and Jordan Valley settlements were being
harassed without respite and without regard to previous armistice
agreements or the cease-fire of the fourth day. In a frontal offensive 'on positions massively fortified in depth, concentrated
armoured forces and mechanized infantry, supported by the air
force, began to negotiate mountainous terrain previously considered impenetrable by tank. Within two days, the entire Syrian
front was broken, and a total Syrian withdrawal effected. A further
cease-fire imposed by the Security Council this time put an end
to all firing on the evening of 10th June.

Israel, fighting for her survival, won a brilliant, decisive victory.
Operationally speaking, she adopted an offensive strategy; yet the
Six Day War was as perfect an example of a war of self-defence
as any ever fought in the recorded history of mankind. The Arab
leadership, and the Egyptian in particular, this time had left the
world in no doubt about their intention: that they were bent
on the total destruction of Israel. They must afterwards have
regretted a little the phenomenal success of their pre-war *jihad*
('Holy War') propaganda. Most of the nations of the world
(except, of course, those whose settled prejudices or ill-will or
both made them incapable of impartial judgement) showed understanding and sympathy for Israel's heroic struggle. Her prestige
was further enhanced by the fact that she had accomplished the
great feat alone and unaided. The attempt by Cairo to explain
it all away by claiming that there had been Anglo-American air
intervention—as if defeat at the hands of Anglo-Saxons were
less discreditable than defeat inflicted by Israelis—was generally
treated with the contempt it deserved.

The Six Day War decisively vindicated certain basic positions
I had maintained during the preceding period.

1. Israel could not be accused of isolationism. She had cultivated friends throughout the world and had sought from them (and herself given to others) political support, economic aid and military supplies. But she had found that, in the last resort, she had to rely on herself alone in her fight for survival. Even so limited an undertaking as that of the maritime powers, given in 1957, to guarantee freedom of shipping in the Straits of Tiran had proved to be unrealizable. The peace-keeping U.N. Emergency Force on Egyptian soil had dissolved into thin air in a matter of hours. The moral was obvious. We could not put our trust in any military guarantees. We had to build up a military strength which would enable us to rely on our own forces for the defence of our country without military assistance from outside. Besides (as I explained earlier), military dependence on a foreign power entailed political dependence, and any major power 'guaranteeing' our existence might well have been tempted to impose on us a totally unacceptable political solution to the Palestinian Question. And when the crisis came, the guaranteeing power might not necessarily have agreed with our assessment of the situation; or if it did, even with the best of intentions its help might have come just too late. This time, accordingly, we had fought alone, avoiding the mistake made in 1956, and as a consequence could show substantial political gains along with our military victory. This was a far cry indeed from our situation after the 1956 Sinai war, when we had had the military support of Britain and France but had lost heavily on the political front, with what were in the long run disastrous consequences for our security and that of the Middle East as a whole.

2. The Six Day War was not only a war between two armies and nations; it was a clash between two conflicting social and political systems. It was a confrontation of a social and political democracy with a military dictatorship exercising its arbitrary political rule over a pitifully backward society. The democracy gained the victory; and this effectively proved the validity of the arguments advanced against the pessimists who had insisted that time was against us. Israel in 1967, even more than in 1948 and 1956, had shown herself to be stronger than all the Arab armies

together. This was, in the first place, because the Arab
social structure, notwithstanding the advances it had made,
had yet failed to advance sufficiently in the vital field of
military technology. Consequently the Arab armies were for
the most part incapable of using effectively the sophisticated,
ultra-modern weapons they had been equipped with: the
Arab soldiers, in themselves by no means cowardly or incom-
petent, failed abjectly in the tasks imposed upon them, which
were far beyond their sociological level and capacity. Moreover, there was still no Arab unity. The Arab states still could
not work together. Nor within each state was there any social
concord or sense of national unity. The prevailing ethos was
one of cheating and lying. The rulers lied to each other.
Ministers engineered the downfall of their own colleagues.
Officers were bent on outwitting their superiors, privates
their officers. The top men in government were incapable
of being honest with one another or even with themselves.

By comparison, Israel was a model of harmony and civilization: essentially united in spite of her fierce internal
quarrels; single-minded in the pursuit of the common goal
of survival; aided and sustained by Jewish solidarity throughout the world and by the sympathy of international public
opinion. In this way democracy triumphed over tyranny,
and quality—of the individual and of the social group—
proved its superiority to mere quantity.

3. The Six Day War also proved conclusively that the
doctrine of anticipatory counter-attack effectively ensured
the survival of this country and of the Jews as a nation. By
wresting the initiative from the enemy, Israel won the
victory and saved herself from destruction. From this she
has learned, once and for all, that in a war with her Arab
enemies she has no alternative but to take the initiative,
firmly rejecting passive defence. She has also learned that in
such circumstances it will be generally recognized that an
anticipatory initiative is not an act of aggression.

4. The personal courage and heroism displayed by commanders and troops alike in the Six Day War are now widely
known. There were fifty-one citations (in a war of just six
days) for acts of extraordinary bravery and self-sacrifice by
individual soldiers which, according to foreign commentators,
would have earned many of them a Victoria Cross in Britain

or a Medal of Honor in the United States.[5] Speaking without
vainglory but also without false modesty, one may observe
that this is nothing new in the history of the Jews. One
remembers their fierce resistance to Roman rule nearly
two thousand years ago; how in the medieval period they
chose to be burned at the stake rather than deny their God;
how against unspeakable odds they survived the assaults of
the Jew-baiters of Christendom in the centuries of persecu-
tion. And in more recent times, one could cite the exemplary
pioneering courage and endurance of the first Zionist settlers
of Palestine; the heroic, hopeless resistance of the ghetto-
fighters against the Nazi terror; the courage and self-sacrifice
of the underground Jewish forces of Mandatory Palestine in
their struggle for independence, and of the first soldiers of
the sovereign Jewish State fighting for the survival of their
national home in the War of Liberation. Jewish history is
indeed, as the historian Namier said, not a history but a
martyrology. But (as Namier perhaps forgot) the martyrs
have always also been fighters; and it is this characteristic
combination of the inextinguishable fighting spirit of the
Jews with their capacity for martyrdom or self-sacrifice that
was unforgettably exemplified in the Six Day War.

5. However, the individual acts of courage and heroism
—as the heroes would be the first to agree—were only one
part of the achievement of the ultimate glorious victor, the
Israel Defence Army (*Zahal*) as a whole. Its distinctive
features, which I mentioned earlier in this book, proved their
value in a quintessential way in the Six Day War. Zahal
owed its brilliant performance to the incomparably intelligent and precise planning of its General Staff; to the quality
of its leadership at all levels; to the excellence of its Intelligence Services; to its superb logistics; to the smooth, effort-
less operation of all its vital services. General Yitzhak Rabin,
the Israeli Chief of Staff in the Six Day War, was able to
claim with justifiable pride the fulfilment of every C-in-C's
fondest dream: 'There was in this war not a single unit that
did not attain its objectives.'

6. The State of Israel has since its establishment been the
strongest element, both socially and militarily, in the Middle

[5] An account of some of the citations may be found in the 31st October,
1967 issue of *The Jerusalem Post*, Israel's English language daily newspaper.

East. The Six Day War decisively confirmed this position. Israel's dynamism and resourcefulness have now been demonstrated as perhaps never before, and are clear for all the world to see and judge at their true value.

CHAPTER VI

Since June 1967

I am writing this chapter in August 1969, more than two years after the Six Day War. As a result of the war, the Israel Defence Forces command improved strategic borders: that is, they have a better topographic posture, greater strategic depth, a much more efficient early-warning system against approaching enemy aircraft. Israel is bound to do all in her power to achieve final borders that will guarantee peace with security. Despite Israel's fervent desire for peace, however, there is as yet no sign of peace. On the contrary, the leaders of the Arab countries insisted, in frantic haste, on tying their own hands at the 1967 Arab summit conference at Khartoum with their three barren commitments, 'No recognition of Israel, no negotiations and no peace with Israel.' Egypt has since supplemented these by further public undertakings of her own: for instance, 'what was won by force shall be restored by force'; she has pledged 'the liquidation of the results of Israeli aggression whether by political or by military means,' and even made such a far-reaching commitment as 'the restoration of the conquered lands to the Palestinian people.' In all these declarations, the Egyptian Government completely ignores its responsibility for the outbreak of the war and Israel's national and international rights.

The Arab governments' threats to renew the war against Israel, despite their own acceptance in June 1967 of the cease-fire arrangements proposed by the U.N. Security Council, are accompanied by a tremendous drive to re-arm and rehabilitate their defeated armies. By the beginning of 1969, thanks to generous Soviet supplies, Egypt's armour had regained the strength it had on the eve of the Six Day War, and her air force was 50% stronger. In 1970, her armour will almost certainly reach 150% and her air force 200% of their pre-war strengths, not to mention other sections of her forces. The numerous terrorist organizations receive direct and indirect aid from all the Arab countries, which supply them with weapons of war, give them moral and political support, and allow them to train on their territory, establish bases there, and operate from these bases. The Arab regular armies often provide logistic support and covering fire for terrorist units in their operations against Israel. Moreover, the Arab armies themselves, especially those of Egypt, Jordan, Iraq and Syria, periodically violate the cease-fire agreements by firing on Israeli forces or villages, by violent incursions across the cease-fire lines, and by occasional air raids. As a consequence, the entire cease-fire system has been brought to the brink of collapse.

It seems that history is repeating itself. The political and military leaders of the Arab states appear not to have learned the lesson of their defeats. Nor have they succeeded in liberating themselves from their characteristically false assessment of the situation. Illusion continues to dominate the Cabinet offices and General Staffs of the Arab countries.

This does not mean that another war is necessarily inevitable. But it does appear to grow more possible from month to month. Even supposing that Arab rearmament and provocations against Israel are meant at this stage only to strengthen their regimes and the morale of their peoples and armies and to fortify their political bargaining position, it is certain that some of the motives for their past aggression against Israel are still operative. These include xenophobia and religious fanaticism; inter-Arab rivalry for hegemony of the Arab world; the wish to divert the attention of the masses of the people from their social and economic miseries to an external 'enemy'; the desire to liquidate the sole example of a social and political democracy in the Middle East represented by Israel for fear that the system might spread. Their motives are intensified by the Arab leaders' sense of humiliation and desire for revenge as a result of the 1967 defeat—the third in nineteen years; and are further aggravated and encouraged by the irresponsible competition between the great powers for Arab sympathy, and by their policy of appeasement and supplying of arms. There is no doubt that if the Arab leaders feel themselves strong enough, or believe (rightly or wrongly) that they have reasonable prospects of even

a partial victory which will produce some change in the territorial *status quo*, they are likely to try their luck again at war.

Israel's policy remains unchanged. She wants peace treaties
with effective security arrangements, with each Arab country
separately or with all of them together according to which is
feasible at the time. Permanent peace with the Arab states is one
of the fundamental principles of Israel's national policy. She
has not in the past, and she does not now, aspire to further
military victory. Nor will she adopt military means for the
attainment of political goals—even such a vital and supreme
goal as the achievement of peace. Besides the moral objections
there are the practical ones: I do not believe that an imposed
peace can be a lasting one. On the other hand, when a war has
been forced on Israel, and new strategic, territorial and political
conditions have been created by her victory, it is surely reasonable that a special effort should be made to find a permanent
political solution by a wise and responsible use of the results
of the military victory.

I have always believed in the saying of the ancient Chinese
philosopher of war, Sun Chu: 'The theory of war teaches us
not to rely on the possibility that the enemy will not come, but
on preparedness to meet him; not to rely on the prospect that
he will not attack, but on the fact that we have made our position
invincible.' Thus Israel has been compelled during the period
since June 1967 to keep abreast of the arms race, at least in
respect of the quality of her arms. She has also—more than
ever in the past—directed her efforts to fortification in depth,
in both senses of the term. The maintenance of a convincing
balance of forces is one of the principal ways of maintaining a
reasonable chance of avoiding a new major war, as well as the
certainty of defeating the enemy if he imposes a new war on
Israel.

Israel's desire for peace, the sincerity of which can be tested
at the conference table, and her will to live, which has been
tested three times on the battlefield, make it imperative for her
to adopt two different but complementary policies at one and
the same time. She works for peace as if peace were within reach,
devoting unwearying effort to the establishment of contact, open
or covert, with like-minded elements in the Arab countries; and
simultaneously she strengthens her military power and maintains
a constant state of military alertness as if war were inevitable.

The unity, stability and basic rationality of Israeli society enable the Government to pursue both courses without inconsistency. Thanks to this imaginative and realistic combination of policies, Israel is less likely to miss any significant opportunities of working for peace with those Arab circles who want it, while ensuring that she will not be taken unawares on the battlefield.

Israel believes that the growth of mutual confidence between her and her neighbours, who are the enemies of today but may be the allies of tomorrow, is no less important than strategic borders. But after twenty years of bitter hostility on the part of the Arab rulers, during which hatred of Jews and Israel has been deliberately implanted in the hearts of the Arab younger generation, she cannot rely on a miraculous change of heart. Consequently, in addition to conscious and persistent efforts to achieve greater understanding and trust, she has to insist on full, contractual peace treaties, accompanied by security arrangements which will be firmly anchored in defensible frontiers. The provisional arrangements of the past have led from war to war. Because she wants the Six Day War to be the last of her wars with the Arab states, Israel will not agree to any temporary settlement as a substitute for real peace. She is therefore determined that the transition from the cease-fire agreements to full peace-treaties shall be carried out in one step, even if she has to wait for decades. Meanwhile, Israel will respect the cease-fire agreements on the basis of reciprocity until they are replaced by peace-treaties, and will honour the cease-fire lines until permanent, secure, agreed and recognized political borders are established.

In view of my present position in the Israel government, I cannot delineate in detail a future map of Israel which will give her the greatest possible security with the fewest political problems, and will also be consistent with the historic bond between the Jewish people and the Land of Israel. I shall therefore content myself with enunciating a few 'algebraic' formulae.

The historic tie is of capital importance. It is the very foundation of the whole Zionist movement and the rebirth as a nation of the Jewish people in its historic homeland after nineteen centuries of exile and dispersion. It is the moral and political basis for bringing under Israeli sovereignty new areas which serve some of the most ancient and ineradicable spiritual needs of the Jewish people, as well as vital strategic and political ends. It is also the basis for the State of Israel's very right to exist within any borders—a right which is denied by its enemies, who persistently violate it by military and political means. If therefore Israel should agree to any particular territorial compromise in return for a durable peace, she would do so not because she abandons her historic ties with the territories in question, but despite her historic rights, and for the sake of such an historic achievement as the conclusion of a peace treaty with the Arab countries.

However, this book is concerned mainly with the development of Israel's defence doctrine, not with national-historiosophical analysis. I therefore return to strategic considerations, to say, first, that I disagree with both of the two extreme views held by some people in my country. The one insists, either on historiosophic or strategic grounds, that Israel must not give up an inch of territory even in return for durable peace. The other argues that Israel must not (apart from Jerusalem re-unified) annex any considerable territory even if it is required for security—either on the grounds of a moral revulsion against expansionism, or for fear that it would put an end to the prospects of peace. But though I repudiate these positions, I take one point to be axiomatic. The armistice demarcation lines laid down in the armistice agreements of 1949 cannot serve as permanent borders. These for most of their length are devoid of any strategic value whatever, and a return to them would be tantamount to Israel's returning to a potential strategic death-trap. Withdrawal to the armistice lines would invite a renewed Arab offensive, involving a fresh effort to wipe Israel off the map of the world. For the most part indeed the armistice lines cannot serve even as a starting-point for the establishment of permanent borders: they were always temporary, and it was the Arabs themselves who, in the years between 1948 and 1967, took pains to persuade world opinion of their temporary character for fear that the world might come to regard them as permanent borders. The armistice agreements and the lines demarcated under their provisions were unilaterally abrogated by the Arab states in 1967. They have been washed away by the blood of the thousands of Jews who died to ensure their people's survival. They have no validity from the point of view of morality or international law, and certainly none from the strategic point of view. Only within the framework of direct negotiations will it be possible, in my view, to arrive at a territorial compromise which will give Israel a firm strategic posture while taking into account reasonable Arab aspirations in regard to territory, population, and national and religious ties.

When Israel's political frontiers are established, they must be strategically defensible. That is to say, they must be based on a strong topographical posture composed of natural obstacles, capable when properly defended of resisting a modern land army, and suitable for the mounting of a major counter-offensive. They must give the country a dimension of depth which will prevent the creation of military *faits accomplis* by hostile armies, air forces, or ground-to-ground missiles. Israel must have a highly developed early-warning system against the approach of enemy planes. All these considerations imply the need for frontiers which will be different from the 1949 armistice lines, though they need not be identical in every part with the present cease-fire lines. Speaking for myself, if I were able to choose between keeping indefinitely the cease-fire lines (with all their strategic advantages) without peace and different secure borders with peace, I would choose the latter.

Some people ask whether in this era of land-to-land continental missiles, sea-to-land missiles and long-range bombers it is of any real importance to have borders founded on topographical obstacles and strategic depth. It is true that artillery, missiles and bombers (to speak only of conventional weapons) can wreak havoc on a large scale. But they alone cannot subdue a courageous people fighting for its survival and independence. The heavy German bombardments of the British Isles during World War II did not subdue Britain. The heavy American bombardments of North Vietnam have not broken its people's will to fight. One has to conclude that until one side's territory is occupied and the resistance of its people and army broken by land forces, whether they arrive by land, sea or air, no war comes to an end: unless indeed it is brought to an end by a peaceful settlement.

The intensification of the fire-power, mobility and rapidity of movement of armour, motorized infantry and mobile artillery, as well as improved engineering methods of overcoming natural obstacles and fortifications, do not reduce the importance of static defences. On the contrary, the greater the improvement in the enemy's mobility and offensive capacity, the greater the need for an integrated counter-deployment: for the strengthening of the defensive system to make it impenetrable by a mechanized army; for the enhancement of general and local offensive capability by the correct disposal of forces and a high level of operational skill. The present, post-June 1967 topography of the land of Israel makes it possible to delineate natural borders constituting a 'defensive wall' which in itself will be a deterrent factor, or will at least considerably improve Israel's defensive capability. In the geo-political and geo-strategic conditions of the Middle East, there is thus no substitute for strategically defensible borders. Israel, in any case, if she wants to survive, must persist in her demand for secure borders in the areas that before June 1967 made her most desperately vulnerable. Defensible borders without peace are preferable to peace without defensible borders. If Israel establishes secure borders, they will finally be agreed. If they are not agreed because they are secure, it is better that they are secure, even if for many years to come they are not agreed. I need not say that the solution we hope and strive for is that they be both secure and agreed.

Israel cannot wait indefinitely to establish her security borders, as if she were a mere caretaker for the Arab states in the administered territories. In view of growing Arab threats and the worsening of the border situation, it is Israel's right, and indeed her duty, to establish settlements and security positions in border areas of vital security importance, making her own decisions about the questions of political policy involved. Such accomplished facts, besides their primary security value, will also make their contribution to the political struggle for permanent political borders, by showing the Arab States that in this sphere, as in others, time is not necessarily on their side. The strategy of 'creating facts' must, however, be shaped in such a way as to leave the various options for peace open while achieving the necessary secure borders.

It may well be that Israel's desire to establish strategic borders different from the pre-1967 armistice demarcation lines will be misunderstood, and perhaps even opposed, by some members of the world body, including friendly ones. What is at stake, however, is Israel's security—that is, her very existence. It seems to me therefore that, while making every effort to explain her position and needs, Israel must not give way to international demands and pressures. After all, although Israel has many

friends, she has no mutual assistance treaty with any power: she
was left to fight the Six Day War alone and unassisted. Accordingly, if she is faced with the choice between withdrawal to the
old armistice lines for the sake of short-term political gains and
the establishment, even unilaterally, of new and secure borders at
the cost of political complications, the second alternative should
be preferred. The political difficulties (one may hope) will
ultimately pass away, but only the capacity for self-defence will
ensure Israel's survival.

The demilitarization of areas of strategic importance may
indeed help to solve the problem, but only to a very limited
extent. Past experience with demilitarized zones does not inspire
confidence in this method of giving a threatened country a sense
of security. It is sufficient to recall the demilitarized zone on the
Rhine between the two world wars, or that in Vietnam, or the
demilitarized zones that for nineteen years separated Israel from
her neighbours, to make it clear why Israel rejects categorically
this expedient as the sole element in a security settlement. On the
other hand, there is no reason to reject the suggestion that in a
comprehensive security settlement, mainly based on the delimita-
tion of strategic borders, several areas should be demilitarized—on
condition that the demilitarization is reliably controlled, and that
mutual alarm systems are established to warn against a threatening deployment of forces for a sudden offensive by either side.

Since no one can tell how many years will pass before there is
peace, Israel must deploy her forces so as to be able to hold her
ground in a state of no war and no peace with alternating periods
of tension and relaxation. The present situation of a legal cease-
fire which is periodically violated is liable to lead to extended
hostilities. It thus calls for constant alertness to prevent surprise
attacks, whether in the shape of commando raids, terrorist
activities, shelling and air raids; or full-scale war, whether in the
form of an enemy crossing of the cease-fire lines in big formations, or marine and paratroop landings in the flank and the rear
with massive air-support. To save the national economy from
being swamped by the burden of military expenditure, it is necessary to maintain the utmost flexibility in the deployment of the
Israeli forces. This is to be based on the maintenance of forward
forces, powerful in defensive fortifications, fire-power and alertness but not over-demanding in manpower, together with mobile
formations in geographical depth to act as reserves for counter-

offensives and holding operations. The Israeli system of rapid
mobilization of the reserves enables the general staff to maintain a
relatively small standing army without endangering the security
of the country.

The Six Day War, which saved Israel from succumbing to a
sudden offensive and brought about a revolutionary improvement
in her strategic position, was yet not sufficient to put an end to
the war of terror, sabotage and firing across the cease-fire lines.
The Arab terrorist organizations had been active for years before
the June war, and indeed contributed substantially to the escala-
tion that led to its outbreak. Since the Israeli victory of 1967, they
have got renewed impetus and more open support from the
defeated Arab countries. They have announced that their primary
aim is to liquidate the State of Israel. It may be doubted whether
they are really under any illusion about their capacity to achieve
results not attained by the regular Arab armies. But it seems certain that they have set themselves a number of intermediate
objectives. These are:

1. Revenge for past defeats;

2. Indiscriminate killing of Israelis and destruction of Israeli
property, as ends in themselves;

3. To demoralize the border settlers, with a view to effecting their withdrawal from the settlements;

4. To frighten away investors, tourists, and (in particular)
new Jewish immigrants, in order to isolate Israel and impede
her economic development;

5. By all these means, to conduct a war of nerves which,
they hope, will ultimately undermine the morale of the people
as a whole;

6. To maintain a continuous state of belligerence between
the 1967 war and the time when the Arab countries may be
deemed to be ready for another full-scale war;

7. To create an atmosphere in the Arab world that will make
it difficult for any Arab country to make peace with Israel;

8. To become a significant factor in internal Arab politics,
both in the individual Arab states and in inter-Arab political
organizations (the Arab League, etc.);

9. To build up, by war and the creation of an heroic myth,
a Palestinian entity aspiring for national liberation.

This is not the place for a full discussion of what is known as the 'Palestinian Entity'. I can only indicate some of the salient points. To begin with, no such entity ever existed as a separate national unit. On the contrary, the Arab population of Palestine, in both Ottoman and British Mandatory times, regarded themselves as an inseparable part of the Arab people as a whole, with special ties with Syria; in those days, the Arab national movement itself defined Palestine as 'Southern Syria'. When the United Nations decided in 1947 on the partition of Palestine and the establishment within its territory of two states, a Jewish state and an Arab one, no Palestinian entity could be found to establish the Arab state—not even one to refuse to recognize the Jewish state and declare war against it together with the other Arab countries. Nevertheless, it may be granted that an ethnic entity such as the Arab population of Palestine *could* take shape as a national unit. Modern history knows of many instances in which tribes or large groups of immigrants have become new nations. Whether a Palestinian entity exists or not, however, can be decided only by the people concerned. A genuine national entity is not dependent upon external recognition. Either it exists, with or without a legal status, or it does not; and if a Palestinian entity exists, there is no reason why it should not appear. If the Palestinian Arabs are fired by the aspiration for national self-determination, it can be realized on the East Bank of the Jordan. This was once an inseparable part of Palestine, and was severed from it only by a British Government decision at the beginning of the 1920's. In addition to the original inhabitants, who were part of the Arab population of undivided Palestine, the East Bank now contains approximately the same number of Arabs again— immigrants or refugees from Western Palestine. A Palestinian nation, if it exists, could therefore be created in Transjordan, either as a monarchy or as a republic, irrespective of its claims upon Israel. The constitution of such a national entity does not require any war of terror against Israel; it is solely a matter for internal Arab decision.

Although some of the members of the terrorist organizations may be credited with patriotic motives and personal courage, they are not entitled to the name of a national resistance movement. First, it is a cold, unpalatable fact that they do not take their orders from the people which (they claim) they wish to 'liberate'; their aim is not to liberate but to dominate. What we have here is not a people with a guerilla army, but fragmented terrorist organizations seeking to adopt a people. Second, they use murderous methods of warfare which are repudiated by genuine movements of national liberation: as the Haganah repudiated them when it was fighting the British mandatory power in the middle 1940's. Third, they endeavour to create a nation by destroying another nation. The duty of the Israel Defence Forces with respect to the terrorists is clear. Along with the other branches of the security services, their task is to defend the cease-fire lines and protect the population under their care, Arab as well as Jewish, against terrorist attacks, sabotage and bombardment from across the lines. By a suitable combination of artificial obstacles along part of the cease-fire lines and the use of scientific methods of detection, penetration into Israel-held territory can be reduced to a minimum. Active defence on both sides of the line, as and when required, can reduce the effectiveness of the terrorist organizations still further.

The terrorists have had little success. They have managed sporadically to kill, to destroy property, and to impose additional burdens. Nevertheless, Israel's border settlements were never more stable than they are in the present situation. Not a single settlement has been abandoned; indeed, new ones have been formed on the borders since June 1967. The national symbol of heroism in Israel today is the mother who refuses to leave her border settlement and brings up her children within the range of light arms and artillery fire, in the uneasy space between the children's bedroom or classroom and the shelter. As to the economic life of the country: so far from its having been undermined by terrorist activities, foreign investment, tourism and Jewish immigration have actually increased, reaching new peaks during this period. The terrorists' only real achievement appears to have been political: they have succeeded in attracting a certain amount of attention from international public opinion, and have up to a point become a force in Arab politics. It seems that in some Arab countries they are a much greater problem to the ruling regime than they are to Israel.

It is thus fair to say that up to the present time of writing the Israeli security forces have been strikingly successful in containing the scope of terrorist activities. It is in the nature of terrorism, however, especially when it receives external aid, to flare up again from time to time even when it has suffered severe defeats and failed to achieve anything. It may therefore be assumed that the war of terrorism, sabotage and bombardment will continue as long as the present situation exists. Since the terrorist organizations are stationed and trained in the Arab states and frequently receive assistance from their regular armies, Israel has no alternative but to place the responsibility for terrorist activities on the Arab hosts as well.

The moral right and the operational capacity of the Israel Defence Forces to launch a pre-emptive counter-offensive are still of the first importance. At the same time, on long stretches of each front and for the land forces in particular, it is no longer a matter of supreme necessity as it was before June 1967. Indeed, in certain sectors (which for obvious reasons I shall refrain from specifying), it would be better to allow the enemy to attack first, thus exposing himself to dense artillery and anti-tank fire before the Israeli forces go over to a counter-offensive. In other sectors, however, it is permissible and sometimes essential to carry out a pre-emptive counter-attack, as strategic necessity and political conditions may determine. It is important to remember that in the new situation created by the Six Day War a number of vital areas in the Arab countries have become exceedingly vulnerable— a fact which opens up to Israel's active defence wide-ranging possibilities of imposing a strategy in accordance with her needs if the present situation should develop into a full confrontation. As far as the air force is concerned, Israel's right and capacity to carry out a pre-emptive counter-offensive remains absolutely vital. She will now also have to take into account the possibility of an attack by missiles from the land or sea, and prepare for such an eventuality.

In my view, Israel in certain situations will be entitled and even compelled seriously to consider the necessity of crossing the cease-fire lines, whether on a small scale or in a large-scale pre-emptive counter-offensive, for a brief incursion or for a more extended action. These are the principal situations:

1. in case of an offensive, local or general; or a concentration of enemy forces in preparation for an offensive; or if it is discovered that the enemy is actively preparing for a large-scale air or missile attack on targets vital to Israel;

2. for the purpose of crushing terrorist warfare conducted from bases across the cease-fire lines when it appears to be impossible to stop it by more limited means;

3. in case of enemy interference with Israel navigation on the open seas, or in narrow straits or passages, such as the Bab-el-Mandab at the southern entrance to the Red Sea;

4. in order to extend aid to open or covert allies, actual or potential, in one or another Arab country;

5. in case of a change in the *status quo* of a neighbouring country definitely menacing to Israel.

In connection with the last point, I ought to say that I am in principle opposed to interference in the internal politics of another country, even when it is one which is in a state of belligerency vis-à-vis Israel—as all the Arab countries have been since 1948. I deny any country's right to initiate war, even with a view to imposing peace, because I believe that military force should be used only for self-defence. However, in the complex situation of an unstable Middle East, far-reaching changes in the uneasy *status quo* may occur which are of vital strategic significance. In such a situation—when a change in the *status quo* definitely and verifiably threatening to Israel's security has occurred—an appropriate Israeli military action is justified.

The fresh tasks indicated above require the further development of the Israel Defence Forces. For obvious reasons again, I can only describe it in the most general terms. In addition to defensive deployment in depth, the armoured formations must be reinforced with a new generation of tanks. The mechanization of the infantry must be completed, and the power of the mobile artillery increased. The paratroops corps must be strengthened, and the effective range of long-range dispatch methods improved. Engineering formations for crossing water obstacles, minefields and fortifications must be fully equipped; maintenance services and logistics must be perfected, and all the services adapted to the fighting methods of the seventies. The air force should remain basically a tactical force. It must, however, lengthen its effective range in order to be capable of attacking ground, sea and air targets and protecting Israeli shipping and aviation. In addition to his regular tasks, the Israeli pilot must develop new surprise methods for day and night fighting, since it may be assumed that the enemy has learned something from the lessons of 1967. Special attention should be given to anti-aircraft defence and the protection of aeroplanes on the ground. It is also necessary to expand the transportation capacity of the air force with many transport planes and helicopters, for carrying both troops and relatively heavy fighting supplies.

The navy's main task is to prevent the landing of enemy forces on Israel's beaches. But it must also be capable, in co-ordination with the air force, of protecting the country's shores from bombardment and missiles directed against her cities. It must develop a capacity to attack sensitive objectives on the enemy's shores. It cannot, for economic reasons, and it need not, be based on heavy and expensive vessels. Light, rapid and manoeuvrable boats, armed with cannon and rockets, along with a number of modern submarines and highly skilled sea guerilla units, will solve almost all the problems of sea defence. In addition, I think that some of Israel's best ground formations should be given additional training as marines to make possible the landing of relatively large forces on the enemy's shores, whether as part of a major offensive or as a far-reaching diversionary operation.

The country's regional (territorial) defence must be further strengthened. It should have the resources to deal with hostile terrorist activities (which might in the future be combined with a regular war); and it should be able to block any local penetrations of limited regular army forces across the cease-fire lines. It is also necessary to improve Civil Defence arrangements and the organization of the population in the rear for an emergency.

Concerning nuclear warfare, I can only repeat what I have already said. The introduction of nuclear armaments, strategic or tactical, into the Middle East should be avoided, if possible for ever, on a basis of reciprocity. But Israel must at the same time maintain a scientific and technological nuclear capacity at a highly advanced stage; she cannot allow herself to be taken by surprise in respect to this most deadly of dangers. I also think that special efforts should be made reciprocally to exclude chemical and biological weapons from the arsenals of the Middle East. But, again, Israel must be prepared to face the possibility of the enemy's using these horrible means of warfare.

To sum up: the Israel Defence Forces, without making any basic changes in their doctrines, must equip themselves with modern armaments, and deploy their strength in accordance with the strategic conditions created by the new territories and the areas of weakness disclosed in the enemy's disposition of forces. Their open and declared purpose is to deter the enemy from starting a new war, or if such a war should nonetheless occur, to ensure a victory for Israel with the utmost speed and efficiency and a minimum of casualties.

Military deterrence, however, is not the only or even the principal means of advancing peace. Without Israel's deterrent strength, war would be inevitable; without the power to win, Israel would be defeated in battle; and a defeat would mean the end of the national existence of the Jewish people. Yet, to achieve peace, it is essential to get the illusory hope of victory out of the heads of the Arabs once and for all. It is to this end, I believe, that the most imaginative, energetic and practical political efforts must be directed, on the part of Israel herself and that of all members of the world body who wish for peace in the Middle East.

I recognize that to make peace with Israel may be for the Arab leaders, for psychological and emotional reasons, a formidable task. Yet it could turn out to be their finest achievement; for what can be finer than to overcome false pride for an end as great as peace? I believe the Arab societies need peace no less than does Israel: for them, as for Israel, only peace can ensure social and economic progress and safeguard national independence. In war there is always a victor and a loser; in a just peace, both sides are the victors. The time has surely come for Israel and the Arab states to be victorious together by concluding a true peace: peace with security for Israel, and peace with honour for the Arab states.

PART TWO

Voices and Documents

The selection of documents contained in this section, though far from exhaustive, may help to give the reader an insight into the sources of the military conceptions of Israel's Defence Army and their ideological basis. They are also intended to give a more immediate, concrete sense of the spirit that inspired the makers of Israel's army and its fighters from the earliest days to the Six Day War and after. He will doubtless be struck by the simplicity or even naïvety of the ideas and emotions expressed in some of them, especially the early, most formative statements. But it was just this simplicity, together with their sincerity, which made an unforgettable impact, appealing directly to our hearts and minds.

Some of the documents are self-explanatory: for instance, the Oaths of the Haganah and the Palmach, and the Foundations of the Haganah, which express the spirit and values that informed the Jewish self-defence organization from the start. Some are of mainly historical interest, like Yitzhak Sadeh's *The Flying Squad*, which recounts a turning-point in the military thinking of the Haganah from a more passive to a more active conception of self-defence. There are accounts of the lessons to be learned from experience: for example, Yigael Yadin's reflections on the War of Liberation and Moshe Dayan's on the Sinai Campaign. I have included outlines of the actual programmes of training and education received by members of the Jewish defence forces to show what specific means were used to develop the military skills, physical stamina, morale, and sense of purpose which mainly accounted for their victories. These schemes and plans are supplemented by reports, some official, some personal, of particular military operations undertaken by the Jewish armed forces, which demonstrate their military powers and accomplishments at various stages of their history and, again, the spirit behind the actions. There are also excerpts from historic addresses by national leaders such as David Ben-Gurion and Yisrael Galili, which set out the political purposes and national strategy of the Zionist movement and its armed force, the Haganah. I have also included some articles, addresses and letters of mainly moral and educational intent, for instance, Yitzhak Sadeh's *The Fellowship of Fighters* and my own letters to Palmach emissaries abroad and my *Profile of a Commander*. The selection ends, suitably I think, with Yitzhak Rabin's *Address at Mount Scopus*, delivered a few weeks after the victory of the Six Day War, which pays tribute, in a definitive way, to the moral inspiration of the Israel Army as well as its military greatness.

I hope that these illustrative documents will confirm also a point particularly stressed in the book: the astonishing continuity and consistency of the growth of Israel's military doctrine and organization. The Israel army, I tried to show, developed by stages from a group of horsemen into first a guerilla force and then a sophisticated modern army composed of well-integrated land, air and naval forces—from an underground army to the regular army of a sovereign state. It did so, and this is the point that emerges again and again from the documents, while remaining rooted in and faithful to its past yet at the same time ever flexible, ever adaptable, ever receptive to new ideas, ever ready to learn from experience—its own, that of the enemy, that of every other army.

Most of the documents are reproduced from *Sefer HaPalmach* ('The Book of the Palmach'), the massive, two-volume collection of writings about the Palmach (reports, eyewitness accounts, memoirs, essays, articles, speeches, addresses and letters), collected and edited by Z. Gilead and M. Meged and published by Kibbutz HaMeuchad in 1953. Where a document has been taken from a source other than *Sefer HaPalmach* this has been indicated. In each case I have prefaced the documents with a brief introductory note of my own.

Y.A.

This important early document is a memorandum written in December 1912 by Yisrael Shochat, one of the founders of *Histadrut Hashomer* ('Hashomer Association'), the earliest organization for self-defence of the Jewish community in Turkish Palestine. It is the most explicit, first-hand statement of the time concerning the aims, problems, complaints and demands of Hashomer, the forerunner of the Haganah and the Israel Defence Army. It was addressed to the Zionist Action Committee, the forerunner of Israel's sovereign Parliament, and sent from Constantinople, where Shochat was at the time studying law at the university.

———◆———

A Proposal for the Defence of the Jewish Community in the land of Israel[1]

Yisrael Shochat

The 'Shomer' Association, which has now been active in the land of Israel for five years, has, since its foundation, set itself a fixed aim—to assist in the defence of the *Yishuv* [Jewish community] against its neighbours. But our function has not been limited to that of a small group of young Jews guarding the property of the settlements. Our aim has been, at the same time, to inculcate in the farmers and workers the feeling and the awareness that they, and only they, can defend themselves and their property. In order to achieve this aim we have done that which we have been able with known results.

Under the present political circumstances the continual need for defence of the Yishuv has been doubled. We are in a period of transition during which the power of the Ottoman government will be weakened and there may also be certain unexpected changes in the near future. There are also those among us who

[1] Source: *Toldot HaHaganah* ('History of the Haganah'), Ma'arachot (1954), I, i, pp. 235–36.

feel that there is a danger of attack by our neighbours. But whatever the case, our weakness and our lack of strength are now very obvious, and we therefore feel that now, at this critical political moment, is the time to pay special attention to this and to strengthen the defence of our settlements in the land of Israel.

It is our direct duty to admit that our physical strength in the land of Israel is very meagre. The various organizations and their leaders have never paid sufficient attention to this aspect, and we have, as a result, suffered, and may suffer more. The first and the only organization which has been active in this field has been the Shomer Association. It is not our intention to overrate the value of our Association. We do not want to boast of our strength or our deeds. On the contrary, all that we have done and all that we possess is but a drop in the ocean compared to what we lack and what has to be done.

We must however remember one thing: it is quality that counts, not quantity. The number of Jewish watchmen in general, and members of the Shomer Association in particular, is still very small, but this tiny group is organized and is accustomed to order and discipline and is dedicated to its work, as it has shown in action more than once. The Shomer Association is the natural focal point, capable of organizing the defence of the Yishuv in the land of Israel. There is another important reason for this, that of conspiracy. Any new organization will be noticeable and will arouse unnecessary fears among our people and our neighbours. One cannot trust the farmers in this respect. Both the government and the local Arabs have become accustomed to the Shomer Association and for years have become accustomed to seeing armed Jewish watchmen without finding it at all suspicious.

The principle of defence which we propose is this: defence has two aspects, active and potential. The day-to-day active defence is, now, in the hands of the Jewish watchmen working in the settlements under orders from the Shomer Association. This Association has, therefore, to take upon itself the leadership of the defence of the Yishuv. But in addition to the active guards who are always under arms, we need a reserve force with which the active force can be strengthened. Our ideal is that in time of danger all the farmers and the workers who are able to bear arms will participate actively in defence. We must direct our efforts to this end; in each and every settlement a local defence association must be organized which will include all able-bodied and eligible farmers and workers, in order to prepare and train them. In addition, there must be a suitable quantity of weapons, corresponding to the number of persons which the settlement can mobilize at a time of danger. Obviously, all these arms, which require special care, will be in the hands of the Shomer Association. Physical and other training will be given by the Shomer Association in conjunction with the settlement committees. We will thus be certain that at a time of danger we will have in every place hundreds of young men prepared to defend their lives and their property.

We hereby propose the following specific plan. In every settlement day-to-day defence groups will be established, on the initiative of the Shomer Association. The number of members in these groups must be limited, because they must be selected, and not taken on randomly. The task of these groups will be to train themselves physically and in defensive tactics, and to organize the general defence of the area in time of danger. Each group will be headed by a committee, and on each committee there will be a representative of the settlement committee. Prudence demands that this representative be a suitable person, therefore the members of the group must have the right to veto his appointment; but there must be such a representative. All defence committees are to be unified and co-ordinated by a single centre.

The day-to-day defence will be concentrated in settlements in which there are a reasonable number of Jewish workers and watchmen. In those settlements in which there are as yet no Jewish workers or watchmen and the number of young men is small, it will be impossible to establish a permanent defence association. Obviously, help will come from a nearby settlement in time of danger.

We have described the general plan for the defence of the Yishuv in the land of Israel, a plan which in the light of our experience and our knowledge of the country we consider to be most suitable. We know that this project will be a difficult one, and will demand great efforts. But difficulties must not impede us; on the contrary, they should force us to make the best use of our abilities.

Our goal is not an ephemeral one, born at a moment of crisis, it is rather a great historical goal, the value of which is timeless. We, on our part, are willing to devote our time, our strength and our labours to defence, and we hereby call upon you to come to our aid in this work both from a material and moral point of view.

We are certain that you will treat our proposal with all due seriousness and that you will discuss the resources you can devote to it. We do not mention specific sums, because you know as well as we do that the sum required is large, and the greater the means available, the more it will be possible to broaden the scope, and improve the quality, of the work.

We attribute special importance to your aid not only in its direct, material sense, but also for its moral value.

As I tried to explain in this book, the Haganah was a rare combination of a military organization, a movement of social and national liberation, and a nation-wide land settlement agency. Consequently, it had to base its discipline and education on well-defined and unusually inclusive ideological principles. The following is the full text of the *Foundations of the Haganah* as formulated by the Haganah High Command, based on a draft written by Yisrael Galili, a member of the High Command for many years and its last Commander-in-Chief. He was later Deputy Minister of Defence, and is now Minister of Information in the Israel Government.

Foundations of the Haganah (May 1941)[1]

1. The Haganah is the military force of the Jewish people building its political independence in the land of Israel (*Eretz Yisrael*)

2. The Haganah is subject to the authority of the World Zionist Organization jointly with the Jewish community in the land of Israel, and stands at their disposal and under their orders.

3. The following are the tasks of the Haganah:

   a) To protect the Jewish population of the land of Israel from all who attack its life, property and dignity.

   b) To protect all activities directed to the realization of Zionism, and to the securing of the political rights of the Jewish people in the land of Israel.

   c) To protect the land of Israel against all enemy action from without, in ways appropriate to the prevailing political conditions and possibilities.

4. The Haganah alone is authorized and permitted to act in all matters of Jewish defence in the land of Israel.

[1] Source: Haganah Archives. The name actually used in the title and throughout the document is not Haganah (membership of which was at the time illegal) but *Irgun Ha-Haganah* (Defence Organization) abbreviated to *Ha-Irgun* (the Organization).

E

5. The Haganah is a unified, nation-wide body administered by a unified, centralized and graded military command, and it alone has sole authority over its members in respect of their duties.

6. The Haganah serves the whole nation, the whole Jewish community in the land of Israel, and the whole Zionist movement. The Haganah does not interfere with internal affairs of the Jewish community or the Zionist organization. The flag of the Haganah is the national flag (blue and white), and the national anthem (*Hatikvah*) is its anthem.

7. The Haganah is open to all Jews prepared and able to fulfil the duties of national defence. Membership in the Haganah, while both an obligation and a privilege for every Jewish man and woman, is in practice based upon the free and voluntary choice of the individual.

8. Membership in the Haganah involves strict military discipline, and readiness to fulfil every authorized order. Discipline in the Haganah is founded upon each member's conscience, and upon the rules of comradeship, freedom of thought and human equality.

9. The Haganah is not subject to the laws of any non-Jewish power. Its existence, its weapons and its activities are to be kept strictly secret. Whoever violates this principle is liable to pay with his life.

10. The Haganah teaches its members loyalty to the Jewish people and their land, love of freedom, independence, courage, the power to withstand suffering and oppression, the readiness for self-sacrifice, and a respect for the value of human life, uprightness of character, simplicity of life, and all civilized values, Jewish and non-Jewish alike.

Tel-Aviv, 15th May, 1941

This Oath was taken by each member of the Haganah on his acceptance, after a period of candidature, as a full member, on the recommendation of other members. It was taken at a special ceremony,
sometimes with, sometimes without, the handing over of arms. The
place varied according to the particular conditions of the illegal
existence of the branch to which the new member belonged: it might
be a school in a town, or a stable at a kibbutz; and it was often conducted under the cover of sports clubs, youth clubs, and other seemingly innocent organizations.

-------◆-------

Oath of the Haganah[1]

I hereby declare that, freely and voluntarily, I join the Hebrew
Defence Organization in the land of Israel.

I hereby swear that I shall remain faithful all the days of my
life to the Defence Organization, to its code of law and its orders
as defined in its Foundations by its High Command.

I hereby swear that I am at the service of the Defence Organization all the days of my life, that I accept its discipline uncondi-
tionally and unreservedly, that I will obey its call to active duty
anywhere and at any time, and that I will submit to all its commands and fulfil all its instructions.

I hereby swear that I will dedicate all my strength, and if
necessary give my life, for the defence of my people and my
homeland, for the freedom of Israel and the redemption of Zion.

[1] Source: Haganah archives.

Major-General Yitzhak Sadeh (1890–1952) was the founder and first commander of the Palmach, Chief of Staff of the Haganah during the anti-British struggle, and in the War of Liberation founder and first commander of the armour brigade. The following is his account, first published in 1944, of the formation and methods of the Haganah's field-companies known as FOSH (*plugot sadeh*) which came into operation during the Arab riots of 1936–39. The establishment of FOSH represented a turning-point in the history of the Haganah in that it marked the transition of its strategy from that of a passive to that of an active defence. Sadeh himself commanded this small force, which developed during the riots into a bigger organization, the field-army of the Haganah, known as CHISH (*cheil sadeh*).

———————◆———————

The Flying Squad[1]

Yitzhak Sadeh

The disturbances developed quickly. We didn't get much chance for planned and orderly training. The first actions involving the 'Flying Squad' were spontaneous and hid within them the elements of tactical changes. The great advantage of these actions for our men was in having a live enemy and not a stage-managed one. Each new 'lesson' was more valuable and laid more stress on the principles. Examples will clarify this.

The first stage: One of the isolated (collective) villages, Hartuv, near a railway station on the Lydda-Jerusalem line, in close vicinity to an Arab village. The plan of defence was based upon concentration of the village's population—if necessary—in a two-storeyed house standing at the centre of the village. The number of villagers was small and would not even have sufficed for defence-in-strength. They were sent reinforcements in the form of a seven-man detachment with an officer. This is how the new

[1] Source: *Meoraot Tartzav* ('The Riots of 1936'), Tel-Aviv, *Davar* (1937), pp. 518–19.

nuance in the planning of defensive action appeared. The officer sent to the spot adhered to orders and saw to the concentration of the inhabitants in the Big House. However, at the same time he sent a small mobile force out of the stockade—two men under his own command (he left the house under his second-in-command). The mobile squad was armed with revolvers and grenades and its task—in case of an attack on the house—was to counter-attack.

The commander trained one of his men for independent action at night (it was later discovered that this man had special qualities for this type of work).

The second stage: At the outskirts of Jewish Jerusalem, in the Bayit Vegan quarter. The usual defence plans called for positions in the houses on the outskirts of the quarter. Attacks on the quarter came from hills some 30 to 60 metres from these houses.

A squad was formed to patrol the quarter. Later on these patrols left the quarter and policed its vicinity. A detail established itself on the hill from which attacks were usually launched by the enemy. When the Arabs arrived at the hill, as was their wont ever night, they were met by small-arms fire from the hill and they retreated to Ein Kerem. An attack on Ein Kerem brought the action to a satisfactory finish.

This method caught the attention of younger officers in Jerusalem. (They held the rank of company commanders but until that time had had no special and additional training.) They volunteered as privates and joined the Patrol Squad which was then being organized, and in its ranks first underwent night-field-training.

One of the settlements, in the vicinity of Jerusalem, was being attacked every night from quarry pits to the east of the village. The squad of Jerusalem officers—the Flying Squad—executed the following manoeuvre.

The whole detail got into a light truck and set out in the direction of Jerusalem, giving the impression they were abandoning their position. Some distance from the settlement the truck slowed down and the men jumped off. The tender picked up speed and continued to Jerusalem. The men advanced under the cover of the abandoned Turkish railway embankment and reached the rear of the quarry from which the attacks were launched on the settlement.

In this case the static defences of the settlement served as the 'anvil' and the Flying Squad as the 'hammer'. We first began to send out ambushes in the same area. It is of interest to note that the same area also served the British Army for trail ambushes (maybe certain places are naturally suited to such purposes).

At a more advanced stage there were exercises at one of the settlements in the vicinity. The idea was to set up an ambush on the outskirts of an Arab village from which it was known that the gangs had withdrawn. At the same time a small unit was sent to patrol the area. Its task was to push the gang back towards the village, towards the waiting ambush.

At this stage the men of the 'anvil' and the 'hammer' began to be picked from the same unit.

This method trained—though perhaps not systematically—a cadre of officers and men, burnishing them in the heat of danger. Most of these boys proved their worth in later actions and even today we are still learning the lesson of those realistic exercises.

This Oath was taken by each member of the Palmach on the completion of his basic military training, which was also the period of his candidature, at a special parade at which he received his personal weapon (a pistol, a rifle, a submachine-gun, or a machine-gun). The ceremony was usually held at night, in a forest or an olive grove, or whenever possible at an historical site: like Ma'ayan Harod, where Gideon tested his army, or Modi'in, the native village of the Maccabees, or Massada, symbol of Jewish resistance to Roman rule.

Oath of the Palmach[1]

With this weapon which has been entrusted to me by the Haganah in the Land of Israel, I shall fight against the enemies of my people for my country, without surrendering, without flinching, and with complete dedication.

[1] Source: Haganah archives.

This is a sketch of the basic field training received by every member of the Palmach. The emphasis is on developing his power to react quickly, to think clearly and logically, to make the best use of his weapons, to know how to exploit to the full natural conditions (terrain, darkness, etc.), and to operate both as an individual and as a member of a group. All this required, of course, maximum physical fitness and mental readiness, and was supplemented by direct instruction in the value of certain moral qualities—in particular, conscious discipline, responsibility, comradeship, and the sense of cause or purpose.

Palmach Field-training Programme[1]

From the end of 1946 this training programme did not include route marches as an item; each man in the Palmach did an average of 15 days' route march in a year.

Individual Training		Days	Nights
General:	learning the subject	–	2
Cover:	cover from observation	2	–
	cover from fire	1	$1\frac{1}{2}$
	camouflage	7	–
Observation:	estimating distances	4	–
	learning the lay of the land	3	$1\frac{1}{2}$
	scouting and photography	$1\frac{1}{2}$	–
Movement:	orientation	10	8
	utilizing lay of the land	5	4
Conclusion:	individual infiltration	4	3
		$37\frac{1}{2}$	20

Training of Soldiers for Independent Action	Days	Nights
Ambush	2	2
Functions of infiltration	2	2
Searching people	2	1
Guarding a limited object	2	2
Guarding an area	2	–
Guarding a line	2	1
	12	8

[1] Source: *Beshviley Machshava Tzvayit* ('In the Paths of Military Thinking'), Ma'arachot, 1950, p. 83.

Training of Individual Soldier in Units for Independent Action

	Days	Nights
Runner (courier) training	3	4
Independent Scout	5	4
	8	8

Training of Individual in Units

		Days	Nights
Observation:	noting and observing	2	–
Movement and fire:	structure of battle and taking of positions	3	3
Fire control orders (given in rifle training)		3	–
Sectional fire discipline (given in rifle training)		2	–
Movement and fire at different stages		6	3
Assault		2	–
		18	6

The Independent Section

		Days	Nights
Movement:	observation	2	1½
	tracking	10	6
Assault:	attack on field position	2	–
	attack on fortified position (house)	3	2
	attack on encampment	3	3
	ambush	9	6
	searching for enemy	3	–
	searching people	2	2
Retreat:	retreat	2	–
Defence:	defending a house	4	2
	defending a field position	4	2
	protecting an area	2	2
	guarding a line	2	2
	protecting workers and a road	3	–
		51	28½

Training of Small Detachment

	Days	Nights
Introductory explanation	1	–
Attack on unprotected object	4	2
Attack on protected object	4	2
Attack on fortified object	4	2
Ambush to destroy armour	3	1
Ambush to delay armour	3	2
Harassment	3	1
Deception	3	2
	25	12

E*

Section Training	Days	Nights
Scout patrol	4	3
Sentry patrol	4	2
Combat patrol	4	–
Silent scout patrol	4	2
	16	7

Two-sided Exercises		
Ambush against protected trek	8	4
Sentry patrol against planned attack	8	4
Scout patrol against combat patrol	8	4
Combat patrol against combat patrol	4	–
	28	12

Platoon Training		
Protected trek	4	1
Attack on field position	2	1
Defence of field position	4	2
Seeking out enemy	4	–
Assault raid	–	4
	14	8

The Palmach attached great importance to the training of its young N.C.O.'s. We regarded the N.C.O.'s course as the basic training for command, for in our illegal underground conditions each N.C.O. had to be capable of operating not only within the framework of a platoon guided by an officer, but also of acting within his section independently of the platoon. He had therefore to be a man who could think for himself, appraise local conditions, and take decisions; and the Palmach accordingly trained its section commanders not only as N.C.O.'s but also as officers: indeed, every N.C.O. was an officer in the making. This, of course, had the effect of raising the level of the officers' course, which was subsequently attended by the best of the N.C.O.'s when they had served for a period (of not less than six months) as section commanders and deputy platoon commanders. To adapt Wellington's famous aphorism, it can be said that the great battles of the War of Liberation, the Sinai Campaign and the Six Day War were won in the N.C.O.'s courses of the Haganah and the Palmach.

Training of Palmach N.C.O.'s at Daliya (Report)

TRAINING THE INSTRUCTOR	HOURS
Principles of training and instruction (lecture)	1
rifle	18
machine-gun (Bren, M.G.-34)	28
Sten-gun	14
field-training	35
drill	4
Total	**100**

LEADERSHIP	
Introduction: use of cover	2
movement	2
utilization of lay of land for movement	2
utilization of land for firing positions	2

estimating of distances	2
indication of targets	2
buildings	2
weapons and explosives	4
topography	36
use of sand-table	2
night field-training	2
firing range	8
independent work	6
the tactical value of light arms (lectures)	2
principles of battle	1
the commander's preparations (battle orders)	2
range organization	2
field exercises	2
Total	**81**

THE INDEPENDENT COMMANDER	HOURS
Security (lecture)	1
examples of planning and execution	5
problems of planning and execution	8
battle exercises A	4
„ „ B	4
„ „ C	8
planned attack (lecture)	2
field positions	9
a bivouacked enemy	4
mobile enemy	4
fortified positions	3
attack on house (night)	2
ambush (night)	2
retreat (lecture)	2
demonstration	4
exercise	4
defence (lecture)	2
exercise	5
searching out enemy	4
protected night trek	2
Total	**79**

PATROLS	
Reconnaissance and scout patrols (lecture)	2
exercise	6
silent patrol	2
defensive patrol (lecture)	1
exercise	6
protection of field workers	6
line security (by night)	2
Total	**25**

THE N.C.O. IN THE PLATOON	
Protected march	4
attack on a fortified position (with live ammunition)	5
retreat	4
defence	6
searching out enemy	6
Total	**25**

TWO-SIDED EXERCISES	
Searching out enemy	5
protection of field workers, attack	4
platoon on protected march, section harassing	4
ambush against protected march	4
night ambush against protected march	2
protection of line, sabotage of lines	4
protection of object and sabotage	4
Total	**27**

FIGHTING IN BUILT-UP AREA	
Personal training	5
section	5
platoon	2
Total	**12**

EDUCATION AND ENTERTAINMENT	
Lectures, discussions and socials (see following)	145
Total	**494**

DETAILS OF EDUCATIONAL ACTIVITIES AT THE DALIYA COURSE

1. The Zionist Movement:	
A. History and aims of the Zionist Movement	4
B. The Zionist Organization, its structure and organizational bodies	2
C. The development of Zionist policy	4
Total	**10**

2. Jewish Settlement in the Land of Israel:	
A. The development of Jewish settlement over the last 70 years	3
B. The organizational structure of the Yishuv (The National Council, the Elected Assembly, Knesset Yisrael and Local Councils)	3
C. The Histadrut[1] and its institutions	3
Total	**9**

[1] Histadrut—The Israel Labour Federation founded in 1920

3. ZIONIST POLICY: HOURS
A. Zionist Policy during World
   War II and its aftermath
B. Problems of Zionism
C. The future of Zionism
   (possibilities and probabilities)

                          Total   14

4. THE HAGANAH:
A. History of the Haganah   2
B. Foundations of the
   organization   3
C. Organizational structure   2
D. The organization during the
   War   2
E. Haganah outside the Land of
   Israel   2
F. Ma'arachot Publishing House
   and the Ma'arachot Magazine   3

                          Total   14

5. THE PALMACH:
A. The brigade, development
   and problems   4
B. Economic factors   2
C. Rules and regulations   3
D. The ideal officer   3

                          Total   12

6. SECURITY:
A. Secrecy and security in the
   brigade   2
B. The Police and the C.I.D.   2
C. Prisons and investigations   3
D. Failures   1

                          Total   8

7. THE DISSIDENT GROUPS:
A. Ideological roots (Revisionism)
   the Irgun Zvai Leumi,
   Stern Group (Lehi)   4
B. Dissident groups: organiza-
   tional structure and activities
   and methods   2
C. Dissident activities in the
   U.S.A.   2

                          Total   8

8. PALESTINOGRAPHY: HOURS
A. General geographic outline
   and population distribution   2
B. Development and absorptive
   capacity   4
C. Forced marches, choice of
   routes and organization   2

                          Total   8

9. THE DIASPORA:
A. Distribution of Jews   2
B. Jewish institutions abroad.
   (the Joint World Jewish
   Congress, national
   congregations, etc.)   2
C. The future of Diaspora Jewry   3
D. Jewish youth in America and
   youth movements   3

                          Total   10

10. ILLEGAL IMMIGRATION
A. Organization   2
B. Illegal immigration from
   Europe   3
C. Practical problems of illegal
   immigration   2

                          Total   7

11. RESISTANCE MOVEMENTS:
A. Conditions leading to
   establishment of resistance
   movements
B. Methods

                          Total   8

12. WORLD POLITICAL PROBLEMS

                          Total   3

13. THE MIDDLE EAST:
A. The Middle East (Outline)   2
B. Our neighbours (Arab
   countries)   2
C. The Arabs of the Land of
   Israel   3
D. Britain and the Middle East   3

                          Total   10

14. KNOW THE ENEMY: HOURS
A. General and tactical
   conclusions to be drawn from
   the Disturbances   3
B. Military potential of the
   Arabs of the Land of Israel   3
C. Arab youth movements and
   gangs   2
D. British armed forces in the
   Land of Israel at various
   periods   3

E. British methods in the Empire   2
F. Military forces and insignia   2
G. Armoured forces, their
   methods and action against
   them   3
                                    ___
                            Total   18

15. TACTICAL ANALYSIS
                                    ___
                            Total   6

Entertainment and social activities: Reports from commanders of illegal immigrant ships (Jossi Hamburger, Ike Yitzhak Aharonovitz, and others); campfire social with Gadna[2] leaders .

Musicale: Mendelssohn's works, with the participation of Menashe Ravina. Theatrical performances: (Klatzkin, Margalit, Rodenski); evening of Alterman's poems (Z. Yosskowitz). Every Friday night: Sabbath Social with readings from Weekly Portion of the Law, a review of events and readings.

Lecturers

Yigal Allon; Shimon Avidan; Baruch Eisenstadt; Yisrael Be'er; Yisrael Bar-Yehuda; Eliezer Bauer; Chaim Bar-Lev; Isser Ben-Zvi; Yehuda Blum; Yehoshua Blum; David Barash; Yisrael Galili; Yitzhak Greunbaum; Eliezer Galili; Yehoshua Globerbaum; Yitzhak Dubnow; Ya'acov Dori; Shlomo Drecksler; Shimon Halkin; Harman; Chaim Zinger; Ya'acov Hazan; Yitzhak Tabenkin; Josef Tabenkin; David Carmon; L. Levita; Dan Lerner; Golda Meirsohn (Meir); Moshe Sneh; Arnon Azaryahu (Dinai); Akiva Atzmon; Y. Klinov; Joseph Karkov; Eliezer Shoshani; Yitzhak Rabin; Gershon Rivlin; Dan Ram; Berl Repetur.

Signed—Chaim Bar-Lev (Kidoni),
23 July–10 Sept., 1947.

[2] Movement for the premilitary training of youth between the ages of 14 and 18.

Yitzhak Sadeh delivered the following short address in 1943 to Palmach troops at an informal gathering round a camp-fire in a wood in the Galilee. It was subsequently printed and reprinted, and circulated to all troops and the general public as a masterpiece of inspirational eloquence. Today it may sound somewhat naive, indeed even a trifle 'corny'; but it was tremendously influential in its time, and helped to develop the tradition of *unconditional* comradeship which became and remains to the present day a distinctive feature of Israel's armed forces.

The Fellowship of Fighters [1]

Yitzhak Sadeh

The fellowship of men fighting for a common cause is surely the perfection of comradeship. Without it nothing can be achieved. The realization of any goal requires a joint effort, a common insight into its purpose and a high degree of individual preparedness. In battle, fellowship is the very condition of success. Fighting as an independent Jewish force we already achieve part of our goal. The rest is the building and restoration of this whole land, and of a better, juster society in it.

The bricks with which we build are the bodies of comrades. The mortar is the blood of brothers who shared the vision. Who is your comrade? He is the man standing at your side ready to shield your body with his, ready to carry you in his arms at the risk of his life, ready to fall at your side for the sake of the building which can be erected only by fighting.

Comradeship has to be nourished. It has to be learned. As you learn to feel that each and every day of the year is the crucial day, so you must learn to know that the friend at your

[1] Source: *Misaviv laMedura* ('Round the Camp-fire'), in the series *Dovrot* ('Rafts'), Kibbutz HaMeuchad (1953), p. 53.

side is your brother in the deepest sense—your comrade in dedication, in readiness, and in act.

You must know also that your own blood may be mixed with the blood of your comrades in the mortar of the great visionary building.

The fellowship of fighters is the foundation of life, the innermost heart and soul of comradeship.

As Commander of the Palmach I wrote the following two letters to Palmach emissaries engaged in organizing the self-defence of Jewish communities abroad and illegal immigration to Palestine. The first letter, written on 1st January, 1947 to Dan Ram, the commander of the Jewish ghettoes in Iraq, indicates some of the problems which the Jewish underground had to face in unusual conditions in an Arab country before the establishment of the State of Israel. The second letter, written on 21st June, 1947 to the emissaries operating in the Jewish D.P. camps and organizing the illegal exodus of the remnants of European Jewry, brings out some of the grave problems faced by the survivors, how they were saved by the Haganah, and how they contributed their share to the Zionist struggle for independence by their very readiness to immigrate illegally to Palestine in spite of the hardships and dangers (of a cruel sea and a ruthless foreign power) to which it exposed them. This letter has the further significance of having been written when the British had begun to deport the captured immigrants to internment camps in Cyprus, and some of the emissaries, as well as the potential immigrants themselves, were doubting whether illegal immigation could be continued in view of the ever-improving methods of the British in guarding the Palestinian coast. In the letter the pros and cons are discussed, and the firm conclusion reached that illegal immigration ought to go on.

———◆———

Letter to an Emissary

1/1/1947

Ramadan[1] My Brother,
From your telegrams and letters it becomes clear that there is grave danger for the Jews in the area under your command. In truth, we never deluded ourselves in this connection. That's what made us begin to organize defence groups in critical areas. I was very satisfied to learn that you have succeeded in starting a group and that we were able to transfer at least some of the weapons

---

[1] *Nom de guerre* of Dan Ram.

intended for you. It is depressing to think that Jews may once again be slaughtered, our girls raped, that our nation's honour may again be besmirched.

From the plans for the defence of the Ghetto that you sent us, and from your explanations, I see that your spirits have not fallen despite the danger, despite the chasm on the brink of which your 'flock' stands.

The great distance that divides us does not enable us here to view your position in the right perspective, and I beg you therefore not to expect us to give you full and detailed orders concerning your operations. All that I can do is outline, in a general way, the line of thought and approach, leaving you to fill in the appropriate details. I do not consider this a bad approach since I well know your sense of responsibility and how capable you are even under stress.

I have studied your plan of defence and have found it well-suited to its purpose. I have only a few remarks which I would like to put before you.

a. It seems to me that the reserve force which you wish to hold back is rather small and that it might be worthwhile to enlarge it even at the expense of weakening the squads holding the positions. You can never know for certain where the attack will be launched, and it is likely enough that it will be the charge of a wild mob; with the help of a suitable and flexible reserve you should be able to close up any break-through. Weakening of your positions need not trouble you too much, since, under the conditions you're working in, one man armed with a sub-machine gun, or even only a revolver, is like a whole squad, especially if he has a few hand grenades in his pockets.

b. Your men had better not be hasty in opening fire so as not to give the other side an excuse to begin a large-scale riot. But should the enemy attack, your reaction must be decisive so as to prevent a massacre.

c. In my judgement, should disturbances break out you will be able to enlarge the circle of defenders and co-opt Jews who have as yet not been organized as members of the Underground. But be warned lest you do this prematurely, thereby endangering the security of your units which are, in fact, the only defence you have against a terrible pogrom.

d. In my opinion your task is to hold out until we mobilize international diplomatic intervention. It follows that you must keep us informed of all that occurs, so that we will be able to act with speed.

e. Finally, a warning: don't let yourselves be persuaded to believe what any policeman says who appears to come to your aid after disturbances have broken out. You will have to weigh up, on the spot, to what extent governmental intervention is really meant seriously. It is obvious that even a government of scoundrels will not be able to allow chaos for any length of time, and the more so if we succeed in mobilizing diplomatic intervention.

I will do my utmost to increase your iron,[2] but I fear that under the circumstances this will take a long time. Good luck with your new bakery.[3] With an enemy as primitive as yours, that, too, is of importance.

From other places the news is worrying, but not to the extent that yours is.

You see, Ramadan, one cannot escape 'soap-box Zionism'. Don't smile. You are doing the right thing by combining your educational-organizational work with the efforts of the pioneer-youth movements there. We must encourage all forms of immigration and I am very satisfied with your efforts in this field. The sooner we bring these Jews over here, thereby assuring their existence and increasing our strength here, the better. (It may be that the rule about 'shortening the lines' is apt here but I don't accept it in regard to our own defence problems.)

I must make do this time with a short letter. I shall try to let you have more news from home and from our organization[4] in the near future. All I'll say now is that we are working intensively and seeing the fruits of our labours.

All the best to you from all of us here, especially the 'old man',[5] who takes a great interest in you and your work.

Be strong and of good courage

Yiftah[6]

[2] Arms.
[3] Primitive production of explosives.
[4] The Jewish Brigade.
[5] Yitzhak Sadeh.
[6] Yigal Allon. Officer-in-Command of the Brigade.

Circular Letter to Emissaries

21/6/1947

To all our emissaries—Shalom!

You cannot imagine how pleased we were to receive the letters of Erez, Arik, Zifzah and Eli[7]. We showed them to some of the others at H.Q. and also sent them to Amon[8]. I know no more important factor in raising the spirits of all of us, you the emissaries and we who sent you, than regular communications, the feeling of comradeship and of our collective destiny.

My visit to Europe was belated but not too late. I have always felt close to our comrades engaged in the illegal immigration operation and have never missed the opportunity of meeting them during their stay here, both during the preparatory period and after it, as the opportunity arose. However, these meetings are not to be compared to those abroad, in the field. The meetings with our comrades, wherever they were, were the pleasantest and the most important of all the meetings I had in Europe, despite the depression that they sometimes caused. This direct contact with comrades increased my feeling of fraternity with each and all of you.

On my return I tried my best to describe what I had seen to my fellow workers and superiors. I reported on the great possibilities for illegal immigration; on conditions in the camps; on the readiness of the Jews to immigrate despite the difficulties in their way; on the condition of the security forces and on the growing strength of the Revisionist forces. I made a number of practical suggestions concerning our part in the operation, but unfortunately I cannot boast of any outstanding success.

One thing I did 'succeed' in doing thoroughly. I managed to spoil our relations with a number of organizations with which we are connected. I was given a lot of compliments for this! But it seems that we had no choice. As for ourselves—we have to continue on the road along which we have been travelling, and that means:

> a. we must increase the number of emissaries engaged in various jobs connected with illegal immigration;

[7] *Noms de guerre* of the emissaries of the 4th Battalion—Abraham Zakai, Eliezer Klein, Zipporah, and Eli Zohar who were active as seamen or wireless operators in the service of the illegal immigration organization in Europe.

[8] Josef Tabenkin, O.I.C. of the 4th Battalion.

b. we must get key-jobs with more responsibility for as many of our comrades as possible;

c. we must put the stress on those spheres of activity directed by our members; and

d. we must try to learn from our activities and pass on our conclusions to comrades in the same field.

There is a good chance that one of our central figures will be given a job at the Centre[9] and that he will be officially in charge of all our emissaries abroad. We hope that he will also be given operational responsibility. The Centre has as yet not given its O.K. to this but there are signs that justify our optimism this time. Personally I put great hopes on this for it will give all our emissaries someone to turn to. Contact will be made with someone who will be able to understand your personal and professional problems. He will be able to advise you about the work itself on the strength of his experience at home and as a result of his connections with H.Q. and the Brigade. He will see to it that all the scattered emissaries are in close contact with the Brigade, thereby assuring the continuity of communication between the Brigade and its members abroad: being sent on a mission will no longer mean a cutting off of bonds of comradeship.

Since Amon and Benny[10] told me that they are corresponding with you and keeping you supplied with up-to-date information, I see myself free to write this time about Resistance[11]—which is today an extraordinary political and moral question. We discussed this problem more than once in the past when we met and I voiced my opinion quite clearly and left orders which cannot be misunderstood. There has been, however, a definitely hostile attitude on the part of some of the escorts[12] to the principle of passive 'resistance': so much so indeed that in the most recent ships it has been almost extinguished, causing us serious harm because of the false interpretations put upon this both by our own people and by the outside world. This being the case, I find it necessary to outline once more the reasons that brought me to the conclusion that unarmed resistance, as drawn-out and vigorous

[9] H.Q. of the illegal immigration organization in Europe.

[10] Benny Marschak, Information Officer of the 4th Battalion.

[11] The resistance of immigrants to their being deported on their arrival in the land of Israel.

[12] O.I.C.'s of illegal immigrant ships and their Palestine-Jewish crews.

as possible, is important and thereby make you understand our view that you should act only in accordance with routine orders.

The following are the points stressed by the escorts opposing passive resistance.

a. There is no sense in organizing P.R. among the immigrants while the Yishuv [Palestine Jewry] is passively looking on.

b. Stopping P.R. will cause an upheaval in the Yishuv and will compel it to initiate and pursue different lines of action in the struggle for immigration.

c. P.R. resulted in casualties. Is the price not too high?

d. P.R., unaccompanied by a plan to beach the ship in order to enable the immigrants to land in this way, has no real value.

e. The immigrants' resistance to their transfer to other ships for deportation causes them shame and degradation; they are dragged along the ground by the British soldiers and insulted.

f. The morale of the immigrants has fallen and they have become faint-hearted.

These six points cannot be ignored and without doubt one could add to them. I do not wish to take them lightly and shall try to answer them one by one.

a. There *is* sense in resistance even if the Yishuv is passive. I would say that as long as it does stand aloof we must fan the flame of resistance so that it will not die out, for it is one of the last embers of the struggle against foreign rule, of the struggle of the Jewish people for its existence. Calling for an end to passive resistance is like setting a stone on the grave of the struggle. This and more: for the immigrants' active opposition to their deportation is one of the sharper expressions of this struggle of which we should not, and may not, despair even if the Yishuv has as yet not found a suitable way to identify itself with it. The continuation of passive resistance is the best surety that such a way will be found.

b. Putting an end to resistance will not cause an upheaval in those parts of the Yishuv who have not reconciled themselves to the struggle (not even to the struggle for immigration). The result would be just the opposite. They would draw satisfaction from silence on this sector of the front. On the other hand we know that from time to time active immigrant resistance to deportation reawakens the public's conscience, and that of its leaders, to the extent that we may yet witness resistance becoming the link between the struggles of the past and those that are before us. And the struggle will surely come as soon as it is understood that, under the circumstances, it is impossible to achieve political aims solely by negotiations, and that if we do not wish to surrender, and this does not come into question for us, we will have no choice and will be forced to increase and sharpen the struggle against the rule which wishes to stifle us.

None of us will be desolate if we find ourselves mistaken and we do not have to take to arms; but, to my regret, the chances of that are not great.

c. As far as casualties are concerned—you are right, my friends, we may not talk lightly about the life of a man and more so of our immigrants. Nothing shocks one as much as the death of these refugees who succeeded in coming through Hell, only to fall at the Gates of Hope. Indeed we must do all we can not to cause loss of life among the enemy while resisting them, thereby giving them an excuse to murder immigrants. But let us not deceive ourselves: as in the past immigrants and escorts fell to the enemies' bullets, so also can they be killed in the future, whether fired at under orders from above (so as to put fear into their hearts), or whether killed by the hand of some murderous soldiers firing without orders. I am fully convinced that these sacrifices are not in vain; their blood is that of warriors offering themselves at the altar of our People's independence. Our grief at their deaths is great, but in the long run we are saving additional lives and directly saving others who are at death's door. In full awareness of the responsibility that I take upon myself, I tell you, Comrades, that we must continue with passive resistance despite casualties. But, Heaven forbid that we should fail to play our part, or that we should antagonize the enemy unnecessarily thereby causing needless deaths and injury.

d. There is no doubt that resistance combined with plans to help the immigrants disembark and escape after beaching the ship is to be preferred to all other forms of resistance.

And had we tried this in the past I am sure we would have succeeded and would continue to succeed and add success to success. But I must make it quite clear that resistance to the capture of a ship by the British is, in itself, an aim, even if there is no possibility that the ship will be able to slip away—as was the case with the *S.S. Chaim Arlosoroff*.

e. I am far from belittling the sense of humiliation felt by those dragged from ship to ship in preparation for deportation. And were we able to find some other popular expression for the Jews' refusal to allow themselves to be sent from their country, maybe we could give up this form of struggle. However, my friends, there is no other expression. Let us not be misunderstood by allowing non-resistance to be seen as the immigrants' agreement to being sent to Cyprus, only because we seemingly wish to save our own honour.

It is better that we be dragged along the docks, that the task be a long one, that we burden the deporters as much as possible. There is no dishonour in this. Should those dragging us feel this to be honourable, they will soon cease to do so (and in truth many of them have already); but if we do not resist deportation we will be giving up our human and national honour.

f. The fact that the morale of the immigrants is low and that they have no fight in them, is justifiably a cause for concern. This is what one of the comrades had to say during one of the discussions on this subject: 'The morale of the immigrants is bound up directly with the state of mind of our emissaries, and their readiness to fight stands in direct proportion to the fighting spirit of the ship's captain.' This being so, my friends, take courage and do not falter.

I have tried to answer the questions put to me by others. I now wish to try to answer some that have as yet not been asked but which must surely trouble many of you.

Two of them are:

a. Why resist at the beginning of the struggle when the end is known—deportation to Cyprus?

b. The public in the Land of Israel and all over the world have become used to seeing, and hearing about, deportations and no longer get upset when hearing of resistance: obviously its political value is declining.

I'll try to answer.

a. If we weigh up resistance on the scales of technical results, the supporters of self-restraint and non-resistance would be justified. The physical might of the British is vastly superior to ours and they will finally overcome every ship and deport its illegal immigrants. However, if we continue with this line of logic we must surely come to extreme defeatist conclusions. According to this line of argument, if one small patrol boat met our ship at sea and ordered it to change course for Cyprus, that would be enough to make the ship fulfil its orders. For should the ship not do so other naval vessels would come to the aid of the patrol boat and they would, in any case, overcome the immigrant ship thanks to their technical superiority. Consider our image and methods of operation should the deportations take place in this fashion. There is a further danger, far more extreme. Who can ensure that the day will not come when the government will force the ships to return to their port of departure in Europe? From a technical point of view there is no doubt that they can do this. Will we then also continue to act in accordance with the logic of those opposing resistance? The practical outcome of this cold logic will lead to the virtual cessation of illegal immigration. I have no doubt that the mere existence of illegal immigration and the fact that the camps at Atlit were crowded caused the government, which opposed us, to give 1,500 certificates of immigration monthly, despite what was written in the White Paper. I do not doubt that it was only our armed struggle that put off the beginning of the deportations to Cyprus and likewise I am sure that the immigrants' resistance today delays the decision to deport them to their port of departure. It follows that resistance, first and foremost, has an objective aim—to defer for as long as possible any additional restrictions on our 'illegal' efforts. It has in addition an historical, educational, political and moral aim, for it is impossible to tolerate deportation of Jews from the gates of their Homeland without our doing our utmost to resist such action—if only to prevent ourselves appearing in our own eyes, in the eyes of future generations and in the eyes of the world, as docile and abject.

b. It is the task of resistance to make the act of deportation as difficult and as unpleasant as possible for the government. It must, from time to time, reawaken the support of those of our people in the Diaspora who are able to come to our aid, and awaken the conscience of those of the nations of the world who have as yet not lost their conscience. They are meanwhile able, even if only in a small way, to stop injustice. The British efforts to publicize any case of non-resistance and to confuse and blur reports of resistance are sign enough of the importance the enemy gives to our struggle.

Our struggle must therefore continue under all circumstances. Accept this letter then, Comrades, both as an informative one and also as an order. I ask you to invest thought and effort in finding even more efficient, more perfect ways of defence and finding ways to adjust these to the reactions of the British Navy. We must learn from the experience of every ship in its struggle. We must try to train and guide our immigrants to struggle and resist.

We have meanwhile received further information about the part our comrades are playing in the organization and operation of illegal immigration. Though we are, of course, not free of fault and failure, in the summing up the way you fulfil your duties is encouraging and promising. Try to keep up the standard. Do your best to fulfil your duties, both great and small, seriously and with a feeling of responsibility. Deal with our immigrants as near relatives, worthy of honour and brotherhood and, above all, continue to be a close-knit group culturally and militarily.

The Brigade will do its best to increase the number of seamen and professional escorts without whom illegal immigration is impossible. We will demand responsible positions for those of us who have the experience and the capability. We will continue to demand the appointment of a supreme commander for the whole continent, and we will try to influence and direct activities in such a way that deliveries[13] will be executed efficiently.

The absence of immigrant ships during the visit of the [United Nations] Inquiry Commission is certainly a political blow. There is, however, no truth whatsoever in the rumours that this was done deliberately. I do not doubt that we are suffering from a lack

[13] The landing of illegal immmigrants on the coast.

of foresight in planning illegal immigration, which was badly prepared for the summer. Who knows better than you that this failure does not stem from those responsible for illegal immigration and that the obstruction is not political? This, however, does not alter the political fact which is distorted and misunderstood by our people at home and by the whole world. It's a great pity, for it will still be possible to remove the stain of this failure if the ships speed up and get here in large numbers.

Yiftah

*The Attack on the Bridges; Sabotage Action No. 9; Allenby
Bridge; The Night of the Radar; The Radar Action*

The following five documents are a record of some typical Palmach actions during the period of the struggle against the British
(1945–48). *The Attack on the Bridges* (p. 146), for instance, shows
how at zero-hour late one night, and regardless of the distance
of the targets from Jewish-populated areas, all the bridges connecting Palestine to the neighbouring Arab countries were blown
up and the whole country cut off from the region. The operations
against two British radar stations on Mount Carmel, described in
The Night of the Radar (p. 162) and *The Radar Action* (p. 165),
were designed to destroy the means by which the British were
enabled to capture ships in the Mediterranean carrying illegal
immigrants from the Jewish refugee camps of Europe after the
Second World War. All these actions were intended to demonstrate
the high military standard of the Palmach's exploits, and thereby to
convince the British policy-makers that Western Palestine could
not be used as a safe base for British strategy in the Middle East,
and that it was within the power of the Jews to determine whether
the country was to be quiet or disturbed beyond British control.
The operations were also designed to impress the Arabs with the
military strength of the Jewish armed forces, in the hope that this
would act as a deterrent.

These accounts of the attack on the bridges were reprinted
in *Sefer HaPalmach* from *Alon HaPalmach* ('Leaflet of the
Palmach'), the illegal news-sheet, edited by Z. Gilead, which was
published regularly by Palmach headquarters and circulated to all
units of the Palmach.

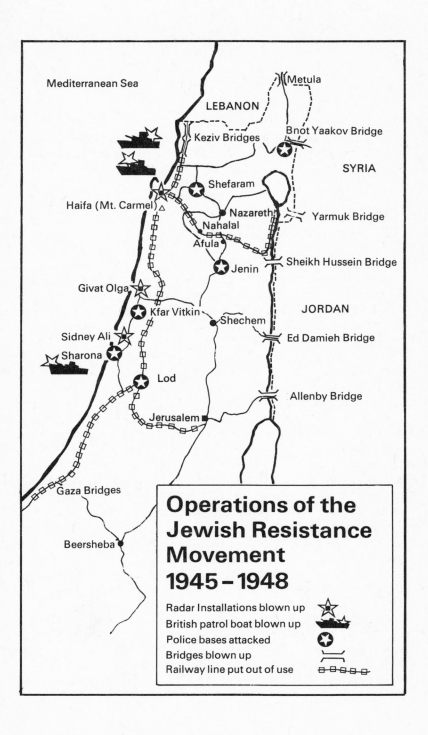

Mediterranean Sea

LEBANON

Metula

Keziv Bridges

Bnot Yaakov Bridge

SYRIA

Shefaram

Haifa (Mt. Carmel)

Nazareth

Yarmuk Bridge

Nahalal

Afula

Sheikh Hussein Bridge

Jenin

Givat Olga

JORDAN

Kfar Vitkin

Shechem

Sidney Ali

Ed Damieh Bridge

Sharona

Lod

Allenby Bridge

Jerusalem

Gaza Bridges

Operations of the Jewish Resistance Movement 1945 – 1948

Beersheba

Radar Installations blown up
British patrol boat blown up
Police bases attacked
Bridges blown up
Railway line put out of use

This was the official bulletin to the units issued by Palmach head-quarters on 19th June, 1946, immediately after the operation which took place on the night of 17th–18th June, 1946.

The Attack on the Bridges

On the night of 17th–18th June, 1946, our forces attacked along the length of the borders of the western part of the Land of Israel in order to destroy the road and rail bridges to the neighbouring countries. Eleven bridges were attacked. Of these ten were destroyed or severely damaged and one was not damaged.

The Keziv Bridges. Two medium bridges over the Achziv River, in the Arab village of A-Ziv, $4\frac{1}{2}$ kilometres south of Ras en Nakurah, one carrying the Haifa-Beirut road and the other the Haifa-Beirut-Tripoli railroad.

When our men got to within a few dozen metres of the target, after a rough, exhausting trek through thickets and orchards guarded by armed Arab look-outs and by dogs, past stone walls and trenches, they were spotted by the enemy who immediately opened up heavy fire from a fortified position and sent flares aloft to call for help. On an order from the commander, Nehemia Shein, the unit stormed and took predetermined positions under covering fire. Yehiam Weitz was hit in the chest by a bullet and fell. He was given first aid, and his last words were: 'Carry on. There's no point in caring for me.' He sent greetings to his family and his friends.

At the same time the road was blocked to the north and the south, both by mines and armed detachments. Some of our men started to evacuate the Arab villagers living near the bridges, who were likely to be injured by the blowing up of the bridges. An enemy flare suddenly struck the main explosive charge as it was being placed under the railway bridge. There was a tremendous explosion, and thirteen of our comrades were killed. It was now impossible to destroy the other bridge. The railway bridge, however, was completely destroyed. Among the dead was the commander of the operation.

Gathering up the wounded, the unit withdrew with its equipment.

It is almost certain that the sentries guarding the bridge had received information about the advancing unit from Arab watchmen, and thus we lost the element of surprise. However, the attack was carried out with great daring. It can be said with certainty that were it not for one piece of bad luck, the operation would have been successful.

The wounded carried their arms with them, and many showed great personal courage. In addition to Yehiam's body, unidentifiable remains of bodies were found by the bridge. It seems that few of the bodies remained whole after the massive explosion.

Metula. Two bridges. One on the road from Metula to Tyre, 2 kilometres north-west of the Metula police station, on the border. Our unit reached it surreptitiously, blew up the bridge, and retreated safely, with its arms. The second bridge was medium-sized, and on the Metula-Vale of Lebanon road, one kilometre north-east of Metula. It is near the guarded gate of the camp of an armoured corps unit. The unit stole up to the bridge and started laying charges. The British guard discovered them and opened fire. The bridge was blown up and destroyed, and our unit withdrew safely with their arms. Fire was not returned in order not to reveal the route of withdrawal.

The B'not Yaakov Bridge. A large bridge over the Jordan, carrying the road from Rosh Pinna to Damascus.

Our unit reached the area of the Jordan surreptitiously. Our men overpowered the sentries, disarmed them, tied them up and removed them from danger. Simultaneously the road from the army camp near Rosh Pinna was blocked with mines and the telephone wires cut. The guard at the police station on the east of the Jordan near the river did not notice what was going on, and the bridge was blown up and destroyed.

Our unit returned safely, with all its arms.

Diversionary action at Mt. Canaan. At H-hour, which had been synchronized with the other actions in eastern Upper Galilee, a diversionary action took place between the Mt. Canaan police station and the Border Force camp. The government forces panicked and fired at each other. The fire continued for a long

time after our men had withdrawn. The army, which thought that
Mt. Canaan was its most vulnerable position, rushed reinforcements there. Thus the diversionary operation achieved its aim.

A number of Border Force men were wounded by shots fired
at them from Mt. Canaan.

The El Hawah Bridge (Yarmuk). Railway bridge on the Zemah-
Damascus line over the Yarmuk River. The longest bridge in the
country (130 metres), it is situated on the border point of the
Land of Israel, Transjordan and Syria. There is a concrete guard-
post near the bridge.

Our unit reached the place surreptitiously. Scouts found that
the guard post was empty and that the bridge was not guarded.
The bridge was blown up and completely destroyed.

During the withdrawal, when the unit reached the border point,
they encountered a mounted patrol of the Transjordan Border
Force. In an exchange of fire two Transjordanian soldiers were
injured, and the rest fled.

The unit continued on its way and returned to base safely,
with its arms.

At the same time diversionary action took place by means of
telephone messages to the Zemah and Tiberias police stations.
This stratagem confused the police and the army who opened sustained fire and thus secured the safe retreat of our unit.

The Sheikh Hussein Bridge. A large bridge over the Jordan,
carrying the Bet-Shean (Beisan)-Irbid road. The bridge was
guarded at both ends by Palestinian and Transjordanian forces.

The unit approached the bridge surreptitiously. The sappers,
helped by the uproar of the River Jordan, stole up to the bridge
and placed the charges; the Arab sentries were ordered to leave
the danger area. The bridge was blown up and destroyed.

Our forces withdrew safely, with their arms.

The Ed Damieh Bridge. Bridge over the Jordan, carrying the
Nablus-Transjordan road, 45 kilometres south of Bet-Shean, near
the Bet-Shean-Jericho road.

The unit reached the bridge surreptitiously, having crossed
populated Arab areas. The explosive charges were placed with a
time-fuse, to enable our men to get away and to secure their long
and difficult escape route.

The explosive charge was supplied with an additional fuse in case the time fuse failed or the enemy tried to defuse the charges. In fact, for unknown reasons, the time fuse did not work.

The following morning, when a unit of the Royal Engineers tried to remove the charge, the second device exploded. The bridge was destroyed and one British officer was killed.

Our unit made the long difficult trek back safely, with their arms.

The Allenby Bridge. Bridge over the Jordan, carrying the main Jericho-Amman road. A large bridge, guarded at both ends by Palestinian and Transjordanian forces.

Our unit got close to the bridge. When the sappers began their work heavy fire was turned on them with light and heavy machine guns by the many guards. The sappers completed their task under covering fire from a specially designated unit that operated under excellent fire control and co-ordination. The bridge was blown up and destroyed.

The withdrawal was long, difficult and dangerous, but was completed safely. All our men returned with their arms.

Two policemen were injured.

The Gaza Bridges. Two large bridges, carrying the road and the railway from Palestine to Egypt, 7 kilometres south of Gaza. The bridges were secured by fixed guardposts and in the surrounding districts there are many army camps and well guarded air fields. The landscape is flat, making secret movement difficult.

Before the task force went into action, cover units held the guard posts under fire. The road, busy with military traffic, was mined and blocked by armed units north and south of the bridge.

The sappers hurried to the bridges, placed the charges and lit the fuses. The railway bridge was severely damaged while the road bridge suffered considerable damage.

During the action diversionary activities were undertaken in the region of the railway line at Dir-Sened.

Despite the length of the trek, the withdrawal was completed safely, and all men returned to base with their arms.

 a. As always in these raids we were true to the ethical code
 characteristic of all our activities: avoidance, as far as
 possible, of loss of life. Wherever possible villagers or policemen were evacuated from the danger area, or warned in good
 time.

F

b. In most cases the actions were difficult and our men showed exemplary ability.

c. There was a full moon, which made things more difficult for our units and forced them to take extraordinary measures that are not necessary on dark nights—silent movement and great care.

d. These extensive operations, which covered all borders of the country, demanded meticulous planning and full co-ordination so that one operation should not defeat another or prevent the withdrawal of another unit in the vicinity. The co-ordination was well handled and the operation as a whole succeeded.

e. We have information that the operations caused much excitement and consternation among the Arabs, and among army commanders here.

f. The Yishuv is proud of the ability and the willingness of its units.

Palmach Headquarters.
June, 1946.

Members of *Hashomer* with their commander Yisrael Shochat (center), Galilee 1904

Yitzhak Sadeh (center) with Moshe Dayan (left) and Yigal Allon, Hanita 1938

Orde Wingate leading members of his Special Night Squads, Ein Harod, 1938

The Jewish Brigade inspected at an Allied Victory Parade, Italy 1945

The Haganah in action during the Arab Riots of 1947

Illegal immigrants are helped from the *Parita* by the Haganah

Bet Yosef, a "Stockade and Watchtower Settlement" in the Jordan Valley

Haganah troops look out over the Arab Quarter of Safad, shortly
after the city's capture

An Israeli machine-gun position at Ramat Naphtali, in the hills
of Galilee

Israeli troops sweep toward El-Arish, November 1956

Tank and armored units on the outskirts of Rafah, June 1967

A forward attack from helicopters in Sinai

Israeli torpedo boats patrol the Straits of Tiran, June 10, 1967

Tank crews rush to take up position after a battle alert,
November 1969

In training for the future

This account of the destruction of Allenby Bridge, linking Palestine to Transjordan, was written by the commander of the units immediately ofter the action on 17th–18th June, 1946.

Sabotage Action No. 9 (Report)

The Force: Palmach units   Date: 19th June, 1946

The Task: Sabotage of Allenby Bridge in order to prevent it from being used for as long a period as possible.

Preparations and Reconnaissance: (a) Preliminary and preparatory reconnaissance was carried out in March 1946. Two night reconnaissance trips; trip to road and the vicinity; day reconnaissance of object itself. (b) Scouting of object and re-examination of road on the nights of the 6th and 7th June, 1946; fixing the plan of operation and last reconnaissance with unit commanders before the operation on the night of the 8th of June, 1946. (c) night reconnaissance before the operation to check possible changes, night of 14th August [sic!] 1946.

General details on the object and its vicinity: The bridge is built of steel bars, supported by four stone and reinforced concrete supports, with an asphalt road running over it. Dimensions: length—35 metres; width—6 metres; thickness of two inner walls —1.20 metres; width of the river-bed—25 metres.

Vicinity of the object: On the Palestinian side, a Customs house, a police station, a number of huts for living quarters, and a hut serving as a canteen and place for the sentries to rest.

Enemy forces: Exact number unknown. Estimate: 15–25 policemen with at least one automatic weapon. Also two watch dogs. On the Transjordan side, a two-storeyed police building.

Guard: Two sentries on the bridge by day and by night, two permanent lookout men in the police buildings. Additional enemy forces in the area: in Palestine, army camps near Jericho; in Transjordan, unknown.

Our forces: 35 combatants (including 14 reservists) and one driver.

Equipment: 8 T.M.T.'s[1]; 3 magazines with 60 bullets each; 19 revolvers, 2 magazines for each—altogether 225 bullets; 1 machine-gun, 8 magazines—350 bullets; 40 hand-grenades; 6 mills bombs; 2 rifles with 50 bullets each.

Division of the force: 1st Squad: 3 soldiers; 3 T.M.T.'s; 6 grenades. 2nd Squad: 4 soldiers; 3 T.M.T.'s; 5 grenades; 1 rifle; 3 mills bombs. 3rd Squad: 3 soldiers; 1 machine-gun; 1 rifle; 1 pistol; 3 grenades. 4th Squad: 3 soldiers; 2 T.M.T.'s; 1 pistol; 6 grenades; 1 mine. 5th Squad: 7 soldiers; 7 grenades; 5 pistols; 6 knapsacks of explosive, each weighing 25 Kg. 6th Squad: 7 soldiers; 7 grenades; 6 pistols; 6 knapsacks of explosive, each weighing 25 Kg. 7th Squad: 2 soldiers; 2 pistols; 2 grenades; 4 mills bombs. 8th Squad: 3 soldiers; 1 driver; 2 pistols; 1 grenade. One O.I.C. of operation (moves with 4th Squad): 1 pistol; 1 grenade. One O.I.C. of sappers (moves with 6th Squad): 1 pistol; fuses.

Method of operation: (night action): (a) silent penetration of area of activities while deploying covering squads. Placing charges (300 Kg) on the two sides of the inner wall (the Palestinian side). Setting of time-fuse and withdrawal. (b) In case of engagement with enemy, covering squads give covering fire while object is stormed and fuse is lighted; withdrawal under covering fire.

Detailed plan: The force will leave base[2] together in a lorry to point of departure. Squad No. 8 will remain to guard the vehicle and to give warning of danger. The force will move towards the deployment point. The force will divide up: Squad No. 1 will move to point A, its task being to secure and give cover to Squads No. 5 & 6 from the western side of the bridge, against enemy fire from either side of the river;[3] Squad No. 2 will move to point B,[4] its task being to hold down enemy forces in the Palestinian police station; Squad No. 3 will move to point C, its task will be to ensure free movement for Squads No. 5 &

[1] T.M.T.—A sub-machine-gun produced by the Haganah.
[2] Bet Ha'arava.
[3] The Jordan.
[4] Ramat Rahel.

6 and to cut off the Transjordanian police; Squad No. 4 will move to point D, its task will be to command and serve as reserve; Squad No. 5 will move to point E, its task will be to transport and place the charges against the wall; Squad No. 6 will move to point F, its task the same as Squad No. 5.

Method of action of Squads No. 5 & 6: After the covering squads have taken up their positions, they will approach by crawling, led by their superiors and the sabotage commander (in the event of a silent operation), or by running (in the event of a storming action); they will put down the charges and withdraw at a crawl (in the event of silent action) or by running and jumping (in the event of a storming action) towards the deployment position. Squad leaders, on instructions from the sabotage commander, will set up and connect the fuse, will activate the time-fuse device ('red pencil') and will withdraw at a crawl. They will inform the operation commander silently of the activation, and he will send messengers to the squad leaders ordering a general withdrawal to the rendezvous (in the event of a silent action).

In a storming action, a 90 centimetre fuse will be ignited, and 'blast' will be shouted. At the same time the operation commander will make an agreed sign with his whistle, in addition to the cry 'blast'. These two signals will be the sign for a general withdrawal to a distance of 100 to 150 metres. While each squad leader remains in charge of his detail, the force as a whole will take cover and will await the explosion. When this is heard, the entire force will withdraw, either in squads or individually, according to the circumstances. The rearguard will scatter pepper all the way back to the rendezvous. If the withdrawal is not made together, the rendezvous will take place up to one hour after the explosion. From the point of rendezvous the unit will return to the lorry which will stop at point A where all equipment will be assembled and taken to the cache where it will be hidden, except for two pistols and three hand-grenades to be kept by the forces for self-defence. The force will continue to point B, and from there by vehicle to point C. There a motor boat will be waiting for them, with knapsacks containing equipment needed for a three-day trek—blankets, food, a change of clothes, books, zoological and botanical equipment for disguise; also water and two one-way carrier-pigeons to take messages to base E. The boat will land the force at point D, and from there it will proceed by night to the daytime hiding place. On arriving at the hiding place, the first pigeon will be released with a short report on the action and the condition of the men. Within two nights, at the most, the unit will reach base E without being observed. If the force encounters enemy forces either while on the march or while camping, the second pigeon will be released to report on the incident. If point D is surrounded by enemy troops, the force will proceed to base F. The men will disperse from base E.

a. *Notes and appendix to plan*: 1. A small squad will be stationed at the point of departure. Should there be any encounter with a small enemy force during the drive there, its function will be to silence the enemy force by threats, brute force, and by tying them up. 2. In the event of contact with a large enemy force, the unit will jump off the lorry while it is moving and will return fire. Scattering will be followed as rapidly as possible by assembly at the first meeting point on the way to the target area.

b. *Medical services*: 1. Detailed instructions will be given to participants in the operation before departure. 2. Every squad will be equipped with first-aid equipment. 3. There will be a qualified stretcher-bearer with squads No. 5 & 6. 4. There will be a medical orderly in the command squad. 5. There will be a nurse with a stretcher in the lorry. 6. Assembly point for the wounded will be by the deployment point. 7. There will be a doctor at the base. 8. Procedure with the wounded: slightly wounded will be taken by the vehicle to a hiding place, prepared beforehand near the departure base; seriously injured will receive emergency treatment by the doctor, and he will decide whether to transfer them to the hiding place or to leave them at the base.

c. *Instructions in event of engagement during the withdrawal by vehicle*: In the event of the withdrawal route being blocked by enemy forces, the river should be crossed to the eastern side and the force will lie low in the undergrowth till the trouble dies down.

Execution of plan: (see attached timetable). We left on 16th June, 1946. The journey to the deployment point passed without incident, according to plan.

Final orders were given at the deployment point. The cover squads and the sapper squads moved to their predetermined positions. When Squad No. 2 got to within 10 metres of the canteen, a sentry noticed them and called out, in English: 'Who's there?' In reply the operation commander shot at him with his pistol and gave the order to take up positions. The sentry jumped into the sandbagged position and started directed rifle fire. At the same time, fire from three additional rifles opened up from the Palestinian police station. Squad No. 4 threw three grenades, and the sandbag position was silenced. Enemy fire was direct but weak. Four Verey lights were fired.

When the first shot was fired, Squads No. 2 & 3 opened up with direct fire against the enemy. Squad No. 1 reached its position in its entirety and opened fire. The squad leader took up a position on the eastern side. Squads No. 5 & 6, with the sabotage commander, broke through to the object and placed the charges. The carriers withdrew to the deployment position and the squad and sapper leaders prepared the detonator and the ignition fuse. The fuses were lit, and the order to retreat— a shout of 'Blast'—was given. The O.I.C. of the operation gave the general order to withdraw. The squads moved out in the previously arranged order, followed by rifle fire from the Palestinian police station and machine-gun fire from the Transjordan one, and by flares. Squad No. 3, whose job had been to cover the movement of the other squads, retreated still covering the whole force with machine-gun fire.

When the explosion was heard, all squads were 150 metres away, except for Squad No. 2 with the sapper's officer, which was only 50 metres away.

a. *Notes on the action*: The commander of the operation controlled the situation well, and gave clear orders and instructions to the squad leaders throughout the operation, and also commanded and directed the orderly withdrawal of the squads. The squad leaders managed their men well, directing them and avoiding waste of ammunition. Conduct of the men: Very good (considering that many of them were under fire for the first time).

b. Stoppages: A slight stoppage of a machine-gun resulted in a delay of two or three seconds in opening fire. 2. A stoppage in a magazine. The return spring was quickly mended. 3. T.M.T.'s did not work. The rest of the weapons functioned well.

c. The enemy used tracer bullets. This helped us.

Continuation of withdrawal: After the explosion the withdrawal continued according to plan, with no incidents, according to the attached time table.

Pigeon No. 1 was despatched on 17th June, 1946 at 06.00 hours; it has not yet arrived.

Having made good progress in the desert in the direction of base E, the O.I.C. decided to return to base the same night.

During the last three hours the force was accompanied by the barking of dogs, and four times they heard shouts of 'Who's there?' from neighbours. Until the last part of the trek, four kilometres from base, no mistakes were made, but in the last section one mistake was made owing to fatigue, and the trek took an extra hour.

Pigeon No. 2, which was released at 05.00 hours on 18th June, arrived at base on time.

a. *General Notes*: The assistance rendered by the managers of 'Achdut'[5] at the base of departure should be noted. All transport arrangements, both by land and water, were carried out well, accurately and faithfully.

b. The lack of training on the part of the reservists was noticeable. This made things especially difficult on the trek back.

c. It became clear that without preparatory reconnaissance, it was almost impossible to find sufficient cover for the whole force in the desert.

d. A debriefing session was held with the squad leaders who made various remarks about improvements in equipment, battle-dress, etc. In conclusion it should be noted that everything went according to plan. The men's morale is high.

Timetable

DATE	TIMES	POSITION
16th June, 1946	20.15 hours	departure parade
„	20.30 „	departure by lorry
„	21.10 „	leaving lorry
„	22.50 „	deployment point reached
„	23.05 „	departure from deployment point
„	23.08 „	the first shot
„	23.15 „	exact time of explosion

[5] The Haganah.

17th June, 1946	00.30	„	getting on to lorry
„	01.00	„	leaving lorry
∷	01.30	„	embarking on boat
„	01.45	„	boat leaves
„	03.45	„	boat reached Royair beach
∷	05.00	„	'En Traibe reached
„	10.00	„	resting under bushes
„	18.20	„	setting out on trek
18th June, 1946	05.30	„	arrival at Ramat Rahel
„	08.30	„	dispersal

SIGNED: THE COMMANDER

F*

The following account of the destruction of Allenby Bridge was written immediately afterwards by one of the participants in the action of 17th–18th June, 1946.

Famous Allenby Bridge

Well, at the beginning there was our song. We stood in the copse, in the departure parade, and while everyone was standing at attention, we burst out singing so that we could be heard for miles. We hadn't sung it that way for a long time. And it's not surprising. . . . Afterwards when we were trekking through bad terrain, when every step was a jump and a dragging of limbs, the words still echoed in our hearts, and sometimes they were confirmed by reality.

Against the enemy our road goes up,
Among the clefts and among the rocks. . . .

Really among clefts and among rocks, not just between them. And add to that, for example, the end. We reached the end when the moon was fully risen. But it only lit up a narrow path, in that thicket of rushes and bushes, in that jungle of the Jordan valley, where once lions roamed and now lads went out to do a deed modestly with a song in their hearts—its words so simple.

Do you know the bridge?
Of course. It's the old kings' road.

It lies between us and the new state, the Hashemite Kingdom. Smugglers of radio sets, plastic bombs, cows and refrigerators use it; sometimes they ford the river, up to their waists in water, and at other times they cross here, protected by their enlightened army. And the armoured cars and convoys of the new king, they obviously pass over the bridge itself. The king once expressed his admiration for that structure of steel and concrete, 'the famous Allenby Bridge', he called it, according to the BBC—and little did he guess. . . .

And because the bridge was important, because it served kings and their armies, it was thoroughly guarded. Whether the guards heard something, or whether they just thought that the bridge between 'Palestine' and the Hashemite kingdom should be well guarded, we'll never know. Anyhow, about sixty soldiers and policemen sat like kings in those buildings, like sentries, at either end, and we, well don't tell anyone, we numbered. . . .

We were about a hundred metres from the bridge, entangled and pushing wearily and silently through the rushes, and we could already hear the free flow of conversation of the policemen. And the reflection of the moon in the water dodged about and peeped through the thickets, menacing us: 'Here, I'll give you away, all of you.' You can laugh, but every time the moon appeared, I cursed it roundly in seven languages.

It was the moon that gave us away; or perhaps it was a startled frog that croaked and frightened the brave sentries? I can't tell you. But one thing I can say. When we heard that ritual response of sentries, 'Halt, who goes there?' we opened fire immediately to give cover to the sappers, in two squads, who were working in the water below placing the high explosives. Fire was opened up on us from all sides, and we were exposed and frightened and dodged through the thickets to hide from the evil eye.

What do you do when they open fire on you? Some people say, hide. Others say, get away and find cover and reorganize your forces. Some say (and they deserve a bullet in the back for saying it, but they too have an opinion) run. And of course, wise guys have lots of good advice for such situations, especially when there are at least twice as many guards as us. Haim didn't think so. He said: 'I'm a Kurd, yes sir, and I don't know any tricks, when I'm told to blow up the bridge, I blow it up, and to hell with them and their shooting.' So we lay down among the reeds; it was quite a party, wow, and occasionally we heard Haim's orders, crisp and clear and mingled with jokes, in the gaps between the shooting.

What does one say, what can I say? I've seen a lot of films in my time, good ones and bad ones, and I've read a lot of books, exciting ones and dull ones, but never have I seen or read anything like that. You understand, here was a real choir of rifles singing, and here the sappers were crawling in the water, bursts of fire spraying the water, and they were doing what they had to do. The bridge had to be destroyed, and they were going to destroy it. They don't want to know any tricks, no, they just destroyed that bridge, and how!

Many of us had learned the craft of war. Perhaps many things are said in books and in lectures on the right way to behave. Perhaps a lot is said about the strategic division of forces. But we did things differently. You ask why? Listen! We had an order to do it, right? And the time of the explosion was part of the order, right? Of course it was fixed; could there be a plan without a timetable? And it would be dawn in a few hours. Do you think we could walk around with rifles and Tommyguns on our shoulders? No, my boy, we don't yet have a Jewish state, and then too. . . . Today, anyway, we're people of the night and in the night we put our trust.

And that's just how it was. You don't believe me? Well, ask any of the boys, they'll tell you how they squatted there under fire, how they planted the stuff with something extra in it, without which it wouldn't explode, and how they made off under a hail of fire with shots of the armies of two states chasing them. And wow, was it hot there in that jungle, wow. It had to be crossed though, especially as we were hurrying and the flares were after us, literally falling between us. How was it that no one was killed, you ask? Perhaps it was just good luck, as some of the boys say. Or maybe it was something else: maybe it was simply that we just had to get back safely, you understand? We just *had* to. We haven't got many people. We've got brains, we've got guts, and we're well trained. But there aren't many of us. But when you don't have many people, they must all get back safely. And when they have to, they do it.

You're laughing at me, a sarcastic, bitter laugh. You say that up there in the action in the north we were few, and even so. . . . Right, I know. We aren't babies and we know what we're getting into. Of course something happens sometimes, and when it does it's in the stupidest, most unexpected and unnecessary way.

I don't know what happened to those on the other side, but when we got to the ruin and drank some water and rested a bit, we counted up our men and found that there were no missing and no wounded. None. Our lives are precious. We're not going to be put into ghettoes or concentration camps here. We don't want to be disarmed and left to the tender mercies of the pillage-happy sons of the desert, or even left to the mercy of Albion Isle's 'civilized' folk.

Do you think that we thought, for a single minute, that right away, the next day, they'd give us our state on a golden plate?

Look, I've been 'preaching' Zionism a bit in the middle, but there's no other way. That's what Giddie says, and he's right.

No, my friend, without Zionism there's nothing. Without it there's no point leaving everything and coming here, to this hail of bullets, no point at all.

And how did we move around afterwards, where did we go and how did we cover up our traces? That I can't tell you. Why? Well, we're going to have to do, many times again, what we did that night.

Will we be pleased? Of course not, who do you think we are, professional soldiers? No, we won't be at all pleased. There are thousands of other things we've got to do, and we want to do them, but there's no other way. So what do you say, there is another way? Let's not argue, you say. O.K. We won't argue. But even so I ask you: Is there any other way? You see, you have no answer.

Two whole nights were allocated for the trek home, a long, long way, but don't you try to guess where 'home' was. First of all, because you won't find it, and second, because you can name any place you like. Any place can be our home, any place I said. In every settlement we'll find a warm bed and food and drink, and kind words, friendly, heart-warming words. In every settlement, I said, in every settlement they toast us, because they know, they know very well, who and what we are.

As I said, two whole nights were set aside for our withdrawal, but we really pushed it, and got back in one. Don't ask how we marched or how we drank water from some stinking pool that on another day we wouldn't wash our feet in. . . . We got back in a single night, at dawn. Why? Perhaps because we wanted a good bed and tasty food? Perhaps. But there was another, much more honourable reason: we wanted to feel how the people of the Yishuv look at us in friendship and brotherhood, we wanted them to tell us again 'it's mutual, brother', and if there's ever a need. . . Well, did you read what they did in Bet-Ha'arava? Tell me, is there any difference between us and those boys who defended their settlements?

Is there any difference?

A Participant.

This was the bulletin to the units issued by Palmach headquarters immediately after the operation, which took place on the night of 20th–21st July, 1947. The commander of the platoon which carried out the action was Haim Bar-Lev, the present Chief-of-Staff of the Israel Defence Forces.

The Night of the Radar

On the 21st July, 1947, in the morning, we were told: The resistance movement attacked the two fortified radar installations on Mount Carmel; one was blown up and destroyed, and a heavy battle took place near the other. Our men who broke in held their own in a tough engagement with the guards and many soldiers who were entrenched in houses and concrete positions. Eliezer Arkin fell. Our men returned to base, taking with them the lightly wounded.

Once again our Brigade has done what was demanded of it. The men stood their own in a very difficult engagement, stubbornly broke through to the target, and damaged it in battle. A military installation serving the British Navy and tracking down immigrant ships has been destroyed.

The expulsion of the illegal immigrants from the Land has not gone without its price.

The time at our disposal to carry out the raid was limited, and was not more than two days. We knew that the task was difficult and very dangerous.

Within two days the men were chosen and the services organized, including armourers and medical orderlies. In a matter of hours all reached the departure base, despite the curfew imposed on the town of Haifa.

The two radar stations are on Mount Carmel, one on the west, near the Stella Maris monastery, and the other to the east, near Hariva.

The unit which operated on the west advanced with its equipment, according to schedule. After prolonged infiltration they reached the perimeter fence. At 10.30 p.m. they broke through the fence and penetrated between the houses near the installation; here they passed a sentry who did not notice them.

Fearing detection, they withdrew and broke through the fence at a second spot. They crossed the road and broke through the second fence, a 'double accordion'. They reached the inner fence 20 metres from the installation. One of the sentries saw them and opened fire. At the same time a military truck approached from the direction of the town, and halted close to our men, at their rear. The officers and men in the truck opened fire on our men. Our men returned with fire in all directions and at the same time proceeded to break through the third fence. A military patrol arrived and it too joined the action. Fire from sundry weapons was also poured from the windows of the neighbouring houses. Our forces continued the battle and prevented the enemy from directing his fire. When an armoured car arrived, and started to attack from the flank with its machine-gun the order was given to explode the charges and to withdraw. The engagement in the courtyard lasted twenty minutes. The area was illuminated by electric lighting and flares.

Eliezer Arkin was mortally wounded. His comrades moved him from the courtyard to the road. Meanwhile the fire was intensified, and two attempts to move him were unsuccessful. Eliezer asked his comrades to take his pistol and to leave him. He felt that he was dying. He asked them to send greetings to his parents and to his friends. Several other men sustained light wounds.

Throughout their withdrawal, till they reached a dead area, our men were under constant fire from two machine-guns, and they moved in the glare of searchlights and flares. The wounded were treated on the spot and at the assembly point for the wounded.

In conclusion, it must be noted that the men and their commander exhibited exceptional self-control and audacity, and the services acted splendidly.

The installation on the eastern Carmel was also reached under cover of darkness, and the unit arranged itself for attack by the perimeter fence. The breakthrough started according to plan, at 1.15 a.m., since the anticipated explosion was not heard from the western radar station. The sappers broke through two fences (one

simple, and the other a double accordion), and reached the installation. The rest of the force was arranged in three covering units,
each one of which had been given a specific sector to cover.

An enemy patrol which approached from outside the camp was
attacked by our covering detail. Several of them were injured,
and the rest fled. On hearing the shooting and the explosion to
the west, everyone in the camp woke up. One of the soldiers in
the camp saw the sapper detail, and heavy fire was opened immediately. The covering squad silenced the enemy fire with excellent fire control and co-ordination and enabled the sappers to
complete their task.

The withdrawal commenced after it was clear that the operation
had been accomplished: a mighty explosion was the sign that
the radar station at Hariva was no longer! The radar station and
the neighbouring tents were blown into the air.

One of our men was lightly injured, but under the medical
orderlies' supervision reached the base with the rest of the unit.

In the two battles we lost a certain amount of equipment.

It is worth mentioning that both the radar installations were
heavily guarded by the Airborne Division and by Arab watchmen,
and the western radar is in a fortified military area surrounded by
army camps.

Palmach Headquarters.

This second report of the same action on 20th–21st July, 1947 was written much later by one of its participants, Haim Guri, now a well-known author and journalist.

The Radar Action

Haim Guri

A lot of time has passed since then. When I visited the place a few weeks ago, I smiled to myself: yes, things have changed. Children were playing, and the first of the winter flowers were blooming; the water in the bay was blue. The sky was blue as well. Rusty barbed wire and abandoned barracks were all that remained of those times. I recalled the days and nights at the end of 1945. I remember that stormy, thundery night when we broke through to the 'object', the people's faces, the battle. A lot of time has passed since then. Some of those who took part in the operation are no longer with us. If you walk through this country and visit one of its many cemeteries you'll find their names inscribed on simple tombstones. I can see them before my eyes now, this band of dead souls, as if they were still alive. Raphael (Ginsburg). I take up my pen, and try to write. To those who loved you, to those who knew you, what can I say that is new. For many you will be just an unknown warrior. Childhood in Germany, death in the hills of Bet-Hanun, buried in Bet-Keshet. I said to myself: we must not forget a single detail of the lives of those who fell in the storm of many battles. . . . I, therefore, take up another stone from the roadside and add it to the memorial.

The country was in a state of siege. The British had strengthened their hold on us. The bright light that seemed to be shining at the end of the war, faith and hope, was extinguished. The occupying soldiers spat a bitter truth in our faces: enslavement. The shadow of a blockade fell on our shores, a dark, menacing shadow. Our hidden arms, our last line of defence, were being sought by brute force. The night of Atlit. The trains and the coastal police station were behind us. But no one was kidding himself about any quick way out. The Palmach was preparing for the future.

Our company's bases were in the valley of Zebulon, some of them near Nahalal. Raphael was a platoon commander at Yagur.[1] There were very few of us, and we knew each other well. We were eager for action, and we were completely convinced that it was necessary. We used to look at each other and wonder who would be called to the next action, who would ever marry. The command tent was on the other side of the valley, the workshop for military planning.

It was a winter's night. Nahum S. and Nehemia Shein (now dead) were sitting over a map of Haifa. A 'sixth sense' made us feel there was something in the offing. Raphael was called over to the tent, and came back after a while. I tried to read something in his face, but couldn't. One of the many good points we found in him was his ability to hide the stormiest feelings behind a calm face, and his ability to keep a secret without letting anyone know that there was a secret to be kept. In those days that was an inestimable virtue.

The reconnoitring stage began. Night after night Raphael surveyed the 'object'. The radar station was on the 'French Carmel', near the Stella Maris Monastery. The area was full of British army camps, check-posts, mobile patrols, and searchlights that made access very dangerous. Raphael crept up by night and lay down by it. He crawled to the fence, and observed for hours, collecting information. Every detail was important. Any detail could determine the fate of the operation. Any detail could seal the fate of our commandos. It was essential to know the exact number of sentries, how they worked, and the times when the guards were changed.

The picture became fuller. By day he would walk around the area with his 'wife' M. They would pick flowers, and enjoy the glory of the world. Indeed it was a beautiful hill, beautiful even to pain. The British had dug into that flowering hill with their nails, they had made that delightful spot on the French Carmel into a base for a diabolical device serving the most despicable role it had ever been entrusted with: guiding the hunters into trapping their prey, which were our illegal immigration boats. In his daytime strolls he would complement what he did by night lying on the bare rocks, in the freezing cold. By day he wore a good

[1] Kibbutz Yagur, near Haifa.

suit, by night grey work clothes. Nobody else did it. Obstinately he would creep up close to the target. Parallel with Raphael's work, our Intelligence was gathering information. The file on the radar station got thicker and thicker. The fruit ripened; it was the fruit of anger.

We assembled in the command tent. Dan L., operations officer of the First Battalion, briefs us. We will get the order to start in three days. But then we heard about the enormous difficulties: the radar was inside an R.A.F. camp in a hut surrounded by a special defence wall. The camp contained the following facilities: a revolving antenna, guards' living-quarters, mess, etc. Everyone in the camp was armed. Around the perimeter there were three barbed-wire fences and a string of lamps that illuminated the inner fence. Two hundred metres away there was a large camp of the British Military Police. The neighbours were mostly Government clerks and suchlike who supported the Mandatory rule, British and Arabs. Four British sentries in pairs, with sub-machine-guns, guarded the equipment and the inner perimeter fence.

There were six men in our task force. The job was to be performed silently, with no battle. Raphael was in charge. There was a mountain of problems, and one of the most difficult was to avoid inflicting casualties on the enemy. This meant either attacking when the equipment was not working, but nobody knew when this was, or overpowering the people inside, which was almost impossible. The final decision was postponed. Meanwhile, Raphael took us to Haifa and showed us the withdrawal routes and the hide-out where we were to assemble at the end of the operation. We were given private addresses in Hadar HaCarmel, a place to go after the thing was over. We prepared our covers and learned the winding route to safety. We were sent by 'Ruthie from the pharmacy'. In various places they would take us in, opening their doors with warmth and understanding.

We returned to Yagur. Raphael trained his men in carrying the knapsacks, in cutting barbed wire, in bringing down sentries. They were the best and the most talented in the company. Arms were taken out of the secret store: well-oiled machine-guns, pistols wrapped up in rags, hand grenades, clubs. Nahum, the company commander, rushed round getting pencil fuses with the right timing. The plan became clearer. They were ready to set out. And a short while later came the order to postpone.

Three times Raphael and his men were ready to move, and three times the operation was postponed. The men got irritable. Raphael, involved and energetic, continued with the preparations. Conditions had changed. The instructions were altered. The date on which the S.S. *Hanna Szenes* was due approached. The task force was at the ready, in case the immigrant ship was caught. The boat reached the coast, and the date of the operation was postponed once again. Meanwhile, conditions became more complex: the enemy had increased his alertness. . . .

But the day did arrive. The departure base was at one of the houses in Haifa. There were seven in the party, including the girl M., and they were ready. In the next room the gelignite was being prepared. Raphael inspected the preparation of the charges. He got a severe headache from touching the material. Time was pressing. The seven climbed into a small car. The car sped up the hill, passing between army and police vehicles. Where the road makes a turn to the left, just when it was dark, Raphael's men jumped out and followed him among the rocks and scrub, up the steep slope to the radar station.

The operation had started. The outer fence was breached. One man stayed behind to give cover, and the rest advanced. In absolute silence, a few dozen metres from the sentries, the second fence was cut. It was evening and the mess was full. They had to hurry, before the moon rose. The third fence was cut . . . nobody noticed. The seconds pass in terrible tension. A military truck drives up the hill, dazzles them with its lights . . . they lie flat . . . it turns away. The sentry approaches . . . stops . . . and returns. Has anybody noticed? Must hurry, the moon will rise soon.

The saboteurs watch their leader; Raphael gives the order. They slip forward, clinging to the wall. The sub-machine-gunner covers them. Raphael presses the time fuses, climbs over the stone wall, catches the knapsacks, and slips them between the defence wall and the wall of the station. Forty kilogrammes of gelignite. Timing of the fuse—45 minutes. The charges are also set with a booby trap which will explode them the minute anyone tries to dispose of them. So there was a double cover: the fuses if nobody caught them, and the booby trap if they were discovered . . . .

Raphael and his men slip out quickly. The party make a rapid retreat toward the car. Speed is essential. Any minute the danger could get much worse. The explosion that was to destroy the hut was imminent. The resistance movement's policy at that time was to avoid loss of life, and accordingly Raphael was instructed to inform a certain person that the fuse had been set, so as to enable him to order an immediate evacuation. The car sped down. The British guards were suspicious and opened fire, and the driver accelerated like a maniac. Raphael calmed him down. At a certain place they all dispersed, each to his apartment or to his hideout. After a few minutes the telephone at the radar station rang and an anonymous voice spoke: 'This is the Resistance. We are warning you that the radar station has been mined and will explode any minute. Evacuate it immediately!' In a friend's home Raphael sat looking at his watch. The lady of the house tried to calm him: 'Don't worry, you are safe!' Little did she know what went on in the lad's heart. He sat and waited . . . and waited. Minutes passed. It was time. The second-hand moved twice round the dial. Why was nothing heard? He went down to the courtyard and rapidly reconstructed his actions. Everything had gone according to plan. Three fuses had been activated, and one of them had to work. But the redeeming blast was not heard.

Next morning there was a laconic official announcement: 'At 8.15 last night unknown intruders placed a mine in the R.A.F. experimental station on Mount Carmel. The mine was removed. No damage was caused.'

From details gathered subsequently the following became clear: immediately after receiving the telephone warning everyone in the hut got out. A courageous British officer risked his life and plucked out the fuses by the ends that were protruding from the explosive charge. The first fuse went off a minute later. Army engineers who came later discovered the booby trap and isolated it from the detonators. The mine was removed.

The raiding party went around like ghosts. Raphael was silent. He wanted to repeat the operation before security arrangements that would make it impossible could be enforced. This was not approved.

Raphael was silent, and it was difficult to know what he was thinking and feeling. It was a mortal blow, to break into the lion's den, to lay the charges, to take the risks . . . the bloody telephone. Who knows what he thought about the affair. He hardly spoke about it. But he was made of tougher stuff. If some people had despaired of the task, he believed single-mindedly . . . the radar was his. He had worked to blow up the equipment. The commander of the Resistance at the time wrote to the com-

mander of the British garrison in Haifa: 'Kindly convey in my
name my respects to the courageous officer who removed the
charges from the radar station. However, I must emphasize that
if the radar station continues in its foul task of hunting down
refugee ships, we shall blow it up without giving you any prior
warning.'

The day arrived. As a result of further reconnoitring by
Raphael, it was decided to make a second attack on the station.
Twenty-two men were assigned to the task, the best of the
fighters. The plan was this: approaching from the opposite
direction, the raiding party was to break in, and cover was to be
given by the rest of the force; the charges were to be set off
immediately; and they would withdraw. If a silent break-through
was not possible, it would be done in combat, rapidly. 'Carry out
the task at all costs,' the order concluded.

The commander of the action was Y.R., and the raiding party
was led by Raphael. We reached the departure bases in small
groups. The force was assembled in a small room: twenty-two
men armed with submachine-guns and revolvers. It was a rainy
night. We set out, led by local scouts. The route was tough and
tiring. Occasionally the rain stopped, and the full moon shone. We
had no battle drill, and we carried grenades in our pockets or on
our belts. We reached the foot of the hill at 02.05 hours, at high
moon. After consultation a retreat was decided upon. There was a
danger that if we were to start late we would get caught by daylight, and there was a withdrawal route of twenty kilometres to
reach base.

We started to withdraw after hiding the charges in some bushes
in the valley. We set out on the road that was no road, stumbling
against rocks. Some were exhausted, so others carried their arms.
At dawn we reached the edge of Ahuza[2], near an old artillery camp
(afterwards it was discovered that there was another radar station
there). There was an arms cache about two hundred metres from
the camp. The group got back to camp exhausted. Once again it
seemed that there would be no operation. Raphael's men,
members of the raiding party, were washed out. The previous
months with the different setbacks had drained them. We all went
to sleep, waiting for more orders.

At 16.15 hours an order was received from Palmach head-

---

[2] Ahuza—a suburb of Haifa, then sparsely populated.

quarters: 'The raid must be carried out at all costs. There are far-reaching considerations involved.'

Once again we arrived in Haifa in groups. Once again we assembled in that small room . . . I glanced at Raphael: his face was composed and serious. Y.R. imbued his men with his own sense of confidence. After we had primed our grenades and heard the briefing, Y.R. said: 'The password is: "I came, I saw, I conquered." ' We grinned and went out into the storm. Raphael and his men led. After a tough and tiring trek we reached the valley where the charges had been hidden. The charges were set up with thirty centimetre fuse wires, meaning a fuse of thirty seconds! We started to approach. After a few minutes we slipped between the houses and lay down on the other side of the road, opposite the fence. The rain was incessant, and silently we were all grateful for the storm. Each man prayed for the storm and the darkness. The squad leaders met and tasks were assigned. The squad which was to cut the third fence crossed the lighted road and reached the fence in the dark. In a few seconds it was breached, and a line of shadows hustled through . . . The rain got heavier, and we were soaked through. Two squads remained outside to cover the withdrawal and to block the road from the nearby Military Police camp. Another squad, inside the fence, took positions against the ATS camp, and the rest broke through the second fence. The first fence was surrounded by a ring of projectors. You could see the figures of the sentries. We knew that the enemy was on the alert. We knew that a few days earlier they had sounded an alert that got all their forces on the hill on their feet within ten minutes. The second fence was cut. The sappers crawling under Raphael's command and the cutting of the first fence are legendary. For almost an hour-and-a-half five men crept that short distance, while on the flanks submachine gunners were ready to open fire in case of trouble. Raphael and his men reached the first fence. The sentries heard a rustling and turned up the powerful projectors, but didn't see the men. They didn't believe that anyone would carry out such a crazy idea twice. At 03.00 hours the last fence was cut. Raphael and his men, the people who had taken part in the first raid, slipped inside and started playing 'hide-and-seek', breathlessly, with the sentries. Suddenly we heard the soft explosion of the detonators. The charges were being thrown in. Raphael and his men slip down as the boom overtakes them. A red pillar of flame and an enormous explosion—the radar was destroyed! Within a minute there was the sound of sub-machine-guns, and Verey lights were fired to call for help. We withdrew rapidiy down the slope. A quick count found everyone present. After a diversionary trek through the valleys, we reached a dark synagogue where we handed in our arms, and hurried on to N've Sha'anan. Before dawn we got to Hariba, and from there along the paths of Mount Carmel to Yagur.

The job was done. Raphael had avenged.

Since then a lot of time has passed, and this story sounds like a dull distant echo. The fellow who played the main role in the operation participated in many battles over the years and faced many dangers, until he lost his life in a heavy bombardment by the Egyptians on the Gaza front. The company commander fell when the 'Yiftach'[3] forces made a hefty onslaught on the enemy's bottleneck near Bet-Hanun, and thereby forced them to evacuate their forces north of Ashdod, Majdal, as far as Yad Mordechai. His dying eyes witnessed the victory of our army.

[3] The Yiftach Brigade of the Palmach.

This is an excerpt from an address, delivered in Tel-Aviv on 30th
September, 1947 to the National Council of the Histadrut (the
General Federation of Labour) by Yisrael Galili, last Commander-in-
Chief of the Haganah. It not only summarizes the tasks of the
Haganah at that critical time, but shows the prescience of the
Haganah High Command in foreseeing the imminent possibility of an
invasion by the regular armies of the neighbouring Arab states and
urging the necessity of preparing for it.

———◆———

Towards a Crucial Decision

Yisrael Galili

In the opinion of a number of colleagues, who are the representatives of the Histadrut working for the Haganah, as well as of those
who are entrusted with the political work of the Zionist movement, the present period is bringing us face to face, as an
increasingly stark actuality, with the danger of all-out Arab aggression. This time its purpose would be not merely to deflect us from
furthering the cause of the Zionist enterprise, but to accomplish
its final liquidation. It needs no oracle or secret intelligence
activity to confirm that. Those groups which mould world policies
are now considering the political future of this country. At such a
juncture the Arabs may think twice about resorting to violence
and aggression. They did this often enough in the past
when the prospects of any gain through terrorism were even
less bright for them than they are at present. From the point of
view of political calculation, the Arab leaders had no reason to
rejoice at the results of terrorism. But then neither had they
reason to regret it, as the British Government never failed to dole
out political prizes as the wages of their terror. From time to
time the violence of Arab terror has descended on us, but it has
afforded no satisfaction to our enemies, for the Zionist enterprise
has not been brought to a standstill. Insofar as this depended on

the Jews, immigration continued, settlement went on, orderly communications were maintained, no settlement was wiped out, and the Yishuv in general did its best to go on leading its life at its usual pitch of intensity. From this point of view the aims of the organizers of terror were not realized, but with the help of the British they did succeed, if only partly, in gaining their objectives after each wave of 'disturbances'. Such was the case after the disturbances of 1920, 1929 and 1936. The prize for terrorism came to them in the shape of various political ordinances that British rule inflicted on us, which culminated in the White Paper of 1939—the fatal blow that Britain struck at the Zionist enterprise.

If this was the case in the past, it is even more so at the present time, when since the World War the Palestine problem has reached a critical point, calling for urgent decision. Whether there are among us those who are satisfied with the present turn of events or those who are not; whether there are among us those who, to further the aims of the Zionist movement, would like to bring the problem into sharper focus and so precipitate the struggle for a decisive solution, or others who would deplore such action—the fact remains that we are all bound to take cognizance of the mounting tension engendered by the Palestine problem among all the parties in the struggle: British and Arabs on the one hand, and Jews on the other. This is the kind of tension that ushers in the days of decision.

The Arabs are fighting to bring Palestine under their rule, to bring the Yishuv to a standstill, with no prospect of further development. All this lends further tension to the struggle—that of a last-ditch battle.

Due to the vicissitudes of the political situation, the defence plans for the Yishuv have undergone serious changes. The Yishuv has never relied for its defence on the authorities, and self-defence has become a sacred principle in its life, one of the basic values in its independence and national freedom. Nevertheless, it is imperative to stress that in the past the basis of our defence plans has always been to keep up the struggle in all settlements or groups of settlements until help arrived, either from the police or the army. Such help was invariably delayed, but the fact is that so far we have not had to confront Arab aggression alone and for long, without some semblance of aid from the authorities. Even if late, support from the police or the army has always helped us in quelling local Arab attacks. Each regional commander, each district or company commander, recognized it as his mission to hold what he had set out to defend until help came, no matter how late. This was the yardstick by which the 'duration' of the mission was decided, as well as the quantities of ammunition and reinforcements of manpower needed.

In the past, in the days of the 'disturbances', Haganah men stood side by side with British army personnel, in different sectors of the front. This cannot exonerate the British of the blame for aiding and abetting Arab terrorism, and Zionists have steadily denounced the British authorities for this. It was usual with them to incite terror until it had exceeded the limit which in the eyes of the Administration was deemed convenient. When it did so, measures were initiated to suppress it. It is worth mentioning in this connection that Government aid to the Yishuv started after the murder of Andrews.[1] It was then that the special Night Squads were formed, under the command of our friend Orde Wingate.

Today, however, we must recognize the fact that the British will not again permit us to move units or hold illegal arms, to station units of mobilized men along continuous lines such as the 'Southern Line', which is the defence line between Kfar Saba and Atlit. Nor will they allow us to form units for purposes of ambush in the Emek and Galilee. No longer will we be able to count on that measure of British tolerance which we enjoyed towards the end of the 1936–39 disturbances. Worse still, our attackers are likely to enjoy military help from the Administration, exceeding anything we have ever received, and it is irrelevant whether this help will be in the form of active connivance in attacks, or of the overt ignoring of violence. What this means is that our defence plans, concerning manpower, arms and ammunition, can no longer be based on watching and holding, or on active defence until the arrival of police help. On the contrary, we can no longer be certain that the Government will fulfil its duty and take the necessary measures to stem Arab attacks or hinder their gaining momentum, stage by stage.

The coming onslaught will not be carried out by the Arabs of Palestine alone. Every day we are deluged by proclamations from different Arab diplomats threatening a 'Holy War' to be jointly

[1] Lewis Andrews, the District Commissioner of Galilee, killed in Nazareth by Arabs in October 1937.

undertaken by the Arab states. There is no need for us to give way to hysteria over this new situation, or to make exaggerated estimates of the extent of the intervention of the Arab armies. Between uttering threats and carrying them out, there is still a great difference. But the fact remains that even if we are not called upon to confront regular armies, the Arabs of Palestine will receive organized and regular help from the Arab countries, even if it is kept secret. There is something extremely serious in these threats, and we must be prepared for an attack from neighbouring countries.

It is not impossible, also, that the British Government may have calculations of its own to stage-manage an evacuation of troops, thereby creating a breach for the Arab countries and making it possible for them to interfere at will. Even if this is not yet a certainty, it is still a possibility which we have to regard as an actuality. It is on the basis of these considerations that we must determine the speed, the extent, and the needs of our defence.

Here and there an age-old argument about what was once known as *Havlaga* (restraint) has been started again. To my colleagues and to me this concept has political and moral implications. We have no intention of uprooting or dispossessing the Arabs, neither do we intend to rule over them, and subdue them by the power of the sword. We have no desire to wage a bloody war between the Jewish and Arab peoples, nor do we regard every Arab as an enemy simply because he is an Arab. We wish to defend our enterprises and preserve our honour, but not by violence and murder, such as the throwing of grenades into Arab markets. We make a distinction between defence and revenge, and our aim is to see the realization of the Zionist ideal going hand-in-hand with the brotherhood of nations.

These values, in the fullness of their political, Zionist, social, and human context still stand, and must continue to stand, as the basic values of Haganah. But there remains one serious question, namely the problem of disturbances in their early stages, and the prevention of their spreading. Disturbances do not begin by someone or other sounding a blast on a big ram's horn, so that all the country gets the tidings: 'The disturbances have started.' More often than not, the beginning is not serious. A few shots are fired; isolated attacks are made. They are sparked off, flare up, and spread by stages, both in space and time. The primary problem is how to show a strong arm at the very onset of aggression while remaining within the limits of a defensive action—preventive and not provocative.

The circles surrounding the Mufti are of the opinion that the Palestinian Arabs are no longer prepared to return to the hardships and the suffering which were their lot during 1936–39; and in point of fact we have no certain knowledge that the Palestinian Arabs are engaged in countrywide military preparations, such as training armed forces, planning operations, and setting up commands. As far as we know, it is the opinion in Mufti circles that the best way to start 'the affair' is by terror—throwing hand grenades into cinema audiences leaving the cinema on Saturday evenings (something which has already been done) and thus starting the ball rolling. They assume that the Jews will react, and in reaction to this reaction, there will be another incident in another spot, and so the flames will spread, until the whole country will be in the grip of violence, and the disturbances will force the hands of the neighbouring countries, which will feel constrained to come to the help of the local Arabs in a Holy War.

It is obvious that we on our part must avoid giving our enemies an excuse for aggression, and must beware of adding fuel to their fire. At the same time we must understand that helplessness can encourage attacks. Therefore, we must not limit our defence to the time and place of the attacks. We must strike at nerve centres, and at specially sensitive spots. Thorough investigation over the years, from 1936 to the present time, has supplied us with information which we can adhere to without going wrong.

To take one typical problem: since 1936 we have become much stronger in settlement, but from the point of view of defence, our lines have become overstretched and cut by Arab population centres that act as separating wedges in the Yishuv. For instance, we have the problem of defending the Negev, the problem of guarding the lines of communication and the vital arteries. Any simpleton knows the key points, and is aware of the paralysing effect that damage to water works, electricity installations and cement works would have on the life of the Yishuv.

The condition of the Haganah is far from satisfactory. In the matter of arms we have become noticeably better off, by acquisition and independent manufacturing. Both because of the present situation, and because of future possibilities, we are now working at more speed and with more energy to improve our store of arms, qualitatively and quantitatively. We have to beware of panic.

We still have time, though all too little of it. This awareness must spur us on to further efforts, to increase the speed of our preparation, and to prevent any sense of slackening and helplessness. Not a day should be wasted; every moment should be devoted to further exertions to acquire what we can, so that we may be better equipped. This is not a question to be discussed in an open forum. My chief anxiety is that we shall not suffer from lack of financial resources in the attainment of this objective, and that we shall have the places of work and the qualified personnel that are so vital for the expansion and increased momentum of our aims.

As to manpower, i.e. the number of front-line personnel in the cities and large villages, the position is by no means satisfactory. Our manpower is inadequate for a period of prolonged and large-scale disturbances. In other words, it is clear that we cannot make our defence dependent on conscripts serving in barracks and permanent camps—our defenders report for duty coming from their work, and return to it from duty. This situation calls for a large number of trained people for the needs of the settlements—for outposts and field duties. For this reason, too, the situation in the cities and settlements in unsatisfactory, since these are the very same personnel from whom we have to draw men for the defence of the country as a whole. We can double or treble the number of trained Haganah men in a short time, for over the last few years we have established a sound basis for a body of commanders and instructors.

Our demands, therefore, from the Council of the Federation of Labour are: to grant the Haganah Command authority to conscript any member of the Federation for guard, command and training duties. I want to point out that the conscription of a member demobilized from the British army is a painful problem. Here you have a man who has served in an army for four or five years, and returns to his country to find, very often, he is without work, has nothing to hold on to. He is tired of war, of camp life, of military discipline; he only wants to be free of the whole business, to find himself a job and his place in society. This war-weariness is the main reason why the Haganah has up to now been unable to benefit from the military experience and the rich resources of skill in training and command developed in the various Jewish units of the British army. Yet we particularly need this type of manpower, to supply the many gaps in the Haganah's strength. Because of the illegal conditions under which it developed, the

Haganah was not able (for instance) to create services, auxiliary forces and units employing special weapons: obviously, not all the branches of an army can be trained illegally.

So we now have to call up scores of members experienced in command and training duties, who received their training in the Haganah and the British army. For this, we must have the necessary authority. I would like you to know that we are struggling, rather unsuccessfully, with this problem. We need the authority to conscript these trained men to instruct new conscripts and strengthen weak spots in the command. Without them there can be no instant 'Open Sesame'. We can no longer train men in cellars with wooden revolvers. Today, effective and intensive training is not only a job, but an art, and must be carried out on a sounder basis. For this we need experienced and qualified personnel.

We demand a return to the form of life that was the rule in workers' settlements in the past: every worker between 18 and 30 must give two days a month (in addition to Saturdays) to training. Moreover, he must devote 7–10 consecutive working days a year for the same purpose. This was done, though rather too late, in 1936–39, and that was perhaps why military standards remained low and defective. It is imperative to return, very soon, to this way of life. We must create conditions for training members outside the cities and in the fields, under camp conditions, and this must be done with the co-operation of both employers and employees. A soldier needs 200 days of training. We are planning mass training of recruits from the cities and settlements for a period of 50 days. This minimal stint has nothing to do with the Conscripted Brigade and the Youth Battalions. We propose to decide on and implement this rule; each employee must devote two days a month at his own expense to training. In addition he should be trained 7–10 consecutive days at his employer's expense. This is the absolute minimum. It is not our way to make excessive demands that neither member nor settlement can meet. The Palmach has reached a maximum of 100 training days a year. The special units are doing even more, not to mention the officers.

Because of a commander's brief period of service, a service-manual for young officers is required. It has become increasingly difficult for Palmach commanders to be released from service. In fact, things have reached a pass when a young officer has to cope with too heavy a burden to be borne unless it is shared by larger numbers. In sum, what is needed is an authority to mobilize, which will ensure the status of the conscript during the period of his service, and bring into the training framework a wider range of the population in the cities, villages, and settlements, including the young. It is also imperative to safeguard the rights of the commanders after their release from service.

If these demands are met, it will be within our power to set up a large and comprehensive force which, with the necessary arms, will enable us to hold our ground for no brief period of time, against the threatened all-out aggression. We would then be able to withstand and keep the aggressor within bounds, so that we may reach violence-prone areas in time. Not only would we be able to protect each settlement within its boundaries, but would prevent the attacker from approaching the boundaries of any Jewish centre.

It should be remembered that conditions in the Haganah are but a reflection of the conditions prevailing in the Movement as a whole; and if we do not create the right atmosphere, we will be unable to stand up to the task. The complacency prevailing in various places is truly astonishing. The fact is that up to this day guard duty is imposed, in many places, on a watchman who has been found unfit for any other work—and this at a time when thefts in the settlements have reached such proportions that they have ceased to be merely criminal and have become a security problem. At times the boundaries between theft and murder have become as blurred and uncertain as those between a criminal and a political act.

On no account must we separate security issues from action against the dissident [Jewish] terror groups. These create disturbances, panic and chaos, and imperil the security front. Not only do these organizations constitute a threat to the inner freedom of the Yishuv, the education of the youth and labour movement and the political framework, but they carry with them, and within themselves, the seeds of demoralization and mob violence. A person walking through the city and witnessing an act of murder cannot distinguish between 'political assassination' and 'simple murder'. These conditions make it possible to drag an Arab from a café in the centre of Tel-Aviv and murder him without a voice being raised against the murderers. This must serve as a warning to us of what is likely to happen in times of greater disturbances and tension. At the time of the funeral of the

Exodus 1947 victims, or the attack on Cafe Hawaii, the main problem of Tel-Aviv's defence was the restraining of the Jews. At such times, guards posted outside the main commercial institutions are not enough—we have to post guards in border areas between Jewish and Arab districts, for one never knows when such an organization can spark off the beginnings of a riot which would end in shooting.

Action against terrorist organizations must be undertaken a) without the co-operation of the British authorities, and without seeking aid from them; and b) since our purpose is not to open a bloody home front within the country, and despite the danger and the threat that the terrorist organizations may start a civil war, we must not be deflected either from curbing their acts of provocation, nor from hindering their activities. We must compel them to reduce and limit their activities and to desist from threats, so that no Jew will be afraid to refuse to rent a room or a cellar to one of their members, or refuse a compulsory contribution, or hesitate to rush to the help of an Arab whose life is threatened in our thoroughfares. Our action will explode the myth of the might of the terrorists, and make it clear that it is within our power to silence them, should we decide to do so. We should not ignore the Haifa incident: this act, and others of its kind (in addition to being a provocation), can serve as an excuse to our enemies among the Arabs.

Comrades, I have touched upon some serious problems, but have refrained from discussing political issues. Any member of this Council is free to make his own assessment of world factors and possible future events. The British Administration is in no hurry to rid us of its presence in this country. The clarion call has been sent out: 'A Jewish State', and before very long it will be a viable reality. But it has its menacing aspects: Arab aggression, and the 'justification' of the crumbling of law and order in the land. The more the transition period is prolonged, the more it will bring in its wake harsh measures to curb the Haganah, and repressive measures against its members. The provocations of the 'dissidents' are likely to serve as a pretext and camouflage to the Administration. We find ourselves on the horns of a tragic dilemma: our preparations must be intensive and widespread, even while we are not permitted to see ourselves as free people in our land, and indeed a massive campaign is to be launched against the Haganah by the Administration.

G

Over the years, an immense potential has developed and flourished in the Haganah, but to a large extent it is still dormant. It can, and will be actualized, if we are imbued with a strong and courageous spirit; if we live this epoch in a constant state of readiness to fight for our lives, anxious, but without giving way to panic; if we rise to the demands the hour calls for without weakening. By virtue of its status as the main strength of the Haganah, as well as by virtue of its prestige in the Yishuv, and above all by virtue of its mission, the Histadrut is called upon to be the spearhead of the struggle of the Yishuv.

On the Eve of the Fight
(Speech delivered to a group of Commanders
on October 20th, 1947)

Yisrael Galili

We have to acquire the faculty of 'brutal vision' and not close our eyes to the near future, even if the events likely to occur may be of the most cruel kind. On the horizon looms a threat to our very existence. The Yishuv in this country is very like the illegal immigrant who, having survived all dangers and reached the shores of the Land of Israel, is tossed between the hope of reaching a haven of safety and the threat of being exiled again to the detested 'camp'.

A clear-eyed view of our situation cannot fail to distinguish an encouraging ray of light and hope beckoning from afar. The world's conscience has not yet been completely stifled. This same ray of hope sheds light on our position: we have been forced into a decisive contest. This is the period in which the fate of the Land will be decided, and with it, the fate of the people. We have to live constantly with the awareness of this fact, and heaven forbid that we lose sight of it, even for a moment.

All the parties engaged in this struggle are concerned to see that the Land of Israel will become theirs to inherit. Time knocks inexorably at our door. The question of gaining control of the country is for us no mere symbolic matter, nor yet a question of Messianic fulfilment: it is a question of the very survival of the Jewish people, now deprived of all protectors, who need the country for their continued existence.

But time is also spurring those among the Arab people who are hostile to us. Their ruling class is aware that they are losing their grip on this country, which is becoming increasingly Jewish. They see for themselves how the Zionist enterprise is striking deep roots—redeeming the wilderness and going from strength to strength, so that its enemies can no longer overpower it; and, with the awareness of time running out on them, they are trying desperately to restore the balance in their favour.

Not only they, but the British, too, constitute a key factor in future developments as in the past, both in the country itself and the neighbouring regions. They too want to hold on to their power here for purposes of exploitation and empire. Their method—the gradual liquidation of our efforts by 'legal' means —has failed; so they too are preparing for another contest of strength. It is clear then that, in the present struggle for mastery over this country, all the separate forces have come together. If we fail to stand up to them, our fate will be sealed.

Under these circumstances, our independent strength carries a decisive weight. The idea of our strength has never been limited to the narrow sense of the weapons at our disposal. Our 'force' in the Land of Israel means the men, the settlements, the economy, the culture, the spirit, the national organization, the Zionist movement, self-defence and self-reliance. This is the strength; this is the primary political factor. The most uninitiated among us know that we have wasted time, that we have not exploited our manpower and material resources to the full. As it is, without the strength we have built up we would never have reached the council chambers of the United Nations. And had we entered these Councils without representing an actual force, not all our political acumen would have been of the slightest avail. Our hopes would have been dashed in no time. Thus the important question remains: exactly what is our strength? Is it in readiness for the coming trial? Are we increasing it? Are we sufficiently on the alert?

Our generation is living at the end of a savage period of history. Many years will have to elapse before humanity recovers from the bestiality with which Nazism has envenomed the world, and before human life can again have meaning, and a child's life any value. The world is still ruthless and prone to war, and the passion for power and influence are still liable to cause the destruction of nations and peoples. We must therefore imbue ourselves with the spirit of the illegal immigrants who fought the British Navy on the very decks of *Exodus 1947*. It is this that can awaken the conscience of the world and arouse whatever humanity is lodged in the human heart.

Zionism, in its efforts to realize its aims, is inherently a process of struggle against the Diaspora, against nature, and against political obstacles. This struggle manifests itself in different ways in different periods of time, but essentially it is one. It is a struggle for the salvation and liberation of the Jewish people. Earlier, we had to defend ourselves in the face of the policies of the White Paper, and the onslaught of the Palestinian Arabs. Now, when the fate of the country is in the balance, we will have to confront a combination of these two forces, strengthening and nourishing each other. Moreover, British policy will encourage Arab countries in an all-out aggression which will help the British.

At our meeting with the members of the United Nations Enquiry Committee, the investigators asked about the military power of the Arab countries, and the ability of the Yishuv to forestall their attack. The answers given by our representatives were honest and truthful, a realistic estimate of the force that the Arab countries can marshall for their 'holy war' in Palestine. Mention was made of the weakness of the Arab armies, of their low military standard, and of the lack of ideological motivation among their rank and file. Inter-Arab rivalries and mutual antagonisms were also stressed. But even if all these contentions are accurate, they must not lull us into a delusive tranquility.

We are approaching a situation in which British policy will attempt to precipitate a decision, while getting its work done for it by the neighbouring countries. We must therefore be prepared to defend ourselves against the military forces of the Arab countries. Our ideas of self-defence must no longer be based on the size of the Arab population in our country and on the estimated force that they can mobilize from among their ranks. We must consider ourselves threatened and attacked, both openly and secretly, by the military forces of all the neighbouring Arab countries.

Even those who contend that this is not a certainty, must view it as a possibility that cannot be dismissed lightly. We have seen the extent of the hostility of British policy and the brutality employed in carrying it through. We belong to the generation that has witnessed the abandonment of the cause of democratic Spain, and is witnessing today the events in Greece and Indonesia. And was it not only yesterday that six million were abandoned to their fate and massacred? In the light of all this, who can stand up and offer us the palliative contention that this possibility will not become a certainty?

At the inception of the Arab League, there were those among us who were far-sighted enough to warn that British policy was covertly and systematically aiming at making the Palestine problem a centre of conflagration in the Middle East, sparking off a bloody encounter not only between us and the local Arabs, but between our Yishuv and the Arab nations.

In academic circles there is room to explore the social and political factors, to distinguish between cause and effect, actions and reactions. We need no such theoretical study to help us gauge the different factors that are combining to present a real threat: British imperialistic interests, the interests of reactionary Arab rulers, the ambitions of certain countries to gain influence in the Mediterranean area, anti-Semitism, inter-Arab rivalries and intrigues, the social and spiritual character of the Arab regions, etc. But whatever the estimates of cause and effect, there can be no difference of opinion as to the outcome, which is as simple as it is grave: the British are preparing a conflagration embroiling the Jews of the Land of Israel and all the Arab countries.

We have heard the announcement of the British withdrawal. During the last few weeks the mask has been lifted slightly and to our eyes certain incidents have provided evidence of the satanic schemes being put into execution in the course of the withdrawal. Such a proclamation about withdrawal without making prior arrangements for the government of the country, leaving it in a state of anarchy, is an obvious act of provocation and an invitation to the Arab countries to take control of the country. It excites the imagination and inflames the instincts, and is likely to frighten the Yishuv into foregoing its political demands and force it to come to terms.

When the High Commissioner[1] was asked at a press conference for foreign correspondents how much truth there was in the information that the British Administration was planning to withdraw from Arab areas into Jewish areas, he replied that if such a plan existed, he was opposed to it. But [Richard] Crossman, a Member of Parliament and a member of the Anglo-American Committee of Enquiry, has publicly announced that such a plan does exist. Such a revelation in itself points to the turmoil which is being stirred up and which we will have to confront. From the offices of the Administration, news leaks out from time to time of details of the discussions and plans. They are debating how to bring about, in theory and practice, the disintegration of law and order, and plans are being scientifically drawn up to reduce the whole country to chaos. They are

[1] Sir Alan Cunningham.

planning a headlong withdrawal, and the destruction of documents necessary for the new administration: a blueprint for anarchy, meticulously worked out down to the smallest detail. One example should suffice: the Commissioner of Prisons asked the General Secretariat for instructions as to what to do at the time of withdrawal with the thousand lunatics and other unbalanced prisoners in the country's jails; he received the liberal and humane reply: 'Let them loose. . . .'

The Jews, the members of the Movement, and the Haganah men, are now looking for help to two quarters. The one is far off—the world's help, if indeed it comes, as a result of the debate in the United Nations. The other is near: the Haganah. And it, the Haganah, is in need of some basic changes:

a. We must draw up plans covering the extent, dimensions, timing, armaments, training, and build-up of our forces on the assumption that they will have to confront not only gangs of Palestinian Arabs, but a general uprising of the local Arabs with the help of the regular armies of the neighbouring countries.

b. We have to wean ourselves, and rapidly too, from the initial assumption upon which our defence plans were based between 1936–39. In other words, from now on we must brace ourselves for a mode of defence which will no longer count on help from the army and police.

c. We must be prepared for the danger arising from a possibility that, while we are occupied in self-defence, the Administration may decide to disarm the Haganah. We have to remember the cynical response the Jewish Agency received when it asked the High Commissioner to reinforce the police force in the settlements. He said in so many words: 'The Government cannot give one section of the population what it is withholding from the other.' And as if this were not enough, after taking this decision he spoke about stopping illegal immigration altogether.

At present we are concentrating armed forces in different parts of the country (yesterday in Upper Galilee and tomorrow in the Negev). These are 'illegal' armed forces, and it would be catastrophically foolish to forget, or ignore the possibility, that the Administration may disturb our preparations by searches for arms.

d. We must note well that in future we shall not enjoy the same measure of independence that we enjoyed during the 1936 disturbances. The Administration will pursue us, whereas the Arabs will enjoy advantages which should enable them to act without hindrance.

We must not treat lightly the numerical strength of the Arab states. The Transjordan forces number between 20,000–25,000 men, including two armoured brigades, and most of the army is mechanized. The Syrian and Lebanese forces are estimated at 20,000. Egypt has 40,000 soldiers in addition to air force units. The whole Iraqi army numbers approximately 25,000–30,000 soldiers. Britain has only to give a nod, and these forces will start marching openly or in secret towards our borders. I am quite certain some of them are already waiting, making their plans. And if it should be said that this is only a manoeuvre meant to cow and put pressure on us, we know full well that what is a political, tactical move today may tomorrow exceed its initial bounds, especially after the humane and liberal brakes of British policy have lost their grip.

It is irrelevant and even despicable to indulge in clever speculations about 'whether', 'can it be', or 'would they dare' to set loose the Arab states against us? Or whether America 'would' or 'would not let them'. We must constantly remind ourselves that we have to defend ourselves. We have to cleave to the tangible. And what is the tangible? It is Jewish land, Jewish economy, Jewish arms, Jewish fighting men in the Land of Israel.

The Haganah has two aspects—the inanimate and the animate. The inanimate is the materials: arms, supply, capital. The animate is: trained people, a trained command, and correct planning. In the field of the inanimate we have acquired what we could, and our acquisitions are growing daily. It is by no means easy to make rapid strides in this field, but we are now doing our utmost to increase our strength in arms and supplies from sources both inside the country and abroad. In this, for obvious reasons, it is wise to abide by the rule: 'Silence is golden'.

Against this, it is possible in what pertains to the animate—i.e. men, training, commanders, mobilization—to make giant strides forward. We need the authority and the conditions to mobilize every man and any number of men, to form them into units, to train them in self-defence, to select commanders from them, and to prepare them for greater responsibility. We need authority, soon, to mobilize materials, technical aid, and any productive forces likely to supply our defence needs. In other words, authority and capital are needed to defend the Yishuv.

We are dallying and delaying, and I have no idea how much longer it will take to organize the Yishuv to meet the coming events. The people have not yet been conscripted. We have not even launched a general fund-raising campaign. The young men of the Palmach and *Chish* (field force) who are posted in the Upper Galilee are still without tents and without overcoats. Anyone looking at what is happening in our public life begins to wonder: what is more important—to prepare to face danger, or to jockey for position in the future administration? Read the papers and find out for yourselves. The Jewish State is round the corner, the air is redolent with the smell of government, and 'political activity' in the Yishuv has increased noticeably. Some bourgeois circles who held the Elected Assembly in contempt and boycotted it, who were completely apathetic in the self-sufficient Yishuv organization, pretend now to have changed and to be deeply concerned and responsible. Be that as it may, there is a lot of thunder, but no rain. That is why I said we need a 'brutal viewpoint', for there is still too much frivolous complacency in the people. Or there are those who lie awake at night, thinking: 'Anyway we will not be able to stand by our strength alone'; or 'After all, the world has not become so wicked that no one will come to our help when they attack us.' Such thoughts or ideas can only fatally hinder us. Of course, we shall not cease trying to arouse the conscience of the world. But we shall not pass the test if we do not free ourselves from the thought of putting our trust in it.

It would be simple-minded to imagine that we can survive at this juncture with only the limited number of comrades that we already have in the Palmach. It would be a bitter mistake to believe that we will be in a position to choose the hour for con-scription, that we will know when and where the trouble will break out, and that we will 'manage' to conscript men in sufficient numbers for that particular day and place. Financial limitations are putting a stranglehold on the Haganah; were it not for these restrictions, we would months ago have had at our disposal a mobilized force of thousands. This would have remained an un-uniformed force until the battle began. The defence force we need

G*

cannot be raised overnight. If we rely on the idea that we shall 'manage', we will not 'manage'.

We still say that it is not within the power of the Yishuv to raise state budgets to establish a mobilized force which only a national treasury can support. That is why we have to build up the conscripted army on the basis of work and military service. The conscripts must alternatively work and be trained. They must earn their own livelihood by work which they must interrupt for purposes of training or defence. The military theory that no efficient army can be built on the basis of both work and training is a theory that stultifies action. Its logical outcome is the liquidation of the existing force and the search for salvation where it cannot be found.

We must not maintain our conscripted forces in closed barracks, but must integrate them into the border settlements exposed to danger. Thus we shall be able immediately to strengthen the Upper Galilee, the Etzion group of settlements and the Negev. Every Jewish settlement must become the base of a mobilized military unit. This demand must be made on each village, and first and foremost on the workers' settlements in the kibbutzim and moshavim. We need an overall and integrated approach. In times of war and emergency we do not forget our concern for the image of the Jewish soldier, for his human and social character and for his pioneer education. Concern for these values ensures the raising of the military standards of our men. Thus, the settlement will provide a base for the armed force, and the armed force will strengthen the settlement.

Not long ago we hurriedly posted field units to Upper Galilee —from workers' settlements. What we have to do, however, is to move manpower from the cities to the villages. We should be able to send infantry at short notice to the Galilee, not from Kibbutz Alonim or Nahalal, but from Tel-Aviv and Haifa. Densely populated areas should come to the assistance of sparsely populated ones.

Is it possible to start a wave of volunteering for the Haganah? Yes, it is perfectly possible, and it lies in our power to do so. During the war against Hitler, there was a positive tide of volunteering in this country. It may be said that these volunteers came because of the pay, the uniform, the opportunity for foreign travel, and other benefits and amenities they received from King George which we could not supply! To this I reply that these may have acted as additional incentives, but they do not explain the volunteering spirit. Basically, it was a remarkable manifestation of national awakening and of Jewish solidarity, which braved all dangers. It is within our power once again to start a great volunteering movement, for the defence of the Yishuv and of Zionism, of freedom and independence, and to augment our forces and our arms.

The Labour movement is the central force in the nation as in the Haganah and in our politics, and it is imperative to organize the Labour movement on a solid base of mutual commitment. The worker who does not undergo training and is not conscripted will make himself responsible for his conscripted fellow-worker. It is from the Labour movement that the challenge against complacency must come, and in its ranks that an exemplary volunteering spirit must be revealed—yes, in its ranks, in the Kibbutz movement, and in our own ranks. Thus shall we be able to fire the imagination of the Yishuv, including the circles of the more well-to-do, among whom, too, a volunteering spirit shall be kindled. It is in this spirit that we will be able to persuade or compel each man in the Yishuv to fulfil his duty. The place of the worker in this mobilization ensures his place in the political scheme. It is so in a time of emergency, and it shall remain so in the days that follow.

Again I must repeat the warning: We shall do no good by telling ourselves that 'we have lost our opportunity and have been overtaken by events'. Let us stop this fatalistic talk, and let our call be for strenuous exertion and for self-defence—while there is time. Let us call on the Yishuv to strengthen its forces. Let us call on the partisans among us, on the veterans who served in the British army, on any Jew who has served in any army. Military experience, from whatever school it comes, is vital and precious to us at this moment. We must be ready with the methods, the receiving centres and the channels for a general mobilization. We must train officers who can convert the conscripted raw material into a daring and well-trained force.

And if some stubbornly persist in asking, Is it within our power to stand up against an all-Arab assault?—our answer is: This is a foolish question! Is it within our power *not* to stand up against them? Have we any alternative? Have we any prospect of survival, other than by facing up to them with our full strength? Ever since we had to stand up against the Palestinian Arab gangs, our strength has been increasing. We have the tools, the nucleus, and the foundations for the building of a great army. Our human material is splendid—daring, endowed with the finest qualities of fighting men. It is said that our men are somewhat deficient in the usual forms of discipline. But, against this, they have the virtues of responsibility and courage. Any loss due to lack of military discipline is more than made up for by the self-reliance, the initiative, and the spirit of our men. They are short of military equipment, but they can inflict crushing blows on the enemy until such a time as the entire force can be organized. Our strength still lies in our potential, and this potential must be actualized. The Jewish fighter must not fail.

The following is a short description and analysis of a typical night operation of a Palmach unit during the War of Independence, 1948–49. It was written by Lt.-Colonel (Res.) Yosef Tabenkin, the commander of 'Harel', one of the three Palmach brigades, which fought in Jerusalem, the Jerusalem Corridor, the Negev and Sinai. Because of the shortage of artillery and the absence of air support, most of Israel's operations in that period had to be carried out at night, in order to use the darkness as a cover for the approaching force, for the 'softening' of the target, and for its conquest—or, if necessary, for a relatively safe retreat before dawn. This kind of operation was used in raids, or for the taking of fortified objectives.

From 'Doctrine of Raids'

Yosef Tabenkin

. . . Our tactics were based on the concentration of the entire force for a night attack; half of the actual force was placed as a reserve at the disposal of the operational headquarters. The plan was designed to allow for the withdrawal of units from the battle at any stage should enemy superiority become evident. The scheme of the battle was generally thus: the storming force reaches the place to be attacked from the rear; the advance platoon attacks and seizes the buildings; two platoons attack from the flank or the flanks, and the advance platoon becomes the company reserve; the storming force has a battery of light mortars and sometimes a machine-gun. The reserve gives support to the storming force and supplies cover from enemy reinforcements or, if necessary, during withdrawal. The supporting forces, armoured cars, mortars, machine-guns, a 'Davidka'[1], act from an independent base or as part of the reserve. The Command Party is usually with the supporting force or with the reserve. A detachment of

---

[1] The 'Davidka' was a home-made mortar.

sappers joins the attacking force, and as soon as the enemy
village is captured, it begins to destroy positions and buildings.
A unit specially chosen by the command, and no one else, begins
to collect the booty. At the end of the attack the entire force with-
draws, the reserve acting as rearguard. Communications are
maintained by walkie-talkies and by runners between the battle
headquarters, the base, company commanders, platoon commanders, and sometimes even section leaders. Medical aid is given by
company and platoon orderlies who move with the forces, at
assembly stations near the deployment point (served also by a
brigade doctor with an 'operating theatre') and at a base hospital.

I shall give as an example of our mode of action the capture
of the villages Beit Surik and Biddu[2].

The mortar was placed on a hill near the radar station, in
Hirbet El-Morn. One company left the Castel and moved along
the ridge to attack the village from the east; the second company
left from Bet-Pfefferman along the road to Biddu, to attack
from the west; one company set out to mine and set an ambush
on the Ramallah-Biddu and the Nebi Samwil-Biddu roads, and
another company set out to do the same on the Biddu-Bet Surik
and Biddu-Kubeiba roads. Armoured cars, the Davidka, the
reserves and the Battalion headquarters followed the company on
the Radar hill-Biddu road. The eastern company encountered an
enemy unit of thirty or more armed men, moving from Bet Surik
eastwards. It permitted them to pass, and continued on its way
to the attack position. The western company lost its way and
was behind schedule. Fire was opened on the company ambushing the Biddu-Bet Surik road from the Bet Surik school, near the
Biddu-Ma'ale Hahamisha road. The plan of attack was changed
on the spot: the ambush company stormed and took the Bet
Surik school; the company was joined by the reserve, and together
they attacked the village from the west, against sparse rifle fire.
The western company which had lost its way took Hill 870, which
controls the area as far as the Biddu-Ma'ale Hahamisha and
Biddu-Kubeiba road and became the reserve company of operation H.Q. The eastern company was ordered to take the village
after a short mortar bombardment, and attacked from the east.
One of its platoons seized the buildings and the other two attacked
at the flanks and began to clear enemy positions.

---

[2] These villages were in the vicinity of Abu Gosh on the main Jerusalem-
Lydda (Lod) road.

The village was conquered and its occupants fled. The reserve company requested permission from headquarters to capture Biddu; permission was granted. The Davidka joined the company. It set out, deployed for attack, and waited for the end of our attack on Beit Surik. As soon as the latter was taken, the demolition of buildings started. Our force in the village became the reserve, and the reserve set out to take Biddu. After a short bombardment with the Davidka the place was captured and its houses were demolished.

The battalion returned to its base in the morning.

The following is an abridgement of a penetrating account of the
liberation of the ancient city of Safad in the Upper Galilee during the
War of Independence 1948–49. Gavriel Cohn was a captain in the
'Yiftach' brigade of the Palmach, which participated in the battle; he
wrote this description, based on his own experience and research,
about a year later. After the War of Independence Cohn became head
of the army's historical department, and subsequently a lecturer in
History at Tel-Aviv University. He was a Member of the Knesset
(Parliament) 1965–69.

———◆———

The Battle for Safad

Gavriel Cohn

The fighting for Safad starting in November 1947 cannot be
correctly summed up or scrutinized except in the context of the
battle for Eastern Upper Galilee as a whole.

Though the Safad area had characteristic and specific problems, most of the problems common to the entire region of
Eastern Galilee also influenced the fighting there. When the
struggle began, the burning problem in all outlying areas of the
country was that of communications with the centre. In Eastern
Galilee, this link depended on a solitary highway ascending from
Tiberias to Jub Yussef and from there to the foothills, up to
Metula. The contours of that highway along the base of hills
that were commanded by the enemy, the dearth of Jewish
villages along it, the presence of Arab Tiberias and of Lubiya and
other Arab villages on the mountains and flanking it, to say
nothing of the unfriendly and unco-operative attitude of the
British with regard to armed escorts for Jewish convoys and
their antagonism towards Jewish acts of reprisal—all these factors
made the problem of maintaining transportation in this area of
paramount importance.

On top of this problem of transportation and of local defence
of the Jewish villages, especially in border zones, and of

lines of communication between them, we were further handi-
capped in defending these footholds of ours in the mountains by
the fact that they were almost completely cut off and access to
them was conditional on British grace and favour. This was so with
Ramot Naphtali, Manara, Misgav Am, Safad and Ein Zeitim, all
of them sparsely populated, without an independent economy, lacking in water, inadequately supplied. But the less their capacity for
defence, the greater their strategic importance, because their
topography made them protective bastions for the valley—predominantly Jewish—which they overlooked.

As far as the Safad area was concerned—which included Safad,
Mount Canaan, Ein Zeitim and Biriya—Arab superiority in manpower was most marked, for the Arab population was large. In
Safad and Eyn Zeytoun alone there were fifteen thousand Arabs;
and the area bordered on Central Galilee, which could be an
abundant source of reserves for the enemy forces.

In the defence of the Jewish quarter of Safad, a great deal of
importance attached to the chain of Jewish points—Mount
Canaan, Biriya and Ein Zeitim—since these prevented its total
beleaguerment. They were also important as jumping-off grounds
for a potential threat to Arab traffic and to the Arab villages in
the neighbourhood. On the other hand, the three settlements in
question laid an extra burden on Safad from the point of view
of supplies. Out of the limited stock which was brought into
Safad under grave hazard in the opening stages of the campaign,
quotas had to be allotted on occasion to these contiguous hamlets
and transported to them, again at great risk.

Harassment and fighting on roads. The signal for hostilities
in the Safad-Ein Zeitim area was given by an attack on an Ein
Zeitim vehicle on 29th December, 1947. The following morning,
a Palmach platoon was already there. A second platoon had gone
to Safad through Ein Zeitim a few days earlier on foot, to
sidestep British interference. Two sections of field soldiery
reached Mount Canaan a few days afterwards.

From 29th December and until the beginning of April 1948,
the enemy was chiefly engaged in attacks, by mines and gunfire,
on Jewish transport using the Rosh Pinna-Safad highway and the
internal Mount Canaan-Ein Zeitim stretch, and in sniping at the
Jewish quarter of Safad and Ein Zeitim.

There was one particularly serious assault on a Jewish habita-
tion at Ein Zeitim on 7th February by local Arabs and Syrian

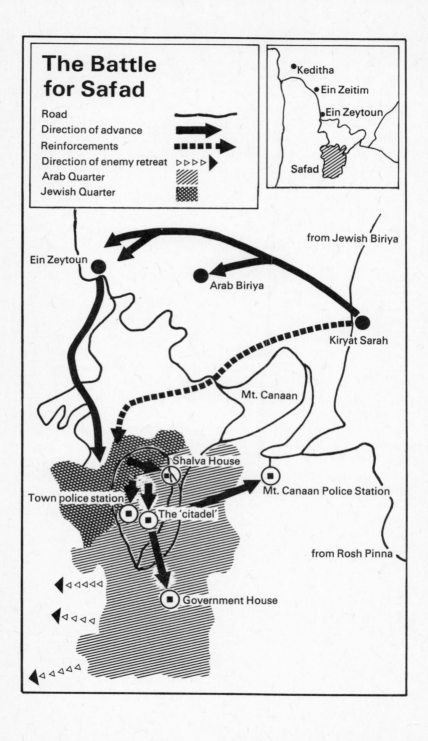

The Battle for Safad

Road
Direction of advance
Reinforcements
Direction of enemy retreat
Arab Quarter
Jewish Quarter

Keditha
Ein Zeitim
Ein Zeytoun
Safad

from Jewish Biriya

Ein Zeytoun

Arab Biriya

Kiryat Sarah

Mt. Canaan

Shalva House

Town police station

Mt. Canaan Police Station

The 'citadel'

from Rosh Pinna

Government House

volunteers under Syrian command. The assault was repelled with the help of British forces, whereafter the enemy apparently resolved to postpone all frontal attacks on Jewish settlements until the British had withdrawn, but, at the same time, to step up harassing actions against them and make it difficult for us to maintain contact with them.

Throughout this period the Jewish forces in the area applied themselves to raids and retaliation against Arab traffic and villages in purely Arab base areas and their approaches. The Palmach battalion posted in Upper Galilee at the time was dispersed in small detachments through a number of settlements, and the interference of the 'third party'—the British—and the need to assign forces for defence circumscribed the frequency and range of these operations. Few though they were, they nevertheless served to check the aggressive designs of the enemy, for he was compelled to deploy considerable strength to shield his traffic and villages. Our most spectacular raid in this area, and perhaps in the whole country, was on Saasa on the night of 14th February, undertaken by two choice Palmach platoons, which were stationed in the Safad area throughout the war. The outcome of this exploit was that all the Arab villages in Central Galilee, until then regarded by the enemy as a 'safe' region, had to draw on sizeable forces for self-defence.

As the time for the British withdrawal approached, the enemy intensified his activities. As in the rest of the country, so in the Safad area, too, the stranglehold on movement to the town became more and more throttling. (Until the evacuation of the Mandatory power, solitary vehicles, especially those carrying supplies and sometimes also passengers, might break through into Safad or get out of it, under British protection.) Several instances of land-mines and the ambushing of Jewish transport between Rosh Pinna and Safad in March led to the restriction of movement on this highway, and convoys had to be preceded by patrols which examined the route ahead and established themselves in covering positions along it. The presence of British troops in the police station on Mount Canaan was not a deterrent to the Arabs of Hareth el-Krad, situated on the way to the Jewish quarter of Safad: their gunfire made it suicidal to enter or leave, and from that time on the passage of Jewish vehicles into the town came to a virtual stop. Communication with Ein Zeitim, however, was kept up by the Rosh Pinna-Mount Canaan road, and from there on—

by the seizure of commanding positions and by returning Arab fire—through the dirt track from Mount Canaan.

On 3rd April a Palmach section seized a commanding position on the Safad-Ein Zeitim road—we called it 'Position No. 1'—to secure the safe transit of a convoy to Ein Zeitim. Half-finished trenches for perimeter defence were found in it. There was no doubt that they had been dug by the enemy the night before, the intention being to occupy the site within the following few days. It was clear to the Area Command that the occupation of this commanding height by the enemy might settle the fate of Ein Zeitim, since it would have isolated completely a settlement already ringed by Arab villages on three sides, north, west and south, and have snapped the only road-link to it.

The size of our fighting force was infinitesimal—a Palmach company consisting of fifty-six combatants, ten men in various services, and fifty girls. Furthermore, its equipment was painfully limited, making it impossible to detach a force of any strength to hold Position No. 1 permanently. The only measures undertaken were the mining of the half-dug trenches, the holding of the site during the hours of daylight by Palmach units from Ein Zeitim, the appearance of a section or so from time to time during the night, and the directing of fire at the village of Taitaba and its forward positions to create the impression of uninterrupted occupation.

On 5th April the site was entered by a platoon of Syrian volunteers of Adib Shishakli's force, armed with machine-guns, who established themselves firmly. At dawn, sniping at the settlement courtyard began, and Ein Zeitim was thus cut off entirely. Besides enemy positions in the villages of Keditha, Taitaba and Eyn Zeytoun, Arab forces were now posted to the west, in the wedge between Haditha and Ein Zeitim, to the south, in the rocky terrain above the Acre-Safad road, to the east, in the land north of the 'old' Jewish Ein Zeitim, to the north-east, in Position No. 1, and to the north, on the ridge between Ein Zeitim and Taitaba.

There was no signalling apparatus in Ein Zeitim. It was a cloudy day and therefore impossible to get in touch with Safad by heliograph. The only way to transmit urgent messages to Regional Command headquarters on Mount Canaan was by runner—a dangerous procedure which reduced still further the small count of fighting personnel, for the runners were not sent back because of the renewed danger to which they would be exposed. It was clear to company headquarters that the only solution was to capture Position No. 1 and hold it.

For this operation, 3-inch mortars and extra Browning machine-guns were brought up from battalion headquarters in the Hula Valley. Two field-unit sections from Safad reinforced the Palmach unit on Mount Canaan, and at 04.15 hours on 7th April that unit launched its assault. Two machine-guns and two 3-inch mortars were mounted in 'Position No. 2', to pin down and soften Position No. 1. The two field-unit sections seized 'Position No. 3', to block any access of Arab support from Eyn Zeytoun and Arab Biriya. A reinforced Palmach section set out from Ein Zeitim on a diversionary attack.

While this three-pronged move was in progress, a Palmach platoon advanced down the wadi from Mount Canaan to Ein Zeitim and at 04.30 hours had reached the foot of Position No. 1 unobserved. A quick charge was successful, and the enemy retreated in the direction of his base in Taitaba.

This turning-point in methods of warfare in the area produced its effect on the enemy and also on the 'third party', which was at that juncture preparing for evacuation and anxious about its line of withdrawal to Haifa. In more than one conversation between the Haganah liaison officer in Safad and representatives of the British Army, the demand was made of us, forcefully and repeatedly, to abandon Position No. 1.

After the capture of Position No. 1, the distribution of the Jewish forces in the area was as follows: in Ein Zeitim—a field-unit section as reinforcement to the men there; in Position No. 1 —a field-unit and a Palmach section; in Position No. 3—a Palmach section.

In the ensuing ten days, the enemy confined himself to sniping at Ein Zeitim and Position No. 1 and mining the track between Ein Zeitim and Mount Canaan.

Intervention by the British gradually lessened. Exchanges of fire between Jewish and Arab positions in Safad multiplied and became more intense. Both sides attempted sabotage and both began preparations for the British evacuation, only the enemy did so more openly and thus more effectively. Concentrations of armed Arabs were observed close to the Mount Canaan Police Station and were seen to be entrenching themselves in its proximity, right under the nose of the British troops in it. The obvious intention was to gain control of the Rosh Pinna highway.

The British evacuation took place in the afternoon hours of 16th April. The Jews of Safad became aware of it twenty minutes before it began, when a British Army unit, equipped with field artillery, appeared on the military road from Rosh Pinna and deployed itself and its guns about 350 yards east of the Mount Canaan buildings, apparently to provide cover for the abandonment of the police station and prevent its being occupied by the Jewish force.

Seeing these manoeuvres, the Palmach detachments on Mount Canaan, not knowing precisely when the evacuation was due and fearing that searches might be made, began to hide what few arms they had. As the British convoy began to move away from the police station, an armed Arab platoon advanced towards it from the Arab hotel—south of the station and about twenty yards from its surrounding fence. At the departure of the last British vehicle, it was already well within the building's precincts. By that time there were no longer any British troops in Safad itself, and the three key positions held by them until their withdrawal —the 'citadel', the town police station and Shalva House—had been seized by the enemy.

When the news became known in Safad, reinforcements were rushed at once to all sectors in the Jewish quarter, and the enemy's attempts—which began all over the town within twenty or thirty minutes of the evacuation—to break through and cause havoc in the quarter were swiftly halted. A runner was sent from Area Command to the headquarters on Mount Canaan and to the Palmach unit in Position No. 1 to ask for all possible reinforcements. A strengthened section under a platoon commander —this was most of our fighting force, with the overwhelming majority of the light arms in the base on Mount Canaan—was taken out of Mount Canaan to occupy the grove south-east of the base which commanded the Rosh Pinna-Safad highway and the paths from Jaouneh to Safad, to prevent their falling into enemy hands and to intercept any movement to reinforce the Arabs in Safad from the direction of Jaouneh. The grove was seized in the teeth of accurate sniping and machine-gun fire from the Mount Canaan Police Station. An Arab unit which tried to reach Safad from the direction of Jaouneh about half an hour after the grove had been taken by our men was routed. At night, reinforcements of about sixty men from different units arrived from Rosh Pinna: every man carried a rifle, ammunition and a loaf of bread, and, with these reinforcements, Hotchkiss and Lewis machine-guns were seen for the first time in Galilee.

At approximately 22.00 hours, the Palmach unit, which had by now organized itself for perimeter defence in the grove, was ordered back. On Mount Canaan, nineteen more men joined it, and at 03.00 hours on the following morning the platoon, led by a battalion second-in-command, moved out. By dawn on Saturday, 17th April, it had managed to enter Safad.

At 05.30 hours, its commander in the town received orders from the commanding officer of Eastern Galilee to institute military administration and to organize Safad's defence.

At the time of the British evacuation, or when boundaries were set and front-lines drawn in the town, the Jewish population of Safad was approximately 1,500, the Arab population practically 12,000. There were countless problems resulting from the low percentage of young people among the Jewish population, the indifferent training of the local Haganah detachment and the generally poor morale of the Jewish male citizens, most of them highly Orthodox and showing little or no interest in questions of defence. As against this, the Arab population was notorious for its courage and national fanaticism and for its fighting qualities. Over and above the civilians, there were in Jewish Safad two field-unit platoons and one Palmach unit. In Arab Safad there were about 700 Syrian volunteers commanded by the Syrian Adib Shishakli and, for good measure, the men of dozens of densely populated Arab villages all around Safad. Quite obviously, the enemy had a considerable superiority in manpower.

The topography of the Jewish part of Safad, too, commanded as it was by the higher Arab quarters, gave the enemy a substantial advantage. Once the British had left, all traffic into the town was halted. The two highways connecting Safad with the rest of the country—the Acre-Safad and the Safad-Rosh Pinna roads—were blocked by Jewish forces, the first near Jewish Ein Zeitim and the other at Rosh Pinna. But the Jews could not use them, since the Arabs had blocked the Acre-Safad road near Eyn Zeytoun and the Rosh Pinna-Safad road near the Mount Canaan Police Station which they held. Entrance to the Jewish quarter was barred in any event by the Arab quarter called Hareth el-Krad, at the turn of the main road into the town. The enemy in Safad had a strong and spacious Arab hinterland with which unhindered and continuous contact could be kept by way of paths leading to Eyn Tinna and Samoueh in the west and thence by the main routes of Central Galilee to Lebanon. Through Marar, the enemy was linked to Nazareth and its environs. Through Akhbara to the south, he had free communication with Syria, and indeed made use of this route to bring in fighting men almost up to the very end of the campaign. In bleak contrast, the Jewish quarter was entirely marooned.

The British, fearing perhaps that for all these advantages the Arabs would not be able to win a speedy and decisive victory, decided to hand over to them all the points of tactical importance in the town which they had held until evacuation. The citadel commanding the whole town, Shalva House, overlooking Hareth el-Krad, and the fork of the roads to the Jewish and Arab quarters were delivered to the enemy on the eve of evacuation; and, a few minutes before the actual withdrawal, the town police station, commanding a large part of the Jewish quarter, then Hareth el-Roumana and, finally, the Mount Canaan Police Station, a fortress that was the key point of the whole area and guaranteed its control.

It will be readily understood that the defence of the town turned primarily on our capacity to solve two interrelated problems:

    a. Defence of the Jewish quarter under conditions of enemy advantage.

    b. Isolation.

Immediately after the British departure, the enemy took possession of a number of key buildings, and the siege of the Jewish quarter became even tighter and more suffocating. Some Jewish positions were evacuated, including the trade school, the most forward position of our defence system on the north-west: the enemy then occupied it. Some buildings on the southern flank of the town, opposite Hareth el-Roumana and the town police station—a block later named 'Stalingrad'—were also evacuated. The enemy scored all these 'successes' effortlessly, yet in the days that followed did nothing to exploit his advantages in earnest. Throughout the weeks of the siege, he pursued a technique of endless harassment by sniping and bombarding us with 60 mm. and 81 mm. mortars. True enough, there were occasional attempts to wreck buildings on the outskirts of the Jewish quarter, but they were ineffectual.

After the enemy's single attempt on the night of 17th April to capitalize on the shock of the British departure and to enter the Jewish quarter from several points at once, which had been broken and beaten back by the stubborn resistance of the Jewish defenders, he made only one more serious effort throughout the siege to penetrate the quarter—on 28th April, launched from the south. Under cover of mortars and firing along all sectors, two thrusts were aimed at our southern defences. The first, meant perhaps as a diversion, was stopped immediately, when the attackers, moving from the town police station towards the Central Hotel, ran into 'shoe-mines'. The second, about twenty minutes later, was carried out by a group of about thirty Arabs, who broke through walls in abandoned Arab shops on the southern border of the Jewish area and infiltrated from the Arab quarter into the Commercial Centre. Our look-out did not discover the approaching force until it was within five or ten yards of him. Neutralizing the fire of our positions by sniping from the Arab emplacements in the northern corner of Hareth el-Roumana, the group tried to break into the Jewish quarter. The first of its members were already at the barrier on the very confines of the quarter, in between the Jewish positions, when the defenders put them to flight with grenades tossed from the courtyard of the Commercial Centre.

The enemy's positions were the briefest distance from ours, at some points less than fifteen yards away. He also had an abundance of weapons and was able to direct his fire at our embrasures and look-outs without interference. One especially perilous spot in the long and tortuous defence periphery of the Jewish quarter was the Stalingrad block below the main street, facing the town police station, the post office and other higher buildings that were in enemy hands. This demilitarized complex—the British did not allow positions to be established in it because of its nearness to the police station—was, on two of its sides, virtually cheek by jowl with fortified Arab areas less than twenty yards away; it was abandoned by its Jewish residents on the night of the British evacuation. The enemy, fully aware that this was one of the most sensitive segments in the whole Jewish defence line, began systematically to blow up the houses. It cannot be said with certainty whether this was part of an aggressive stratagem to drive deep into the Jewish quarter by successive demolitions, or a defensive tactic to provide an open field of vision and fire around the town police station, or simply a wanton urge to damage and destroy Jewish property.

To meet these seemingly insuperable problems of defence, to stand up to the combat techniques of the enemy, to maintain the life of the town and, with all this, to endeavour to break out of the encirclement—these were the responsibilities of the commander of the Palmach platoon, who took control of Safad on the morrow of the British departure.

The Jewish forces adopted the following line of action:

a. The entire Jewish quarter was surrounded by a close 'circumvallation' of positions and barriers.

b. Since there was no possibility whatsoever of establishing a fortified stronghold in the Stalingrad area and of permanently occupying its wreckage, a Palmach section would go out each night and man the whole of the debris-littered space until daylight; in that nocturnal ambush, it was hardly more than fifteen or twenty yards from the enemy's fortifications.

c. From time to time, the Jewish positions directed punishing fire at the Arab areas, and two Palmach sharpshooters were at the trigger throughout the day.

d. Several acts of sabotage were carried out, not only to dynamite dangerous forward positions of the enemy, but also to demonstrate our own aggressive mood. Thus, the Safad Hotel and Ramzi House, adjoining Stalingrad, which threatened our southern flank on the right, were blown up during the night of 22nd April. On the evening of 28th April, Arab shops bordering on the Commercial Centre in the southern sector of the Jewish quarter were blown up; they had provided cover for the enemy's advance to the barrier.

e. 'Shoe' and electrical mines were laid in areas of risk.

f. Our troops at the foot of Mount Canaan regularly harried areas in Safad, Hareth el-Krad and the area of the Seraya with automatic and 3-inch mortar fire.

The supplies of food and water were limited and had to be rationed out sparingly, but they were, in the end, enough to last out the siege: Safad's water source, the spring of Eyn Tinna, two kilometres west of the town, was in enemy hands. There had been no ammunition, no grenades or explosives at all in the town, and everything had to be brought in, on their backs, by relays of infantrymen from the company on Mount Canaan, which would steal into the town from the north. Nor could we contemplate any act of counter-sabotage, even the minutest, unless the explosives were smuggled in from Mount Canaan.

The battle for the liberation of the town. On 28th April, the British evacuation of Galilee was wound up by the abandonment of the police station and military camps in the Rosh Pinna region. In the first days of May, as military actions began in the area of Safad (Operation 'Yiftach'), the Tiberias-Rosh Pinna highway was cleared by our men. After this preliminary action, occupation of the Arab quarter of Safad became the primary objective. Not only was Safad the Arabs' largest and indeed only political and economic concentration of real consequence in Eastern Galilee, it was also the topographical nerve-centre of certain key communications, and its capture would therefore affect the whole campaign in Galilee.

It was clear that as long as the enemy continued to command the Arab quarter of Safad, the Jewish quarter of the town, Ein Zeitim and Mount Canaan could not indefinitely hold out against the double pressures of invading forces from outside and of local Arabs from within. The collapse of Jewish Safad would have allowed the Lebanese columns to manipulate another arm of the pincer movement that would bring them to Safad by way of Malakia-Saasa-Meron and on from Safad to Rosh Pinna.

Intelligence of how important Safad was for the enemy's overall plan was confirmed by a reliable report we received that Kaukji was getting ready to transfer his guns to Meron to 'blot out the Jewish quarter'; that, reinforcing Shishakli's 700 men, the Druze Abdul-Wahab had also arrived in the Safad area with the remnants of his force after the fighting for Ramat Yohanan; and that more Arabs from round about were trickling in.

It was now vital to free the Jews of Safad from an ever-tightening encirclement, and the Command came to a momentous decision: to conquer the Arab quarter of the town, as the first act of Operation Yiftach.

For this strike, most of the Palmach battalion in Galilee was concentrated at the foot of Mount Canaan. Here, for the first time, our troops encountered the problem of battalion organization and form. The sizeable numbers involved gave rise to acute problems of supply as well. First and foremost, feeding the troops meant that rations had to be transported from Rosh Pinna night after night, again on soldier's backs, and this held up and hindered the assembly of equipment for the action planned—for that, too, had to be conveyed in the same slow, laborious fashion over difficult paths during the hours of darkness. Reasonably sustained though this supply line was, the stock of food at the base was beginning to run out and the troops were showing the first signs of exhaustion. As soon as news of the big impending offensive reached the base, it was decided to organize a break-through with a transport column. On 25th April, a convoy was gathered on the military road near one of the bends on the Rosh Pinna-Safad highway. All commanding positions were occupied by us in advance, and during the break-through a machine-gun from the Mines' House on Mount Canaan pinned down the police station on the hill. The convoy succeeded in climbing Mount Canaan and then in descending to the town almost without being fired on.

The occupation of Safad depended upon our seizing the sole key-point outside it, the Mount Canaan Police Station, which overlooked most of the Arab quarter and was actually higher than the second key-point, the one that mattered most in the town itself: the citadel. Although the police station was close to the Jewish positions on Mount Canaan, and on lower ground, it was felt that it could not be successfully attacked, not merely because of the strength of its walls and of the fortifications around it, but also because we simply did not have the arms to take the fortifications—a lack that had cost us dear in two bitterly abortive assaults against the Nebi Yusha Police Station. To venture an attack on the town from outside, from another point of the compass, would call for deployment of large forces and passage through Arab-held areas, along mountain-slopes hard to negotiate and with virtually no possibility of getting proper support.

Alternatively, control of the area might be gained by transferring the Jewish force to Safad itself and then using the Jewish quarter as a springboard for attack. To achieve this, we had to break the encirclement. The weak link in the Arab chain of siege was the northern flank, resting on the villages of Eyn Zeytoun and Biriya, at the foot of an extension of Mount Biriya, and this was the determining factor in our choice of the first stage of the action to liberate Safad.

Occupation of Eyn Zeytoun. Action began at dawn on 1st May. At 22.00 hours, a Palmach force of two platoons left its base on Mount Canaan, and advanced along an extension of Mount Biriya (Position No. 3) in a south-westerly thrust towards Eyn Zeytoun. But an error in the direction of the advance delayed the force and zero hour had to be put forward approximately two hours. From its starting point of attack, about 400 yards north of the village, on the slope of the ridge, the force could look down upon the battle area, spread out like a stage before battalion headquarters and the supporting troops.

The attack began at 03.00 hours on 2nd May. The holding force—a Davidka mortar, two 3-inch mortars and a battery of eight 2-inch mortars—opened up a heavy bombardment of the village, well beyond the assembly area of the assaulting unit. At the same time, one section, under a platoon commander, took up a position on the same slope, facing Biriya, to block any approach of reinforcements. Strong fire was directed from all our positions in Safad to draw off the enemy forces in the town and divert their attention from the real objective of our attack.

After a short spell of concentrated shelling, two platoons charged the village on a forward axis from north to south, one moving on its east flank and the other on the west. Their purpose was to break through from house to house and attain the Acre-Safad highway. The western platoon, meeting strong opposition from the grove north-west of the village, retired a little distance and asked for covering fire; the resistance was duly beaten down and the platoon, now unopposed, could break through into the village. The eastern platoon overcame some scattered resistance in quick grenade fighting, and the two platoons were soon at the highway and posted themselves in the houses alongside, in accordance with the original plan. Forthwith, they set about clearing the village, whose inhabitants appeared to be in a state of shock from the intensity of our bombardment and the infantry's speed of penetration. The search for weapons began, prisoners were rounded up. By dawn the entire village was in our hands.

At daybreak, the section covering the action area from the direction of Biriya was spotted by an enemy look-out on Mount Canaan and was at once brought under accurate automatic and rifle fire. Seeking cover, the section leader decided to try and establish himself in the first row of houses of the village. After a swift exchange of fire, the whole of Biriya was occupied and the eight men of the section were in unchallenged control.

While fighting for Eyn Zeytoun was in progress, news came of the heavy attack by Lebanese forces on Ramot Naphtali; this was the 'probing' action that preceded the full-scale invasion. On the morning of 1st May, the situation there was described as still desperate. Telegrams arriving between 08.00 and 10.30 hours made us apprehensive that the days of Ramot Naphtali were numbered. Nevertheless, the headquarters of Operation Yiftach did not alter by one iota its plan to set Safad free. Help was sent to Ramot Naphtali from the front-line reserve, but the whole of the Galilee battalion was kept in the neighbourhood of Safad.

On 2nd May, the battalion, fully manned and equipped, was moved to Safad along the serpentine path between Eyn Zeytoun and the town, equipment and arms borne by the men themselves, the heavy material on donkey-back. No force was left in Eyn Zeytoun, but, for two days following the occupation of the village, patrols were sent in from time to time to blow up and burn down its houses with the twofold aim of destroying an enemy base and shaking the morale of the Arabs of Safad. On the same day, some villagers tried to re-enter Eyn Zeytoun, probably to take away part of their property, but were observed by a Jewish patrol and driven off, not without loss.

Thus the first phase of our plan was accomplished. The ring that had gripped Safad was broken from the north and a whole battalion made its way into the Jewish quarter of the town. The seizure of Eyn Zeytoun and Biriya and the advent of the longed-for reinforcements gave a tremendous lift to the spirit of the Jews of Safad.

First attack. The attack on the Arab quarter opened at 01.00 hours on 6th May. Its objective was to seize the citadel, on the assumption that once it and the 'nipple' on top of it were in our hands, the enemy would be obliged to give up the town police station and Shalva House beneath it, and that these would, in the second phase, become a spring-board for our conquest of the whole town. The plan was for the attack to begin with heavy shelling of the citadel, while one platoon from Mount Canaan would stage a diversionary drive on the Mount Canaan Police Station and a second occupy a small house and the trade school (which the enemy had seized on the night preceding the British evacuation) on the eastern flank of the citadel, between it and the

Arab quarter, Hareth el-Krad. As soon as the trade school had been taken and was firmly held, a breakthrough platoon of veteran soldiers of the battalion, standing by at the Citadel Hotel, would climb from the direction of the trade school up to the citadel, guided by a Safad resident familiar with the terrain, and would storm and capture the 'nipple'.

At the foot of the hill, several reserve platoons were in readiness, to fight, to transport any wounded, and to entrench.

The trade school was taken as planned. The break-through platoon climbed the slopes of 'Citadel Hill', but once there was involved in an exchange of fire with a strongly fortified Arab position; only at a later stage, after it had withdrawn, did it trans-pire that this position was, in fact, the 'nipple'. The guide, Zeev Cohen, was killed, and the platoon commander could not get his bearings on the terrain without him. To make matters worse, the platoon came under fire from heavy and light machine-guns and from rifle and hand grenades on its flanks, from the town police station and from the Mount Canaan Police Station.

It stood fast in combat for nearly three hours, under an incess-ant fusillade of heavy close-range fire from three directions, but could not storm the enemy position. Reinforcements were despatched, and units to evacuate its casualties, but at dawn the 'nipple' was still not in our possession and the order was given to withdraw—and from the captured positions as well.

An analysis of the failure showed up a number of factors which were taken into due account in the planning of the next action. Thus:

a. The attacking force, almost a whole infantry battalion, was not fully exploited. More could have been attempted in view of the fact that this was a night operation, which, it is recognized, calls for smaller forces. The attack was con-centrated on a single target.

b. No suitable diversionary and pinning-down actions were undertaken against tactical points on the flanks, the town police station and Shalva House, and this was respon-sible for the many casualties caused by flanking fire from these points.

c. There was excessive clustering and crowding together of personnel on the citadel sector when that had been overrun.

d. We lacked a decisive weapon—the Piat gun—capable of silencing a fortified position. Our men had lain for three hours in the open, not dug in, at a distance of less than fifty yards from the unsilenced enemy position.

e. The shelling on which most of the action hinged—and here the success at Eyn Zeytoun had been the example—was sparse and sporadic, on account of defective shells and imprecise ranging.

f. We lacked sufficient information on the operational area.

g. The advanced zero hour prevented the finishing of the job before daybreak.

After withdrawal from the citadel, our forces continued to hold the trade school, but when that too was subjected to ceaseless fire and it became evident that its walls could not stop bullets—two men in it were killed and several wounded—it was abandoned by our unit on 7th May. But this was done by stealth, and a large electric mine, wired to a nearby position, was first placed in the building. The enemy did not detect the withdrawal and went on firing, but eventually sent in a unit of ten men: the mine was sprung, and the trade school, with everybody inside, blew up.

The enemy had done well in the attack, and in the days that followed went on strengthening his positions against the next trial. On 7th May, Kaukji transferred to this area part of his artillery that had previously been in action on Mount Meron, including two 24-pounders. These guns began to pound the Jewish quarter of Safad. On 8th May, a Syrian company forded the Jordan near Batiha to reinforce the Arab fighters in the town, which, all this time, was an arena of intermittent firing and shelling.

The plan of our second effort was devised in the light of the experience gained in the first. In the preparatory stage, more armament was brought up, including 'fleas' (small Davidka mortars) more ammunition for the Davidka mortars that we had, and three Piats as well. (Training in the use of the Piats started immediately.) A platoon, until then stationed near Rosh Pinna, where it had taken over empty British barracks and was protecting traffic, was moved to Safad for what would be a large-scale military operation. Two days before it was to be mounted, the 3-inch mortars were already ranged on their targets, working on reports radioed from an observation post on Mount Canaan: it was impossible to find a site in the town itself from which range-finding observations could be made effectively.

At 21.30 hours on 10th May, the second attack began with a

heavy and concentrated artillery barrage. A platoon on Mount
Canaan was detailed to carry out a diversionary attack on the
police station there. A heavy machine-gun was placed at the
Central Hotel to block communication between the citadel and
the town police station and another at Bussel House, with Hareth
el-Krad in its sights. At the same time, a unit from the 'Emek'
battalion, which had reached Galilee two days earlier to pursue
Operation Yiftach, would attack the village of Akhbara, south of
Safad, through which the enemy was maintaining contact with
Syria: this was to prevent the arrival of Arab reinforcements and
to complicate the enemy's problems of defence. Three platoons
would attack Shalva House, the citadel and the town police station
simultaneously: each was to seize and hold its objective. To
guarantee efficiency and flexibility of supporting fire, the town
engineer sat in the operational headquarters with his maps of the
town and could, by telephone to the mortar positions, direct and
instantly alter their fire-plan as circumstances on the spot might
dictate or headquarters decide. There were also runners and
carriers at headquarters, youngsters of the town, who acted as
messengers and also as reserve 'porters'. The battalion quarter-
master was there, too, so that supplies of equipment, food and dry
clothing could be hurried out whenever the need arose on that
rain-swept night. And, finally, there was also a battalion reserve
unit of entrenching personnel.

The citadel. Our information, before the first attack, was that
the 'nipple' was held by forty well-sheltered Arabs, with connecting trenches and reinforcements at hand. This time, the assault
was delivered from the direction of the Jewish quarter. Three
platoons were assembled in the Citadel Hotel. The objective was
to capture the citadel in a swift succession of storming infantry
sections, one behind the other, so that the charge should not be
halted or its momentum lost. If the first section encountered fire,
the Piats and machine-guns would provide cover and the two
other sections would go forward, wave after wave. If the action of
the break-through platoon went awry, the reserve platoon would
take up the charge, section by section, wave after wave. If it, too,
were unsuccessful, then the picking up of wounded would be
stopped and the 'collecting' platoon would proceed to charge in
the same way. The break-through platoon had three sections, each
with a light machine-gun, a Piat crew as platoon adjunct, and a
heavy machine-gun crew in the reserve platoon.

H

When our shelling ended, the break-through platoon crossed the road that ran round Citadel Hill and began to climb up. Straightaway, three light machine-guns on the 'nipple' opened up on it and other fire was directed against it from the direction of the Mount Canaan Police Station. Fully exposed to the enemy now, the platoon came under a hail of lead and its advance was held up; the platoon commander was wounded, but carried on. The battalion second-in-command then sent forward the Piat crew which, with its first two projectiles, completely silenced the Arab position. The gun-crew approached, but encountered no resistance, whereupon the platoon occupied the position, with its network of emplacements and communication trenches for peripheral defence and a good telephone line. The reserve platoon was brought over and occupation was stabilized and all-round defence was organized.

At about midnight, workers and building materials were transported from the town to the citadel and fortification of the site was put in hand.

Shalva House. Here, according to our information, about sixty well-equipped Iraqi volunteers were posted, with at least three light machine-guns.

Our force was established in Segal House, to the west of Shalva House and about fifty yards from it: the Piats and light machine-guns were concentrated on the upper floor, riflemen on the second, and a demolition squad on ground level. Shalva House was built into the slope of the hill and, from the direction of our imminent charge, its ground floor was on a level with the second floor of Segal House. Under cover of strong fire from machine-guns, rifles and Piats directed at its upper floors, our demolition squad advanced and placed explosives against the wall of its ground floor. The dynamite, dampened by the rain, burnt without detonation, but the flames that went up misled our men: assuming that the explosion had taken place, they charged what was still an unbreached building. All the same, they managed to pierce into the lower floor, but there, not knowing their way about inside, had to light a torch in the total darkness to get to the upper floors. On the second floor, the platoon commander, Avraham Licht, was killed by Arabs who were seeking to break out and escape. Then, suddenly, all was quiet, and the last Arab had fled. A working telephone installation, a good store of foodstuffs, arms, rifles and light machine-guns, with ammunition for them, were found; there were twelve enemy bodies, most of them badly burned, probably the effect of the Piats. Without loss of time, workers were summoned to fortify the building, and establish a telephone link with battalion headquarters.

With the occupation of Shalva House, the second key position in the town, dominating the whole of the Arab quarter of Hareth el-Krad, was ours. During that day, all movement in the quarter was harassed unremittingly and at noon the enemy quitted the place.

The town police station. The longest and hardest battle was for possession of the town police station. The building and its pill-box were the most strongly fortified positions in the town and, according to our intelligence, there were about a hundred Lebanese volunteers in them and ample supplies of arms and ammunition.

After a preliminary reconnaissance by the company commander and other commanding officers, the following plan of operation was decided upon: a section with two light machine-guns under a platoon commander would be posted in Stalingrad to draw the fire of the police building and to feint a break-through; on the third floor of the Central Hotel, a light machine-gun would be mounted to pin down the enemy on the sandbagged roof of the building. The assault force would consist of two sections. A rifle section would remain in reserve at the Central Hotel, and another, with a Piat crew and a demolition squad, would move from the hotel through the debris of the Protestant church up to the masonry fence of the ruined Biriya bakery, about thirty yards from the town police station. Under cover provided by the rifle section and the Piat crew, our saboteurs would demolish the barbed-wire fence with 'Bangalore torpedoes', would then shatter the masonry fence of the police station with explosive charges set only five yards away from it, and finally, with another and heavier explosive charge, would breach the building itself and permit the entry of the break-through force.

The assault force was equipped with twelve loads of explosive, two Bangalore torpedoes, twelve Piat projectiles and a light machine-gun. As the shelling of the 'nipple' started, the drawing-off force from Stalingrad and the Central Hotel went promptly into action. The assault force moved unseen through the wreckage from the hotel up to the first masonry fence at a distance of thirty yards from the police station.

The Piat crew fired four projectiles into the pill-box, and silenced it for a while. Orders were now given to breach the barbed-wire fence with Bangalore torpedoes. The first failed to explode and the two men who had handled it came sadly back; the second was equally futile, and this time the two handlers were wounded.

It was therefore decided not to wait but to cross the barbed-wire fence without first breaching it and then blow up the masonry fence round the police station. Part of the force got through the barbed-wire fence, and four consecutive attempts were made to blow up the masonry one, but again the explosive charges could not be detonated in the downpour. Ten men suffered wounds in these attempts. At the same time, the Piat crews suffered shoulder wounds, for they had not learned the art of firing their weapon over a fence. It was sensed, moreover, that the drawing-off fire from the direction of Stalingrad was becoming scattered; it was realized afterwards that all the men in the section had been wounded, possibly by the fragment of a Davidka mortar shell that exploded in the air: both the platoon commander and the first-aid man had gone on firing a light machine-gun.

At 03.30 hours, another saboteur, a field-unit man, made his appearance, and it was decided to renew the attempt to breach the fence round the police station. Explosives of another type were used, and this time with success. All trained demolition personnel had, however, by now become casualties, so, there and then, the riflemen were told how the charges were to be set off. Six charges, each of fifteen kilograms, were laid against the walls of the police station, the explosions opened two large breaches in them, and the advance could continue. The combat force, its strength now only fifteen rank and file, split up into two groups: one seized the pill-box forthwith, mounted a machine-gun in it and directed its bullets at the second floor of the police building, from which a deadly light-arms fire was coming; the other entered a room on the first floor and from it exchanged fire with the enemy defenders. In this close engagement, the company commander, Itzik Hoch-man, was killed; his second-in-command, at that moment in the pill-box, at once rushed to the police building and, after a brief set-to in which a number of Arabs were killed and four taken prisoner, the whole of the first floor was taken.

All the Stens were by now out of action, and the fighting on the first floor was done by the three section commanders themselves, equipped each with a Thompson sub-machine gun and trained in house-to-house combat. With control of the first floor finally

secured, a guard was placed near the stairway and a message sent
to battalion headquarters that the company commander was dead
and that it was not possible to proceed with the clearing up of the
building because of the small number of men and their utter
fatigue. The battalion second-in-command arrived at once,
organized a field-unit section at the Central Hotel from regular
Haganah soldiers stationed there, and systematically combed the
upper storeys of the police building. It was already daylight by the
time the third floor was cleared, and it could be seen that thirteen
Arabs had established themselves on the roof. Grenades, 2-inch
mortars, heavy machine-guns and a flame-thrower were used
against them, but to no avail. In the ensuing hours, ten of them
surrendered, but the last three went on sniping at our troops
throughout the entire day and got away at nightfall, roping belts
and blankets together and sliding from the roof to the ground.

The storming and occupation of three key positions on the
night of 10th May not only broke the encircling strangulation that
had almost choked life out of the Jewish quarter of Safad, but it
gave the Jewish forces a springboard for attack upon the Arab
quarters of the town. But the job was not by any means done yet.
The Mount Canaan Police Station was still in Arab hands, and
the situation of the Arab quarters no worse than that of the
Jewish quarter throughout the siege.

Accordingly we started to plan the occupation of the whole
town. But now the strange phenomenon occurred which is peculiar
to the Arabs of the country and to the foreign volunteers in the
Arab gangs: the last stage of the battle was not fought at all. The
large Arab contingents in Safad decamped, abandoning the
Mount Canaan Police Station fortress without any further bid to
hold on and offer final resistance. The paths from Safad towards
Eyn Tinna and Samoueh were black with fugitives, and it was
evident that the whole town was being deserted.

At noon on 11th May, Safad looked bare and derelict, and we
began to occupy every part of it. A covering force of Davidka
mortars and heavy machine-guns was placed on the citadel. Our
forces moved in two columns: one, under a company commander,
marched down from the citadel, advanced through the town to
the Seraya and the Government hospital; the other, under a
platoon commander, moved through Hareth el-Krad towards the
Arab Hotel next to Mount Canaan.

The plan was to draw off and soften the enemy, and follow up with a charge, if either column ran into trouble. But the advance into the town proceeded swiftly and unopposed, and by evening our forces were in full possession of the entire town. The advance towards the Mount Canaan Police Station was slower, because of the many mines along the route, but no resistance was met there either. When our troops reached the Arab Hotel, opposite the station, they halted and waited, and, no movement being visible, the three fences were breached by Bangalore torpedoes. An opening was made in the wall, in case the gate and doors had been booby-trapped, and through it our troops entered the police fortress.

Our flag was hoisted on the roof of the building. The operation to liberate Safad had ended.

This is the historic Order of the Day which the first Prime Minister and Minister of Defence of Israel, David Ben-Gurion, speaking on behalf of the Government, issued to the Israel Defence Forces on 31st May, 1948. It deals with the transformation of the Haganah into the legal, regular defence army of the newly created State of Israel, the historical significance of the change, and the heavy debt the new state and the new army owed to the Haganah.

Order of the Day

David Ben-Gurion

With the establishment of the State of Israel the Haganah has left the underground to become a regular army.

The debt owed by the Yishuv and by the Jewish people to the Haganah, at all stages of its existence and development, is great indeed. It has grown from isolated buds in the earliest days of its foundation, in Petah-Tikva, in Rishon LeZiyon, Gedera, Rosh Pinna, Zichron-Ya'acov, Metula, by way of the Shomer organization and the pioneers of the Second Aliya, the Jewish Legion in the First World War, the defenders of Tel Hai, the continual growth of the Haganah organization in the period between the two world wars, the establishment of the Jewish Settlement Police at the time of the 1936–38 disturbances, the establishment of the Palmach and the Field Units, the large-scale volunteering in the Second World War and the establishment of the first Jewish Brigade, to become the Haganah which has been engaged in the mighty struggle of the present war against us, from 30th November, 1947 to 31st May, 1948.

Without the experience, the planning, the ability to execute and to command, the loyalty and the spirit of heroism of the Haganah, the Yishuv would not have been able to withstand the terrible trial of blood of the last six months, and we would not have attained the State of Israel. In the chronicles of the People of Israel the chapter 'Haganah' will shine with a glory and splendour that will never dim.

Now a new chapter has opened. The regular army of the State of Israel, the army of Israel's freedom and independence in its own country, has been established, in accordance with a decree on the Israel Defence Forces published by the Provisional Government.

This army is now entrusted with the security of the people and of the homeland. The words of Israel's Declaration of Independence will be inscribed upon the shield of all armies in Israel:

'The State of Israel will be open to Jewish immigration and for the Ingathering of the Exiles; it will foster the development of the country for the benefit of all its inhabitants; it will be based on freedom, justice and peace as envisaged by the prophets of Israel; it will ensure complete equality of social and political rights to all its inhabitants irrespective of religion, race or sex; it will guarantee freedom of religion, conscience, language, education and culture; it will safeguard the Holy Places of all religions and it will be faithful to the principles of the Charter of the United Nations.'

In taking to battle to crush the forces of evil which are striving to destroy our existence, our growth and our freedom, the army of Israel will bear in its heart the vision of our prophets of old: 'Nation shall not lift up sword against nation, neither shall they learn war any more.'[1]

The regular army of Israel will be made up of land, sea and air forces, including appropriate military services.

All those who until June 1st served in the brigades and other branches and who participated in the defence of the Yishuv and in our war for the freedom of Israel, and all those who will now be re-enlisted by order of the Government of Israel, will make up the Israel Defence Forces.

Every male and female soldier serving in the army will swear the following oath:

'I swear and undertake, on my word of honour, to remain faithful to the State of Israel, to its laws and to its legally constituted authorities, to accept without reservation the discipline of the Israel Defence Forces, to obey all orders and instructions given by its authorized commanders, and to

[1] Isaiah, 2, iv.

dedicate all my strength and even to sacrifice my life in the defence of the homeland and the freedom of Israel.'

The moral and physical strength of every soldier and commander, and his dedication to his duty, will make the Israel Defence Force a bastion of the people and the homeland.

31st May, 1948, Year One of the Independence of Israel

D. Ben-Gurion,
Prime Minister and Minister of Defence

H*

This is a brief summary of the major lessons to be learned from the War of Independence (1947–49) by Lieut.-General Yigael Yadin, now Professor of Archaeology in the Hebrew University of Jerusalem, who during the war served as Chief of Operations on the general staff and afterwards became the second Chief of Staff of the Israel Defence Army. It was written as an introduction to the collection of essays entitled *Beshviley Machshava Tzvayit* ('In the Paths of Military Thinking'), published by the Ma'arachot Publishing House in July 1950.

Learning from Experience

Yigael Yadin

The military history of a war written shortly after the end of that war is generally unsatisfactory because the silence demanded by considerations of security outweigh the benefit to be derived from publication—even if the scope is limited to recording the lessons learned. If military history is to have any real scholarly value from which something may be learned, it must be comprehensive, exhaustive, complete and objective. Writing that is distorted by bias or subjectivity, or is unable—for reasons of security—to give all the facts, will not be of lasting value nor will it make a significant contribution to miliary science, though it may arouse ephemeral interest.

The Ma'arachot Publishing House is thus remarkably courageous in printing, even on such a modest scale, the lessons of our recent war; and all the more so because there are several reasons peculiar to our case which make it especially difficult:

    1. Our political and military situation is still such that security considerations outweigh the value of publishing secret material.

    2. For this reason, it is impossible to publish the original orders and plans and to compare them with the results

achieved; it is often necessary to restrict oneself to the publication of the 'plans' which are, in fact, no more than reports—the interpretation and expression of what actually happened—which do not permit the study of the relationship between planning, execution and results.

3. We are still too close to the events to draw conclusions from the large quantity of material.

4. It is difficult to free a large number of commanding officers whose current tasks in the army are still onerous to set down their views in writing.

Nevertheless, after reading this collection, I think that the editors have succeeded, and have laid the foundation and established the methodology—despite the difficulties, and despite the need to remove whole articles and delete sections of others. This success is partly due to the fact that the editors were able to 'conscript' various officers whose direct knowledge of the subjects of their articles cannot be doubted, as it is derived from their wartime activities.

I am obliged to include myself in the category of officers mentioned above, because to my regret I cannot find the time to write fully on the lessons of the war as I might have done, drawing upon my experience in the Operations branch of the general staff. However, having glanced through this collection, I think that the following can be said to be the major lessons:

1. The capital importance of the morale of the Yishuv in the war against an enemy that was superior in number and in equipment.

2. The total exploitation of the Yishuv's forces in the war.

3. The enormous importance of the unified command over all forces (including staffs, corps and services).

4. The great contribution of the agricultural settlements, both on the borders and in the lines of advance, in enabling the Yishuv to halt an invasion and to conceal mobilization and concentration for attack.

5. The superiority of the Israeli command—especially in the middle and lower echelons—over that of the enemy, in its sense of responsibility, its capacity for independent tactical thinking, its maturity and its leadership.

6. The success of the command in overcoming the technical and psychological difficulties of the transition from fighting at platoon, company and battalion strength to bat-

talion, brigade and divisional strength, and in establishing these formations as permanent operational frameworks. (The transition point was, without doubt, 'Operation Nachshon', which accelerated the slow natural process and by the sheer force of circumstances led to the change-over to fighting at reinforced brigade level.)

7. The great advantage resulting from the training of our soldiers in night fighting, a factor which helped more than any other in achieving tactical surprise.

8. The great importance of correct, one could almost say scientific, knowledge of the use and operation of various kinds of arms, and the occasional failures due to the lack of such knowledge.

9. The great importance of the fact that our commanders personally knew the battle area. (An illuminating example: Our success in the battle of Mishmar Ha'emek is to a large extent attributable to the fact that the officers' training courses of the Haganah were held in the vicinity at En-Hashofet, and that in fact all the officers who fought at Mishmar Ha'emek including the battalion commander, were graduates of these courses and had participated in various exercises to capture Hirbet er-Ras, the capture of which was of decisive significance in the actual battle.

10. Full utilization of the 'strategy of the indirect approach' in planning the war.

In conclusion, it must be re-emphasized that, of all the major principles of war, surprise is the most important; compared to it, all other principles are either secondary or are means to achieve it. The three most important of these are: a fighting spirit, concentration and mobility.

When these three means are achieved, surprise is achieved; when surprise is achieved, the battle is won.

Two major streams of military thought and experience exercised a formative influence on Israel's Defence Army. One stemmed from the Haganah underground army, with its spearhead, the Palmach; the other, from various Jewish military units, with the Jewish Brigade at their centre, serving in the British army. The reciprocal influence of these two elements was already felt during the years of the pre-State period when they were co-ordinated by the Haganah General Staff, which, besides its direct control over its own forces, also exercised through its emissaries some indirect control over the Jewish-Palestinian units in the British army. After demobilization at the end of the war, most of the Jewish troops were reabsorbed into the different units of the Haganah, bringing back with them invaluable military knowledge and experience. The integration of these two major forces into the newly created Israel defence army proved very fruitful.

The following is an abridged article on the legacy of the Jewish Brigade in the British army during the Second World War, written by two officers who served in the Brigade, Brig.-General Avraham Tamir and the late Brig.-General David Karmon. It analyses the specific contribution of the Jewish ex-servicemen of an old, experienced army like the British to the young, unconventional army of the new State of Israel.

———◆———

The Legacy of the Jewish Brigade[1]

Abraham Tamir and David Karmon

Now that Israel's War of Independence is ended, we must look back and try to discover the causes of our victory. Such an enquiry will do much to guide us in building our army in the future. It would be impossible to uncover all the causes in one short article. Each period of our defence activity in the last twenty years has to be summed up. Only a series of such enquiries will clear the ground for the major task of summarizing and drawing conclusions.

[1] Source: *Beshviley Machshava Tzvayit*, pp. 67–74.

The aim of this article is limited: it is an attempt to analyze the lessons to be learned from the service of Palestinian infantry units in the British Army, and to assess their contribution to the establishment of our army and to our War of Independence.

Three stages can be distinguished in the organization of the Palestinian infantry units, which finally brought about the establishment of a reinforced brigade with the incorporation of such other elements as an artillery battalion, an engineers' company, medical services, a transport company, and communications and military police units.

Stage One was the organization of Palestinian volunteers into companies incorporated into the 'Buffs' (the East Kent Regiment) for guard duties, both their equipment and training being in line with that generally given to British units destined for service in the various colonies. A considerable part of the command was British, determining to a large extent the nature of the units. However, thanks to the human material of the units they enjoyed a marked internal cohesion, which was maintained despite the rear echelon functions they were forced to perform at the height of the most decisive battles of the war.

Stage Two was the inclusion of the 'Buffs' companies in the Palestinian battalions of the new Palestinian Regiment. This slowed up the ceaseless flow of Jewish soldiers from the companies into the Jewish service units which were allowed to be active at the front (this process was especially marked at the time of El-Alamein). Even though the Palestinian battalions, after they had been formed, left the borders of Palestine when the threat of Rommel had passed, their tasks were basically unchanged. The *esprit de corps* grew (partly as a result of their being away from home), and their battle fitness improved. At this stage we see the continuous and more efficient training of officers and N.C.O.'s of all ranks, both within the units and in schools and courses of the British Army. At this time too, almost all British officers up to company level were replaced, and an internal discipline was established, based mainly on a deep awareness of the task and mission ahead. It was now possible to see something of the initiative of officers and N.C.O.'s who sought, at all times and in all conditions, to acquire knowledge and to integrate this knowledge into their nature as Haganah-men turned regular soldiers.

Stage Three was the organization of the Jewish elements of the

Palestinian Regiment as the infantry units of the Jewish Brigade, and the formation of the Brigade itself. It began with the organization of the various staff functions followed by the establishment of an infantry brigade and the incorporation of supporting weapons and the various other services. It finally operated as a reinforced brigade, with winter manoeuvres in the mountains of Italy, prior to its being sent to the Italian front.

During this last stage the team spirit grew, as did battle discipline. The officers underwent training at various schools and courses, and received battle training (prior to the Brigade's entering the front). N.C.O.'s and men were trained in various technical skills, individual and unit initiative were enhanced by tough exercises, and high levels of battle fitness and technical ability were achieved. The units were exercised together and in co-ordination with other elements in the Brigade.

It is not our intention to describe the internal developments at each of these stages, or the interrelating influences which brought about many changes in the character of the volunteer Jewish forces during the Second World War. However, in a comprehensive survey of this development, with emphasis on the fact that direct battle experience was limited and was contingent on specific conditions of terrain and military factors, it is possible to isolate certain elements which will help us to understand the lessons to be learned from the activities of the Brigade and their contribution to the War of Independence.

With the recruitment of Brigade veterans to the Israel Defence Forces, or, to be more accurate, at the dissolution and demobilization of the Brigade by the British authorities, it became apparent that the possibility of activating the best-trained and most cohesive formation we ever had had been lost. We were unable to exploit, in a concentrated way, the organizational and tactical coherence that was the fruit of years of labour; consequently, the acclimatization of every individual Brigade veteran in the I.D.F. was dependent on his personal ability to adjust himself to combat conditions in the country and to the military bodies that arose on the foundations laid by the Haganah. It is impossible to know how things would have developed had the Brigade framework been retained and activated in that form in our war. Probably it could not have been retained because of the need in an army-in-the-making to make broader use of the command and training capabilities of the Brigade. Thus in the I.D.F. the experience of the Brigade veterans was utilized only on the individual level, and it is possible that this method of integration led to the practical grafting of the Brigade's experience onto the Haganah stock. But it is hard to shake off thoughts of 'if only', and to wonder what the Brigade could have done had it entered the campaign in the Land of Israel when it was at the peak of its training, organization and cohesiveness. ·

At this point we must call attention to an interesting fact. In certain European countries (France, Italy, etc.), for a certain time, there was a clash of two schools of thought, both of them born of the war. One, the 'partisan' approach, flourished under the Occupation, developing the ability to deploy on a broad basis and invisibly, allowing for hit-and-run attacks on the enemy's logistic and communication routes. The soldiers became accustomed to battle and operational patterns that fostered the development of the lone fighter, and to logistic and command patterns that were not based upon a stable rear, or on communication routes that could be harassed by an ordinary enemy. On the other hand, there was the purist 'military' school of thought, derived from the national armies of the countries which acted in the framework of, or in association with, the Allied forces. The adherents of this approach were trained to think in terms of organizational structures that made possible the training and equipping of a 'large', official and recognized army, mobile and efficient in battle. In such armies there is a degree of patterning in the methods of training and battle routine which facilitates the fighting arm in its deployment, even when on the move, and in the rapid development of its maximum strength.

The clash between these two schools of thought in several of the countries mentioned had serious consequences and caused friction and changes in the top echelons. In Israel, fortunately, the War of Independence helped to obliterate similar differences, effecting the successful integration of British ex-servicemen and Haganah men, with the result that the sharp clashes which occurred in some European countries were avoided, both during the war and when peace came and with it the reorganization of the army.

The direct battle experience of the Brigade—the only Jewish unit in the British army—was limited. This was due to two main facts: that it was activated so late, when the war in Italy was already drawing to a close, and that only its sub-units were used. (There was a single exception, when the entire Brigade fought as an organizational unit in the crossing of the Senio; but even then it hardly ever engaged in motorized, mobile, drawn-out fighting). Nonetheless, in those combat actions in which units of the Brigade did take an active part many opportunities arose for the development and study of those elements which without doubt made such a heavy contribution to the organization and activation of the I.D.F.

As far as direct battle experience is concerned, the lower levels of command had far more of it than the higher echelons, from company commander up; the latter certainly had experience in organizing a 'front', in planning it and planning its activation, but their units hardly ever participated in their entirety. It was thus in the smaller units that our junior officers had a chance to show their ability in handling men in action—and this led, among other things, to an excess of patrolling duties for the Brigade.

It would be incorrect to say that the Brigade's experience was gained in the battle-field. Its skills—and also the major part of its contribution to our own war—were derived directly from its having acted within the framework of the British war-machine. The function of the Brigade in Italy was basically one of pinning down and diversion. The Brigade, even though trained in large-scale warfare, was placed in a static sector of the front, while the major push of the Allied forces took place on a different part of the front. This was, in fact, quite a 'fair deal' for a unit that had been formed so rapidly, and which—from an internal, Jewish point of view—was a unit that contained some of the best sons of a small people who had volunteered for the war. But as a result, it was denied real, large-scale battle experience—not only a baptism of fire, but also bloody, sustained warfare. In addition, the Brigade was concentrated on a more or less continuous front. This was almost entirely absent in our war and the war conditions in our country; thus the Brigade's actual battle experience, that of holding a continuous stretch of front, was not very useful from the point of view of its contribution to Israel's War of Independence. The major contribution of the Jewish Brigade to Israel's War of Independence was not in battle experience—although the lessons learned in patrolling should not be underestimated—but lay in several other spheres to be mentioned below.

The period and the scope of the training of the Brigade were more extensive than its actual fighting. The period preceding its entry to the front line in Italy was one of exhausting, ceaseless training, and it was during this period that the Brigade, its battalions, its units and men, obtained their principal training—though it was in fact only the last stage, coming on top of the training and service of previous years. During this period training was multifaceted. Whereas at the front the only experience was in maintaining a sector of the front-line, with all the associated functions, battle training was for all other types of battle activities as well. Thus the Brigade learned a great deal about a wide range of military skills and know-how, techniques of battle-control, command patterns for companies and battalions, the use of a variety of specialized arms, the use and care of battle equipment, co-operation with other arms, such as armour and aircraft—in fact everything required by a unit and its officers for battle. At the same time, the battalions and their headquarters—the entire Brigade—achieved organizational and tactical cohesion. But above all they learned, especially the officers, how a military unit is built up, how each part is established and systematically added to the whole, according to a previously drawn up schedule. The units in the 'Buffs', which were initially capable of no more than guard duty, grew into fighting units. In addition to actual knowledge, the Brigade men acquired a sense of pride, an awareness of their national mission, and a consciousness of the value of their knowledge for the task of establishing an army.

The knowledge acquired was broad, and parts of it were of major importance for our army. But the process of establishing the Israel Defence Forces and its various units was very different from the setting up of units in the British army. Any attempt to organize our formations by copying the techniques used when the Brigade was created was doomed to failure. The Brigade was formed at the time when the Allies were on the offensive, yet, in spite of this, time was found to organize new formations. This time was also available owing to the conditions of the war—a world war covering enormous areas. By the time the Brigade began to be organized as a reinforced brigade, all its men had been soldiers for a long period. The equipment it was allocated was delivered punctually and in full, and there was no need to take into account a shortage of equipment and ammunition. The organizational apparatus and the skeleton command more or less existed already, and any deficiency could be filled from other units of the British army.

On the other hand, the Israel army was formed in an almost

impromptu fashion during the most difficult periods of the war, when the enemy was at our throats. We had no time. Often we had to put together units 'administratively', and to send them into battle practically untrained, sometimes with inadequate or unsuitable equipment, and sometimes even with officers who were not fully trained.

These differences demanded of the veterans of the British army rapid and flexible adaptation to the conditions under which the I.D.F. was being set up. Consequently, it was not always possible to make full use of their knowledge in the building and training of battle units, especially in spheres like the auxiliary services, supporting arms, artillery, etc., and in the organizing of headquarters and of service functions. The great task of establishing regular and organized units and preparing them for battle—a task demanding time—was to a large extent left over for peace-time.

Fortunately, many of the veterans of the British army, and not only the Brigade, had a correct vision of their role at that time. They succeeded in adapting their experience to the conditions of the building of the Israel Defence Forces, making an invaluable contribution to its 'overnight' creation.

During the period immediately preceding the Sinai Campaign of 1956 terrorist incursions on almost all the armistice demarcation lines, directed mainly against civilians in their scattered villages, had reached intolerable dimensions, and when it appeared impossible to put an end to them by passive measures, it became necessary to resume the tactics of active defence. Priority was given to the development of the small paratroop force, to expand numerically and to raise the level and intensity of its training, and it was this force which carried out most (though not all) of the reprisal actions. After a relative decline, the paratroopers' standard of combat performance and daring was revitalized, and soon became a model for the rest of the army. The following report of a typical paratroop raid of the period was written soon after it took place by Uri Milstein, a Galilee-born paratrooper and author, who participated in the action.

A Paratroop Raid.[1]

Uri Milstein

In accordance with the decision of the United Nations of 29th November, 1947, Nitzana and the areas to its north and west were to be included in the 'Arab State'. In 1948 units of the invading Egyptian Army reached Nitzana and continued to advance toward Beersheba, digging in on the heights along the Nitzana-Beer Mashabim (Bir Aslug) road. During 'Operation Chorev', in December 1948, units of the Israel Defence Force Southern Command, the 8th and Harel Brigades, advanced south and on 27th December captured Nitzana. The brigades split up and advanced separately upon Rafah (Rafiah) and El Arish. Nitzana then served as a base for raids on Kusseima, Bir Hassne and Bir Hama. The Armistice Agreement, signed at Rhodes on 29th November, 1949, stipulated that El Ouja village—that is, Nitzana, and its surroundings—be demilitarized and that neither

[1] Source: *Milchamot HaTzanchanim* ('The Wars of the Paratroopers'), 1968, pp. 55–60.

the Israel nor Egyptian armies be permitted to enter it. In addition, the agreement stipulated that on the Egyptian side of the frontier there should be no positions nearer to Nitzana than to Kusseima. Interpretations of the Armistice Agreement and developments in the relations between the two nations caused the Mixed Armistice Commission to permit entrance of armed forces to, and the establishment of, strong points in the Egyptian demilitarized zone, without permitting a similar move in the Israel demilitarized zone. The only settlements at the time in the demilitarized zone were Keziot and the Beerotayim Control Point. The nearest kibbutz settlements were Mash'abbe Sade, Revivim and Sede Boker.

Under the first agreement, after the Armistice, between Israel and Egypt, signed on Friday, 24th February, 1950 at Ouja El-Hafir, the demilitarized zone of Nitzana, from Bet Hanun to Dir Sunir, was divided between Israel and Egypt. For a certain period mixed Israeli-Egyptian detachments patrolled the area.

On the morning of 26th October, 1955, units of the Egyptian Army crossed the border and overcame an Israel border control post, one kilometre south of Beerotayim, which was held by a small detail. Reinforcements sent from Keziot tried, with the aid of U.N. observers, to remove the Egyptians without force but did not succeed. As a result the reinforcements attacked the Egyptians and drove them from Israel territory.

The bases for Egyptian activities were at Sabha and Ras Siram, five kilometres south of Beerotayim on the road to Kusseima, in Sinai. It was decided to teach the Egyptian army a lesson and preliminary orders were given to prepare for the capture and destruction of the positions. It was also decided to take diversionary action in another sector, and as a result the Kuntilla raid took place on the night between 28th and 29th October, 1955.

Background information to the raid. The Sabha area is cut by Wadi Siram and the Sabha valley into three blocks:

a. The Azuz Ridge and its northern foot-hills going down towards the Rivka strongpoint.

b. Jebel Sabha, a block of cliff-like hills, divided from the Azuz Ridge by a deep gorge, and rising above and controlling the saddle and its surroundings, across which the Nitzana-Kusseima road passes.

c. Jebel el-Amar, a ridge of low hills crossed by dry river courses, which together with the northern foot-hills of the Azuz Ridge closes upon Wadi Siram and controls it.

The hills are rocky, and many are sprinkled with large flinty boulders. It is difficult to dig in here and as a result the enemy's entrenchments were not deep. The fortifications were mostly earth-works which do not give protection under shelling. The ground is exposed and there is little possibility for concealment, apart from the vegetation along the bed of Wadi Azuz, in the vicinity of the Nitzana-Kusseima road.

It was known that in the area between the Beersheba-Nitzana road and the Azuz Ridge lone Bedouins were to be found and they were liable to report our troop movements to the enemy. In addition there were U.N. observers in the area.

Regarding the disposition of enemy forces, it was known that the Rivka strong-point was situated on both sides of Wadi Siram, each post surrounded by barbed wire and with a barbed wire fence connecting the two parts of the strong-point. The area was mined and the position was held by a platoon of *fedayeen*. A small post in Wadi Siram was held by a section. Strongpoint Tamar, on a hill 372 metres above sea level, was occupied by two sections. The Small Sabha post was empty. The Big Sabha position, composed of strongpoints Big-Sabha, Lili, Tova, and strongpoints in the Israeli demilitarized zone was held by a battalion. Reinforcements were liable to arrive from Kusseima and Abu Ageila. D-day was set for 2nd November, 1955 with H-hour to be as early as possible.

Forces and tasks:

1. E-Company under Raful was to capture strongpoint Lili.

2. A company of Nahal troops, fresh from a section-leaders' course and commanded by Z'vika, was attached to the paratroops: it was to take strongpoint Tova.

3. Meir Har-Zion's Reconnaissance Unit was to capture the Big Sabha strongpoint and then dig in on the Sabha Ridge.

4. D-Company under Tibi was to block the Sabha-Kusseima road some eight kilometres to the south of the main battle area in order to prevent the arrival of reinforcements.

5. A platoon of jeeps and a platoon of medium machine-guns commanded by Levi was attached to the attacking force.

6. Two 'Miluim' (reserve) units of paratroopers, under Elisha and Yehuda, were held in reserve.

7. The Wadi Siram, Rivka and Tamar strongpoints were to be overcome by units of the Golani Brigade under Kalman's command.

Sergeant Shimshon Kochav of Meir's Reconnaissance Unit writes of their preparations. 'After the mid-day meal we sat in the *Shekem* (Naafi) canteen passing the time with some of the girl parachute-folders. Suddenly we were ordered into full battle dress, and after half an hour we were on our way south. We knew we were going on a raid, but where to, what target, we didn't know. We discussed the possibilities until we reached Avedat and turned west. That's when we realized that we were out to attack the Egyptians. In the afternoon we reached the Kedem water-holes and unloaded.'

For Raful's company this was to be their second full-scale mission, his men having captured an abandoned strongpoint during the Khan Yunis raid a month and a half previously.

Mussa Ephron's men were new recruits, who had not had basic training let alone a parachute course, and just about knew how to handle their small arms. Mussa had decided to give them shock treatment and 'forge' them in battle. Their junior officers were all good fighting men (Dan Ziv, Dubik, Yoav Sha'ham, Uri Simchoni and others). The main task at the beginning of the action was to calm down the recruits. Tibi's D-Company were a good lot, with experience, having borne the brunt of the main task during the Khan Yunis raid.

At 5.45 in the afternoon, the whole force reached the Azuz area where security was achieved with the aid of a forward scout patrol. The officers went out on reconnaissance and climbed the Azuz Ridge, from where they had a good over-all view of a large part of the enemy's positions. At approximately the same time a Piper parachuted the latest aerial photographs for Battalion H.Q. From time to time vehicles were seen to leave enemy positions and to stop to drop off some soldiers who took up listening posts. These positions were well noted and at night during the action our forces did not encounter even one of them.

At seven in the evening the forces left the assembly area at Wadi Azuz in a very long column. The Blocking Force went first and were followed by Meir's Reconnaissance Unit, then the force under Raful, the Force's H.Q., the Nahal section-leader company, and Mussa's unit. The men of the veteran companies marched easily and quietly, but the recruits who had not been trained in night marches stumbled from time to time and made a lot of noise.

The radio men also made a lot of noise and caused some hold-ups. They were not paratroopers and night fighting was new to them. They made vain attempts to establish communications while on the march and did so far too noisily. When the tumult got too loud Arik forbade all use of radios, a step which caused a great deal of nervousness among the radio men who did not know if they would be able to re-establish contact.

The boom of desert artillery was heard. The men did not know who was shelling whom. The shriek of the shells played on their nerves. One of the commanders quietened the men explaining that this was our softening-up process. As in most of the reprisal raids, there was a full moon.

As the force approached the target area, the Egyptians opened up inefficient fire with machine-guns and anti-tank weapons and filled the night air with tracers. Mussa's recruits came to his second-in-command, Biro, full of fear, saying, 'Sir! look the Egyptians are firing big red bullets.' Biro calmed them down. It was obvious that the Israeli force had not been discovered and that all the shooting was just a sign of nervousness, but it enabled the paratroopers to locate the exact positions of the Egyptians.

The column moved on and at 9.45 p.m. reached the forming-up area some 800 yards from strongpoint Lili. Arik tried to contact the Artillery in order to ensure their support, but failed to get through. Only after some time was contact re-established and five minutes later the force moved to the attack. At 9.55, without stopping his men, Arik gave the order to concentrate the artillery fire on the enemy positions so that at ten exactly the shelling began. With the beginning of the shelling the various commanders received their order to advance and assault. Owing to faulty communications between the Forward Artillery Observer and the batteries, shelling was continued for ten minutes more than was needed while Raful's men waited a hundred and fifty yards from their target and Z'vika's men some three hundred from theirs.

Avraham Ben-Yehuda who was in Raful's force takes up the story. 'We spread out in preparation for the assault and began to advance. 120 millimetre shells and 25-pounders continued to fly over our heads and to fall and explode noisily within a short distance of us. We were not a little confused. At this stage, Davidi, Arik's Number 2, appeared among us, walking upright between the shells. Without raising his voice he ordered the leading men in the assault line to take cover and to wait out the softening-up. Davidi's calm behaviour and the way in which he took control of the situation at a critical moment left a deep and unforgettable impression.'

Raful's force, fully extended, advanced upon the command-post and the mortar positions. The final assault was launched from about a hundred and fifty yards. As the last shells exploded, his men were some fifty yards from the target area's barbed wire fence which they reached through the smoke and dust raised by the shelling. As they went through the smoke they found themselves face to face with an Egyptian unit advancing upon them. The latter, on seeing our men, turned face and fled. This was the moment when most of the enemy's losses were inflicted.

The force continued to advance quickly and in a disorderly fashion. The problem now arose of how to control this human flood which had left behind it areas not completely cleared of enemy soldiers.

Machine-gun fire opened up on the force and its advance slowed down. The source of the firing was at the mouth of a cave serving as an ammunition dump. The bazooka-man silenced the machine-gun and in so doing set fire to the camouflage nets covering the mouth of the cave. The fire spread and caused stacks of ammunition to explode. A chain of loud explosions shook the air for some two hours.

The force combed the positions and during this operation some of the men were wounded. Meanwhile, information was received that enemy tanks had broken into the strongpoint. Davidi sent part of the force to prepare for the defence of Kusseima.

Mussa's force attacked the northern extension of strongpoint Lili. During the first assault the recruits met no resistance and continued to advance. This time they met with determined opposi-

tion and hand-to-hand fighting broke out. Biro gave orders to fire
a bazooka at one of the dug-outs. The foresight of the bazooka had
been damaged and the inexperienced bazooka-man asked if he
should fire from above the waist, knowing that the flash-back
would almost certainly burn his face. Biro hesitated a moment
and he said quietly, 'There's no choice!' The bazooka-man
fired and was badly burned in the face. A new immigrant from
the Argentine fired at a position at short range and wiped it out,
advanced upon another position and was killed.

The recruits were brave, but their shooting at night was not
efficient.

The second target was wiped out and the force swept on to
the next position which was taken in a short time. At the end
of this fighting the company took up a defensive position and
collected their wounded. 'Katza' had a bad stomach wound. Biro
organized the lowering of the wounded to the foot of the hill
on which the strongpoint stood in order to enable them to be
sent back to hospital in Israel. Katza was laid on a stretcher and
the bearers were on their way. Suddenly the men carrying the
wounded were ambushed and fired upon. The stretchers were
set down and the men turned to rush at the Egyptians and wiped
them out. They then returned to the stretchers and continued
on their way.

The Nahal Commanders' Company had a high level of physical
fitness but, unlike the paratroopers, had no previous battle
experience. This explains why it was given the task of capturing
strongpoint Tova which had been considered an easy target.
Zvika's force divided into three sub-forces: Sub-force A was
entrusted with the capture of the southern end of the position,
sub-force B with the northern end, while sub-force C was to wipe
out the perimeter posts.

During the advance towards the battle area the force was at
the tail end of the column. After a two-hour march the Nahal
company arrived at a position one and a half kilometres from
their target. They continued to advance in two files with a five-
man detail leading, spread out in rank. On reaching a point some
seven hundred yards from the enemy positions they spread out
in battle formation and waited for the artillery fire, which began
at ten o'clock. The force continued to advance and Zvika asked
for additional support—'To be on the safe side'. When Sub-force
A was some sixty yards from where the shells were exploding

they attacked and swept through the target area without opposition. The Egyptian soldiers did open fire from tents and trenches but this resistance was unorganized and easily overcome.

Sub-force B, advancing towards the centre of the enemy position, encountered a series of medium machine-gun posts and overcame them one by one in hand-to-hand fighting. During the fighting the troops used mainly hand grenades and sub-machine guns. There were a number of wounded but the fighting soon ceased.

Sub-force C lost its way to the target and ended up at the northern end of the stronghold, opposite an enemy force surrounding medium machine-gun positions. The men attacked. Firing broke out from the left but the soldiers answered fire and continued to advance. Suddenly, five steps in front of the advancing rank, a low dug-out appeared. The commander of the force jumped upon the Egyptian soldier in the trench, driving the butt of his rifle into the enemy's face and falling with him into the trench, but jumped up immediately and ran on. From behind, one of the men shouted out an order to straighten the advancing line, another shouted 'Grenade' and threw one into another dug-out. The detachment halted and took cover. The commander and his No. 2 did not hear the call and continued to advance. The grenade exploded and hit them. The section went on lying down and awaited the order to advance. Time passed and the order didn't come. One of the men shouted, 'Is there an officer here?' No answer was forthcoming; a soldier cried, 'Get up fellows— forward!' The men jumped up and in doing so another man was hit. In that part of the stronghold which had not been cleaned up the men continued fighting without an officer. In random groupings they fought in hand-to-hand combat and wiped out the last signs of opposition in the remaining three trenches. In less than ten minutes all fighting had stopped. There were some casualties. In accordance with orders the force organized for defence against tank attack. But it was soon transferred to the Big Sabha where it began to re-organize.

The Reconnaissance Unit left the column of advance soon after leaving the assembly area. Shimshon Kochav writes: 'We crossed the Sabha valley with speed, bending down low. When we reached the foot of the rise we began to crawl. As usual the crawling was horrible. The artillery firing stopped. We reached Jebel Sabha from the south and began to comb the area. Not far away we saw some Egyptians fleeing for their lives. We reached the enemy positions and overcame all resistance. We got orders to go down into the valley. The scene there was awful; our guns had done a good job and had been accurate in their shelling. There were dead bodies all over. The Egyptians were stunned, bewildered. In one of the tents we found a wounded Egyptian officer who begged for his life. We gave him some sweetened milk and a pill for his headache and called a doctor. In our advance we came across a Beza machine-gun position. They opened heavy fire on us which made us all dive for the ground. Even before I reached cover I felt as if I was flying, my leg began to burn. On my left I saw that Yankele Golan was in a bad way. I believe that generally I like the human race, but at that moment I felt a strong sense of hate for all the world, of people, of war and above all of that Arab who had had the audacity to wound me. How did he dare? I tried to get up, but couldn't. I emptied two magazines at the Arab but, it seemed, without success. Suddenly firing stopped. The Egyptian shouted that he had run out of ammunition. Out of the dark Meir's voice shouted, "What's going on?" Someone answered, "They wounded two of our chaps." Meir shouted, "Finish him." There was a shot. I felt a lot easier.

'After the fighting, I was taken to the first-aid station. All night I heard noises. Our chaps returned home. The lightly wounded had to stay on in enemy territory and wait till dawn. At five in the morning we were put on trucks and transferred to hospitals on the other side of the border. People at home had got to hear about the raid and many of them stood at the roadside to greet us. We received a hero's welcome and the pains passed. We reached the hospital and peace of mind reached us! Yankele Golan lay next to me in the hospital—unconscious. When he woke up he asked for my forgiveness, "Shimshon, I'm sorry they treated me before you!" '

After Meir had completed his mission with comparative ease it became clear that the Golani units were having difficulties with theirs. Meir immediately rounded up those of his men still fighting-fit and prepared to move off. Arik also asked for permission to send reinforcements but permission was not granted, because 'they also have to do something!' Meanwhile, though a little late in the day, Golani finished their task.

As the column passed over the Azuz Saddle, the Blocking Force, under Tibi's command, broke away and moved separately to their appointed place, some six kilometres from Sabha and three kilometres from Kusseima.

One of the men belonging to this force tells his story: 'It was ten o'clock at night. To the north we could hear explosions and sporadic firing and the night sky was illuminated by tracers. The two platoons making up the Blocking Force took up positions along the road. We set up road-blocks in order to trap any Egyptian forces coming to aid their fellows. We lay down and waited. The Egyptians, it seems, sensed the fact that the force had reached the road and approached very cautiously.

'An hour before midnight the men at the first road-block saw a column of tanks approaching slowly. There were six bulky, black figures, without lights, with their tracks creaking, advancing one behind the other like a convoy of elephants groping in the dark. Four of them passed us by. We kept quiet, feeling both depression and curiosity, inspecting the black masses rolling along the road. As the fourth tank passed over the mines of the road-block Tibi blew it up. The tank stopped. The mines in the first road-block were immediately set off and the leading tank also stopped. It was as if the four tanks were in the jaws of a vice. A bazooka finished off the first tank and the fourth was also put out of action. The other two tanks began to turn about. The second tank approached the first, seemingly wishing to save it. We fired an anti-tank grenade and the Egyptians opened up with machine-guns, both in the direction of our road-block and in the direction of the second road-block. That left Tank No. 3. We called it the 'Crazy Tank'.

'The tank turned and made its way between our platoons, its crew firing at us with machine-guns. The bazooka crew began to chase it. It got away and began to open up at our other platoon. They fled. The machine-gunner of the tank exposed himself in the turret, firing from the waist at the other platoon. I saw him. It seemed like a film in which a man from Mars was firing with all sorts of machines at fleeing hordes. The tank commander exposed himself in the turret and shouted something. He was killed by our machine-gun fire. The tank rolled on without its commander. Our nerves were on edge. We were scared. The whole scene was queer. Now we fled in face of the solid steel machine firing at us and then it fled from us with us chasing and firing at it. During the chase Lerman (now Zvi Shmilowitz, a taxi driver) was wounded and we had to carry him with us.

'Our anti-tank grenadiers and bazooka-men missed the target a number of times. Ammunition ran out. We retreated. The tank continued its chase and we dug in. Suddenly it disappeared from view, this time for good. From afar, from the desert, for some time we still heard the rattle of its tracks.

'We got orders to return. The action had ended. The jeep unit evacuated our wounded. At three in the morning we began to return after five strange hours of fighting and confused running around.'

Levi's jeeps and medium machine-guns took over from Tibi and held the road-block until they too were recalled.

Statistical Summary. Our losses in the Sabha raid were six killed and thirty-seven wounded. The Egyptians had seventy killed and many wounded. Forty-eight were taken prisoner. The spoil was heavy. Two 30-millimetre anti-aircraft guns, one 57mm anti-tank gun, four 120mm mortars, six 52mm mortars, three 52mm mortars, four 60mm mortars, twelve Browning machine-guns, eighty-three Browning automatic rifles, fifteen sub-machine guns, two 87mm bazookas, two hundred and twenty 120mm shells, one hundred and seventy 60mm shells, forty 30mm shells, three trucks, two jeeps, fifteen light-trucks, two half-tracks, four Bren-gun carriers and a large amount of small-arms ammunition.

At the opening of the library in memory of Assaf Simchoni, the Senior Army Education Officer, Aluf-Mishne (Colonel) Mordechai Bar-On said: 'The battle of the Sabha was a short and clear military victory. But, to the surprise of many, when dawn came the Israel military victory was turned into an Egyptian propaganda success. The Egyptians staged a solemn counter attack on a massive scale to recapture the empty positions. At the end of the futile 'attack' the world was told of two hundred Israeli dead. Foreign newspapermen and military attaches were flown over the battle-field and the Egyptian dead, still scattered over the terrain after the night of battle, were presented as the bodies of the Israeli dead.'

The following are two extracts from the book about the Sinai Campaign of 1956, written by Moshe Dayan, then Chief-of-Staff of the Israel Defence Army and at present Minister of Defence in the Israel Government. The victorious campaign ('Operation Kadesh') was commanded by the then C.O. Southern Front, Major-General Assaf Simchoni, who died in an air-crash immediately after it. The first extract, dated 8th October, 1956, describes the Orders Group in which the aims and objectives of the forthcoming campaign were set out. The second, dated 26th October, 1956, describes the modifications of the original plan made during the eighteen-day period between the two dates. They are important documents because they were written by the top man in the army at the time, and show the strategic approach and the major factors that determined high-level policy decisions on a vital problem.

From 'Diary of the Sinai Campaign 1956'[1]

Moshe Dayan

8th October, 1956

This morning I held an Orders Group on the Sinai Campaign. Its code name is to be 'Operation Kadesh', and the first planning order is marked 'Kadesh'-1. (Kadesh was the biblical site where the Israelites sojourned long—probably organizing themselves before taking on their enemies—during their wanderings through the wilderness *en route* to the 'Promised Land'.) After reading the order, I answered questions and explained some of the points which required elaboration. I ended by underlining the following principles which will serve as directives in this campaign:

Our task is to bring about as quickly as possible the collapse of the enemy forces and to achieve complete control of the Sinai Peninsula. We should try and capture what we can of the enemy's weapons and equipment, but we have no interest in killing a

[1] Source: *Diary of the Sinai Campaign* 1956, by Moshe Dayan, Weidenfeld & Nicolson (1966), Sphere Books ed. 1967, pp. 42–43, 62–65.

maximum number of his troops. Even if Egypt suffered thousands of casualties, she could replace them fairly quickly. Manpower for the forces is not a problem either to Nasser or to the other Arab rulers, and any advantage we can gain over the Arab armies will not be secured through numerical superiority.

Our units must stick to 'maintenance of aim', and continue to advance until their objective is gained. They must therefore be self-contained, carrying with them all they will need to reach their final target, and not be dependent on outside supplies. Once the roads are clear, they must press forward and not stop to clean up isolated enemy positions. There is no need to fear that Egyptian units who are by-passed will launch a counter-attack or cut our supply lines. We should avoid analogies whereby Egyptian units would be expected to behave as European armies would in similar circumstances.

To make tangible my intention, I set the following order of priorities to our operations:

First, paratroop drops or landings; second, advance through bypassing the enemy positions; third, breakthrough. The point about this 'order of priorities' is that, if at all possible, it is preferable to capture the objectives deep in enemy territory right away, by landings and paratroop drops, than to reach them by frontal and gradual advance after head-on attacks on every Egyptian position starting from the Israeli border and slogging it out all the way to Suez. By the same token, our infantry and armoured forces should advance, wherever they can, by going round the enemy emplacements, leaving them in the rear and pressing on. They should resort to the assault and breakthrough of enemy posts only when there is no way to by-pass them, or, at a later stage in the campaign, when these posts are isolated and cut off from their bases in Egypt.

In accordance with this approach, I stressed that our first task is to capture the enemy heights in the vicinity of the Suez Canal, which is our final most westward objective. This of course can be done only by a paratroop drop. Then we must go for El Arish; after that, Abu Ageila and Sharm e-Sheikh; and only towards the end of the campaign should we deal with Gaza, which is right on the Israel border.

Under this plan, our paratroopers will have to carry out two operations within a very short time: dropping near Suez and capturing their assigned objective; and then, when the infantry column reaches them, reorganizing and making another parachute landing behind the enemy lines on the route to Sharm e-Sheikh, the most distant of our targets geographically and the most important of the campaign. The capture of Sharm e-Sheikh will in fact mark the completion of our control of Sinai.

I also underlined the need to plan the operation of each force in such a way that none is dependent on others, so that if one gets stuck, it will not hold up the advance of the rest.

25th October, 1956

After numerous internal conferences, and contacts and clarifications with people overseas, which started about two months ago, we can sum up the situation today as follows:

1. The Prime Minister and Minister of Defence, David Ben-Gurion, has given approval in principle to the campaign and its aims.

2. Our forces will go into action at dusk on 29th October, 1956, and we must complete the capture of the Sinai Peninsula within seven to ten days.

3. The decision on the campaign and its planning are based on the assumption that British and French forces are about to take action against Egypt.

4. According to information in our possession, the Anglo-French forces proposed to launch their operations on 31st October, 1956. Their aim is to secure control of the Suez Canal Zone, and for this they will need to effect a sea landing or an air drop with, no doubt, suitable air cover.

At 13.45 I met with the senior officers of Operation Branch. For this meeting I prepared directives for the operational order which replaces those in the previous order 'Kadesh'–1 of 5th October, 1956. Apart from the time-table, which lays down the day and hour of the start of the action, today's order contains several changes from the previous order. The first occurs in the paragraph on aims. Stress is now placed on the creation of a threat to the Suez Canal, and only after that come the basic purposes of the campaign—capture of the Straits of Tiran (Sharm e-Sheikh and the islands of Tiran and Sanapir) and defeat of the Egyptian forces.

I

On this question of the defeat of Egypt's forces I have had several talks with Ben-Gurion. It is clear that we have no interest in 'destroying the enemy's forces', the customary directive in the framing of war aims, and it is better that as little blood as possible should be shed. I therefore used the formula 'to confound the organization of the Egyptian forces and bring about their collapse'. In other words, we should seize the crossroads and key military positions which will give us control of the area and force their surrender.

The second change in the operational order affects the phases of our action, and the third concerns the employment of the Air Force.

I hope these are the final changes. Only four days remain to the opening of the campaign.

At the beginning of the meeting I transmitted what I could of the political conditions within the framework of which we would be conducting our campaign. From the operational point of view we had to distinguish between the period up to the start of the Anglo-French action and the period after. It may be assumed that with the launching of their attack, the Egyptian Air Force will cease its activity against us. Egyptian Army units in Sinai will almost certainly be ordered to withdraw into Egypt, and those remaining in their positions will find their morale lowered. Therefore what it may be possible to do after the Anglo-French assault we need not try to do before.

I stressed that the Minister of Defence is worried about the heavy casualties we may suffer in the opening phase of the campaign, before the Anglo-French action, which, we hope, will indeed take place. He believes that as soon as we start our offensive, the Egyptian Air Force will attack Tel-Aviv and Haifa with their Ilyushin bombers and cause considerable destruction to our civilian population. I do not share this apprehension. Of course we may not be able to 'pass between the raindrops' and emerge completely dry, but I think we can manage to avoid getting too wet. I believe that in the early phases we can give our operation the character of a reprisal action, and even though we shall have quite a strong force close to the Suez Canal, the Egyptians are not likely to recognize it as the opening of a comprehensive campaign, and will not rush to bomb civilian targets in Israel.

I explained that it was in conformity with this intention that I had introduced changes in our original plan. Our first action will therefore not now be the capture of objectives on the northern axis, but the landing of a paratroop battalion at the Mitla Pass (Jebel Heitan). The earlier plan called for the opening of the campaign with the seizure of objectives which dominate the main route between Israel and Egypt. This route extends across the northern edge of Sinai, running along the Mediterranean coast, and is served by railroad, an asphalt highway, an airfield, and sources of sweet water. The surrounding area of course holds concentrations of the principal Egyptian forces assigned to the Israeli front.

The Mitla Pass, on the other hand, is close to the southern end of the Suez Canal, and its geographic link with Israel is an unpaved desert track which bisects the Sinai wilderness. This track is defended by small units of the Egyptian Army, and the pass itself is quite uninhabited. I hope therefore that the Egyptian military staff will interpret our paratroop drop at Mitla as just a raid. I do not believe the possibility will occur to them that a campaign to conquer Sinai can start in any way other than an attempt to secure control of the two northern axes, those of El Arish and Bir Gafgafa. Moreover, I assume that even next day, when the forces of our mobile brigade capture Thamad and Nakhl, points of defence on the Mitla axis, the Egyptian High Command will think we are doing so to rush reinforcements to our unit cut off at Mitla, and that our intention is to enable it to withdraw and return to Israel.

The second change I made, concerning the employment of the Air Force, is that it will not open the campaign with the bombing of Egyptian airfields but will confine itself in the first two days to providing air support to our ground forces and protection to Israel's skies. This change is also designed to strengthen the impression at Egyptian GHQ that we are engaged in a limited reprisal action and not a full-scale war.

There is naturally some risk in basing ourselves on my assumptions, and if they should prove wrong and the Egyptian Air Force reacts to our seizure of Mitla by bombing Israel's cities, we shall pay dearly for having passed up the opportunity of surprise and failing to knock out the Egyptian planes while they are still on the ground.

But I think this can happen only if the Egyptians secure intelligence of our plans. In the normal course of developments, I doubt that the Egyptian General Staff, on the first night of our

I*

action, will have any precise idea of what has happened. True, they will receive information from the units under attack on the Israel border; but these units report the presence of Israeli battalions and brigades even when they are faced only by sections and platoons, and Egyptian GHQ is already used to false alarms. Only next morning when the alarms will be found to have been valid will the Egyptian High Command consider how to react. They will certainly not hesitate to throw all their forces into action against the Israel units which penetrated into Egyptian territory; but I do not believe they will hasten to send their planes to bomb Tel-Aviv.

It is almost certain that on the first day of the fighting, the battles will be confined to the Nakhl–Mitla axis, the location of our units who will have broken into Sinai. A day later, at dawn, it is expected that the British and French forces will launch their campaign. If this really happens, we shall then be able to develop our operations in two directions—continue our advance to the south, to Sharm e-Sheikh, and open an attack on the north, on Rafah and El Arish. If, however, things go wrong and for some reason or other we have to halt the campaign, we shall evacuate our unit at Mitla through the Nakhl-Thamad axis, which will then be under our control, and claim that this was only a reprisal action and with its completion, our forces were returned to Israel.

The following essay is from my book *Massach shel Chol* ('Curtain of Sand'). Proceeding on the assumption that in Israel's army, as in every other, the community of commanders is the backbone of the entire army, I have attempted to define and describe the type of commander that Israel needs. Experience before and since the essay was written has proved that Israel's army, based on Haganah legacy, enjoys a remarkably high proportion of first-class commanders, junior and senior, who, I hope, approximate to the picture I have endeavoured to sketch.

Profile of a Commander[1]

Yigal Allon

The commander is the backbone of the military unit. The command personnel constitute the skeleton which holds the separate limbs of an army together and supports them as a single, closely-knit military organization. The capability, devotion and courage of the combatants—in other words the practical ability of the army—are related directly to the ability of their commanders, of each of their commanders individually within the limits of his particular responsibilities, of all their commanders together in so far as they are collectively responsible for the army as a whole and all its undertakings.

Whatever rank he may hold, and whether or not he be assisted by others in his various duties, the man in command is personally and entirely responsible for the unit or operation under his charge. He may, indeed must, delegate authority to his subordinates to enable them to do their work more efficiently and responsibly; but from the very nature of his position he and he alone bears the ultimate responsibility for everything that takes place within the bounds of the legitimate authority conferred upon him.

[1] Source: *Massach shel Chol* ('Curtain of Sand'), first ed. 1960, pp. 300–319.

Among his subordinates the commander is the representative of a democratic, political authority which has been delegated in accordance with the law; at the same time he is the representative of his men and their spokesman on all practical and operational problems. Where soldiers are entrusted with a mission it is not sufficient to hand down orders and directives; it must be possible to communicate their moods, opinions and needs while strictly preserving all forms of discipline.

The lives of men, and under certain circumstances the outcome of a battle or campaign, are to a decisive degree dependent upon the calculations and decisions of the commander. Even the gravest errors made in civilian life, though they may cause damage and loss, are generally rectifiable. But a large-scale military defeat can never be redressed. Israel, in her unique situation, may under no circumstances lose in war, neither in great battles nor in minor actions. Thus Israel's command personnel—whose task it is to prevent defeat and achieve victory in war—are entrusted with a responsibility the gravity of which has no parallel in any administrative authority in the country's civilian life.

Sun Tzu, the ancient Chinese military theoretician, says in his treatise *The Art of War*: 'The commander stands for the virtues of wisdom, sincerity, benevolence, courage and strictness.'[2] If this indeed be the supreme responsibility of the commander it follows that he must be drawn from among the finest human material available. In choosing a candidate for a post of command there is one criterion: his personality. For the man who possesses a complete, harmonious and gifted personality, lends himself to instruction, guidance and education: his character may be moulded into that of a leader in battle.

There are certain attributes a commander must possess: an able mind and depth of understanding, powers of discrimination and deduction, a wide range of intellectual interests, organizational ability, aggressiveness and flexibility, a natural tendency to leadership, and the ability to grasp a situation, weigh the pros and cons and come swiftly to a decision. A commander's work is varied and complex. He must not be content to accept orders from his superiors: he must think for himself, whether it be on tactical questions, on administrative matters, on social problems or on questions of psychology and education. The right

[2] From the translation by Lionel Giles included in *Roots of Strategy*, edited by Major Thomas R. Phillips, The Bodley Head, London, 1943.

man for the job of command will arrange his unit's affairs well and will fulfil his duties sensibly and successfully.

Courage in the commander is a prior condition for courage in his men and for their ability to carry out orders promptly and well. It takes courage and daring to overcome the fears of battle and the trials of armed combat. The commander must also have the courage of his convictions, defying when necessary entrenched, conventional ideas. He must dare to make his views heard in front of his superiors and among his colleagues when permitted to do so, notwithstanding the contrary opinions of those he is addressing. It is incumbent upon him to take risks by seizing the initiative and adopting bold tactics when these are necessary in order to achieve the objective. He must know when the situation calls for withdrawal or avoidance of the enemy and must be prepared to adopt such tactics without hesitation. Victory is rarely achieved without grave risk. And even in defensive actions, it is the commander's coolness and resolution which inspire the men under him to remain level-headed and stand their ground.

'Here my strength is scant, there it's a bit grim,' Pampilov said, pointing to the map. 'I have my staff at this point. Now here the staff should be moved along a little but then the brigade staffs would automatically and immediately move. The battalion commander would also move and find himself a more convenient location. Everything would be as it should, everything according to regulations. Yet . . . yet in the dug-outs there would be a whisper: "the staffs are withdrawing". And so the men would lose their calm, they would become unsettled.'[3] Every commander who has experience of battle must surely find in these simple, direct words a basic truth and must be reminded by them of situations he has himself been in at one time or another.

Generally speaking, there is no more sincere or inspiring form of courage than that which shuns display and seeks the modest, unostentatious way. Under certain conditions, however, the most modest of commanders will be compelled to make a show of courage either by paying an unexpected visit under fire to the front line or by taking the lead when advancing upon the enemy's positions. Yet one point must constantly be borne in mind: courage comes of cool thought and knowledge, never of hot-headedness or lack of knowledge. The kind of courage needed by

[3] *Pampilov's Men* by A. Bek, 2nd edition, p. 294; published by HaKibbutz HaMeuhad, Tel-Aviv 1954.

a commander is serious and purposeful, not rash and adventurous.

Knowledge and breadth of outlook and interest are precious qualities in any man. The military commander endowed with them will carry out his duties and shoulder his responsibilities all the more competently. In modern warfare innumerable factors are brought into play: scientific and technical, social and political, strategic and tactical, educational and psychological, administrative and organizational, cultural and even artistic. For all this, however, formal educational qualifications should on no account be the condition for appointment to positions of command. Personality must at all times take precedence over academic knowledge. The latter is no guarantee of command ability, whereas the man who is gifted, has a strong personality, is endowed with natural wisdom, common sense and qualities of leadership will probably turn out to be a first-rate commander—whether or not he has had a good general education. Appointment on the strength of certificates of education will automatically exclude from the ranks of command most of Israel's youth who, coming from the economically lower strata of the population, have been unable to complete their secondary school education. Not only would such a condition restrict the area of choice and so cause considerable damage to the army; it would also create a new social problem since formal selection of this kind would almost certainly lead to a strictly limited élite providing the sole source of officers. On the other hand, of course, lack of general education is not to be commended in potential officers. The solution to the problem would seem to lie in choosing officers in the first instance according to their general qualities and then providing them with the facilities to expand their general or technical knowledge— should this be necessary—during the course of their service.

Military skills and military science are in no way narrow fields: they embrace the widest and most diverse spheres of learning and technical know-how. Pure, specialized military study, therefore, is not sufficient in a well-trained modern army. Military service is a purely social function whether or not it reaches the stage of war. It follows, then, that in addition to strictly military subjects both junior and senior command personnel need to be given at least a broad introduction to the social sciences, literature and art, to general and Jewish history, and to geography (especially of the Middle East and Israel); the study of at least one European language and Arabic should be compulsory. The importance of a basic knowledge of education and psychology for commanders has already been pointed out.

Though straightforward instruction by means of lessons and lectures cannot be dispensed with, the most desirable and most suitable method of increasing the general and academic knowledge of the command personnel—in view of their age and the conditions of their service—is by stimulating their desire to learn and by encouraging them to form such habits as reading, writing essays and participation in study circles. Officers, particularly those in positions of command, must at all times be urged to expand the scope of their knowledge; nothing has a more damaging effect on the quality of an army than a hard core of commanders whose minds are narrow and inflexible. Educated, enlightened commanders will produce soldiers equally enlightened and thirsty for knowledge, soldiers who will understand why they were recruited and for what they must fight.

A commander worthy of the name must be loyal to certain moral principles to a degree above the average accepted by society and at the risk of being suspected of 'puritanical' tendencies. This means that the commander must regard his title, status, rank and insignia not as pleasing outer adornments and the means to acquiring special privileges but as accessories necessary for the execution of his duties. It is the practical purpose of command which counts, not the 'social standing' it can confer on those vested with it. 'Command is not an honour; it is hard work, responsibility and duty.'[4] This statement, made before the State came into existence, retains its force today; changing circumstances have only affected ideas on the place and function of the officer in Israeli society.

The good commander is a man of sincerity and truth in his relations with his men and his fellow officers. This would seem to be obvious, yet it must be stressed since the cases in which officers forget this elementary precept are by no means rare. Mutual trust—the basis of comradeship among the soldiers of any army—demands complete honesty. A commander who is not honest with his men cannot expect to win their trust. Instead of telling him the truth, especially when to do so would be unpleasant, they will concoct stories—with possibly disastrous consequences. The same goes for the commander's relations with his

[4] Yisrael Galili, military head of the Haganah, addressing a gathering of Palmach commanders: Sefer HaPalmach, Vol. I, p. 297.

superiors. By concealing his failures behind false arguments and excuses, he may affect the course of events to the detriment of his own side, though this may be far from his intention. The commander bears the responsibility both for his successes and his failures. As Karl von Clausewitz[5] so aptly put it: 'There are two kinds of courage: the courage to face danger and the courage to face up to responsibility.' The commander who has the courage to revoke a misplaced or mistaken order will win the respect of his subordinates and the sympathy of his superiors. The more obdurate commander who for the sake of prestige tries to cover up his errors will forfeit the confidence of those above and below him.

The worst of commanders—however able he may otherwise be—is the man of intrigue, the trouble-maker, whose true intentions are always a mystery to his fellows: this is a dangerous phenomenon even in the relations between a leader and his section; and the higher the rank the graver the consequences. Vicious gossip among senior officers about one another, the exploitation of subordinates or personal discrimination against them, and the formation of 'cliques' among officers in order to further their own interests or damage those of another—these and similar manifestations are as poison in the army's blood stream. Sooner or later they must have their effect on the moral standards of the higher command personnel and therefore, inevitably, on all other ranks down to the lowest.

Together, the officers of an army have control of enormous quantities of the nation's material wealth: vehicles, spare parts, fuel, arms, ammunition, clothing and a host of other items of merchandise. Many officers and NCO's are employed in administration and storekeeping and are faced daily by a thousand temptations. It is therefore necessary to create and maintain a high moral level (in addition, of course, to the usual instruments of control and supervision) in order to help those open to temptation to avoid its pitfalls. But the problem is not wholly solved by preventing theft and pilfering from army and civilian stores for which the military authorities are responsible. The same principles must be applied to the booty of war as to the state's property:

[5] Prussian general and celebrated writer on the theory and tactics of warfare (1780–1831).

theft is a crime no matter where or from whom. It is often from small beginnings that the rot sets in: a soldier 'lifts' a few oranges from an orchard and gets away with it; an officer, held in the highest esteem, takes a revolver as booty from the enemy, carries off a few 'finds' from an historic site, or in supposedly innocent mischief sends his wife a souvenir 'from a house in occupied territory' or 'found on an infiltrator'. In this way the dam of army morals is burst asunder and the officer is powerless to prevent the spread of corruption to which he has himself succumbed. No distinction can be drawn here between the penny and the pound; petty or large-scale, crime can be called by no other name. No commander can demand discipline and honesty from his men if he himself does not serve as an example. And plainly the higher the rank the graver the crime—and the more rigorous the punishment must be.

The commander at every level of command is expected to show extreme restraint in his personal conduct, avoiding any tendency to loose-living or promiscuity. For otherwise he will find himself the centre of gossip, jealousy and intrigue. Loose behaviour on the part of junior officers—the more so on the part of senior officers—towards the young women who have been put in their charge is not only a violation of the moral code but also an infringe-ment of discipline and duty. The exploitation of rank in order to take advantage of innocent young women is a disgraceful act which disqualifies its perpetrator from any position of command or instruction. This does not imply intervention in the individual's personal affairs. Positions of responsibility in the army carry with them numerous obligations. And the military unit is no private domain in which the individual may do as he pleases.

The limits which must of necessity be set to the behaviour of junior officers will apply all the more rigorously to their seniors. For the senior officer is answerable among other things for the moral standards of those in his charge. The junior officer is expected to show self-restraint, at least within the confines of his base or camp and among the men of his unit. Yet more is expected of the senior officer, whose habits and activities are often common knowledge among all his subordinates. A commander who can no longer exert the necessary degree of self-control, who is no longer able to overcome his weaknesses and desires, cannot remain in his position of authority and responsibility. He must leave his post—and the sooner the better, lest in the end he be forced to do so by

I**

the pressure of public opinion or as the result of hints dropped to him by his superiors.

The commander must serve as an example of modesty and reserve, qualities commendable in every man, the more so in a soldier. Exaggerated publicity and display may easily cause him to lose his sense of proportion; they upset the balance of his thought, adversely affecting his ability to appraise a situation and make a decision, and they disrupt the inner harmony of his unit. A distinction is to be drawn between information needed by or helpful to the public and disproportionate self-advertisement.

Official announcements—for public or internal consumption—should be signed by all or none of the officers responsible for their contents. Such a method of publication is not only more accurate and balanced but also averts the internal disagreement and jealousy which occur when the official spokesmen and news services single out one or two personalities for special praise, setting them up on a pedestal and ignoring the vital part played by their comrades-in-arms. The problem becomes all the more acute when senior officers begin to hand out compliments to one another in public and appoint 'press-officers' for themselves.

A responsible commander will never seek publicity at the expense of his colleagues or subordinates. It is a very good thing for senior officers to visit their men in the front line at the height of battle in order to examine the position at first hand and to give the soldiers added confidence. It is altogether undesirable, however, that a senior commander should do this if he is not accompanied by the man in charge of the sector, formation or unit being visited. In the absence of their local commander the men will be given the mistaken impression that 'he is back there at headquarters though the chief himself has the courage to visit us in the front line.' The men are not to know that 'the chief' may permit himself the luxury of a tour of the front line only because the sector commanders are at that moment concentrating their every effort on conducting the actual battle. There is indeed no more distasteful sight than that of a group of high-ranking officers visiting their troops, pursued by a horde of photographers and reporters who will of course record every 'historic moment' for posterity, though the visit has no specific purpose and the local commander has not been invited. Sun Tzu put it succinctly: 'The general who advances without coveting fame and retreats without fearing disgrace, whose only thought is to protect his country and do good service for his sovereign, is the jewel of the kingdom.'[6]

To honour or otherwise enhance the prestige of junior officers or men in secondary positions of command—when this is their due—is to the army's benefit. This rule is not, however, to be applied solely to commanders. The whole unit deserves a word of appreciation or praise no less, sometimes more, than highly-placed or outstanding individuals. Yet since military activity is not an end in itself but rather an imposition which is to be thrown off as soon as conditions permit, the myth of military valour must be played down and a constant attempt made to give a rational account of the army's triumphs. In this way experience may be more realistically instructive and the soldiers educated towards a healthier and more relevant approach to their future in the army, an approach devoid of the complex of superiority, self-importance and thoughtlessness so common in some armies.

There is no contradiction between team-work among commanders and the cultivation and development of talents and ability in the individual. Warfare is necessarily a collective activity. Military success is wholly dependent on co-operation between individuals, units, services and battle-formations, between one commander and another at all levels and at all stages of any operation or campaign. The command personnel of every unit is bound to work as a team, bearing its responsibility to the whole unit collectively and led by its commanding officer. The command staff is answerable to the army as a whole in the same way as the management of any major national undertaking is answerable to the whole community. It is up to the corporal to accustom his men to regard themselves as responsible for the standard and the fate of their section. It is up to the platoon commander to regard his section leaders as a team responsible for the whole platoon; and the same goes for the company, the battalion and the brigade (or parallel units) up to the highest level of the armed forces. The commander must share with his assistants the planning and implementation of an action, while at the same time retaining for himself the authority and the time needed to think, to supervise, to exhort, to encourage and to co-ordinate. In a nutshell: he must command his unit while keeping before him the general picture in its true perspective.

⁶ *Op. cit.* p. 27.

Competition between units under the guidance of their commanders is undoubtedly a desirable thing as long as it is kept within the limits of good taste and responsibility. Two-sided exercises and manoeuvres add realism to the competition, and eagerness 'to win' is most commendable. By fostering teamwork, and making the command personnel a more compact body collectively running the whole army, healthy limits will be set to competition, greater unity of the armed forces will be attained, and co-operation in combat will be made more efficient.

The commander is the father of the unit; that is to say he nurtures the unit as a family of soldiers, small or large, in accordance with his position and the number of men under his command. He sees himself responsible for those men in the same way as a father would regard himself responsible for his family. The commander naturally makes great demands on his men. On occasion he will demand of them the supreme human effort. It is only to be expected, therefore, that he will do more than make demands: he will concern himself with the men's every need and show the same regard for them as for himself. 'Regard your soldiers as your children and they will follow you into the deepest valleys; look on them as your own beloved sons, and they will stand by you even unto death.'[7] The remarkable thing about this sentence is not so much what it says; many would agree with the idea expressed, though not so many practise it. The remarkable thing is that it was written 2,450 years ago. In ancient China Sun Tzu understood the duties of the commander towards his men and the value of morale among soldiers.

Concern for his unit does not imply that the commander must do everything himself. But he must have an organizational ability which ensures that everything is done as it should be done, whether he uses his assistants for this purpose or relies solely on himself, depending on the conditions and the means at his disposal. It is always best for a commander at any level to delegate authority and allocate work to others, leaving himself sufficient time to ponder and think things out. For the commander 'to think is to act.'

Since the ultimate purpose of military training, when all is said and done, is to prepare soldiers to do battle, the commander

[7] Sun Tzu, op. cit. page 27.

must inevitably be responsible for the training process which his men undergo. Concern for their material needs, their accommodation, food, medical treatment and entertainment undoubtedly falls within the bounds of the commander's responsibility. It is not enough for a commander to concern himself solely with the military and technical training of his men and their introduction to disciplinary habits, even though this aspect of their service takes up—and so, logically, it should—most of their time as recruits.

Battle is more than a combination of fire and movement. It is the integration of fire, movement *and* consciousness. The commander, therefore, cannot rest content with guiding the fire and directing the movement; he must guide the soldier's mental reactions to battle. Hence the commander is responsible for the mental preparation of his men no less than for their physical and technical training and their being brought to battle. Paternal concern for the soldier and his welfare does not mean pampering him; far from it. Soldiers wrapped in cotton-wool will fall helpless victims to the terrors of war, being unprepared to meet the most terrible of all dangers. Sincere concern, on the other hand, will win the soldier's confidence and will prepare him to face the most trying experiences.

The Jew has always held human life to be the most precious of possessions; traditionally he has likened the existence of one soul to that of the whole world. In Israel today the most acute shortage is probably that of manpower. For these two reasons—the moral and, as it were, the material—the most serious thought must be given to any activity which, once embarked upon, may endanger human life. Yet from Israel's war experience a double lesson is to be learned: her soldiers must be withheld from unnecessary risk; at the same time they must be risked unhesitatingly if the issue facing the nation is life or death.

The great tragic crisis of practical command occurs at the moment the commander sends his men—his 'family'—into battle. Only the commander whose attitude towards his men is that of a father to his children has the right to send them into action. The men who know that their commander values their lives as his own and will not lightly expose them to mortal danger will comprehendingly and willingly accept any task he may impose upon them, be it the most difficult and hazardous.

Soldiers who know that their commander values them and has

implicit faith in them, that he will spare no effort on their behalf and will evade no risk which they must take, that he has the ability to plan and conduct a battle well and that he at no time takes unfair advantage of his rank, will understand the limitations he imposes upon them and will reconcile themselves to the rigorous discipline he expects of them. They will go into battle knowing that it is unavoidable and that everything possible has been done to ensure its success. They will give of their best in executing their mission.

What is the source of the authority the commander wields over his men, compelling them to discipline in their daily routine and leading them out onto the battlefield? Does his authority spring merely from the official recognition accorded his position? The commander's formal appointment—in itself indispensable of course—will give him effective control only when he first takes up his post. But as soon as he takes over full command, his official position alone will no longer enable him to retain control if he does not succeed in convincing his men that authority in the unit is his and that he is capable of wielding that authority and is deserving of the honour given him. Plainly, he may insist that his orders be carried out. For this purpose he is backed by the law—and the law is necessary. But he will not be able to force his men to honour him, to believe in his ability or to value him as a companion. And if he fails to do these things he and his unit will be doomed to failure. A commander is appointed by the appropriate authorities; but his appointment is given effect only by those who are subordinated to him. This does not mean that the men should be allowed to choose their commanders; it means that the most desirable situation is one in which the men recognize and appreciate their commander as if they themselves had elected him.

The men have a highly developed collective sense. They are almost never mistaken about their commander, and are the people best qualified to judge him. It is possible to mislead them by propaganda and publicity stunts. It is possible to create a cult of admiration for some military figure who rarely comes in contact with them. But it is quite impossible to deceive them as to the character and qualities of their direct commanders with whom they work day by day.

Once he has won their confidence the commander no longer needs to resort to the law and the gruff command. And should he be compelled to mete out punishment this will be accepted by his subordinates as fair and justified. The force of law and the power to punish can never be dispensed with entirely. But it is a sign of the good commander that he is only seldom obliged to apply these powers.

There are no bad units, only bad commanders. The unit for the commander is as clay for the potter. In his hands the recruits are moulded into an army unit worthy of the name. Failure in this task is the fault of the man in command, not of the troops.

Much has been said and written on the problem of the 'distance' which is to be maintained between officers and men. Some advocate one extreme, some the other. The truth would appear to lie midway between the two.

The advocates of aloofness on the part of officers claim that this improves discipline. The commander who holds himself suitably remote from his men will not give them the opportunity to observe his weaknesses, and will gradually become a kind of mysterious figure wielding supreme authority against which there is no appeal. Those who favour a closer relationship between officers and men claim that such an artificial separation conflicts with the principle of social equality which must be upheld if true unity and solidarity are to be achieved by the men in combat.

In point of fact, the fear of exposing a commander in his true colours is exaggerated. If he is indeed a weak personality and lacking in certain essential qualities, it is best that this should be discovered in good time so that he may be removed from his position of responsibility. But if he is a man of more sterling stuff, everything is to be gained from the educational influence of his direct contact with the men in his charge. Some degree of 'distance' is desirable, but there is no need to induce it by artificial means: it comes about quite naturally. Respect—if that be the aim—is not acquired by setting a barrier between the commander and his subordinates; it is created by the commander's behaviour, his personality and his competence. The commander who does not possess these qualities and must go out of his way to affect 'distance' between himself and his men is not worthy of his position.

The commander should, of course, be given accommodation and a place of work away from the hubbub and activity of his unit so that he is able to apply himself to his work, which often calls for concentration and secrecy. One may even agree to separate clubs for officers, where they may meet together, get to know one another and discuss common problems undisturbed. But there can be no justification for separate dining halls, and certainly none for officers having food different from that served to the men.

Apart from those officers serving in the regular army, who must be paid (like any state employee) a salary sufficient to provide for themselves and their families, there should not be great differences in pay between the various ranks of men doing national service. Equality of sacrifice, irrespective of rank, is one of the basic principles upon which a good army is built. The commander must not set himself up as superior to his men. He must be inseparably one of them, leading them naturally, *unus inter pares*.

Besides these universally accepted qualities, the Israeli commander needs 'a talent for making friends'; he also needs 'a measure of discretion, so that his talent for getting along with others will not interfere with the exercise of his other necessary qualities.' Whatever the commander may do, he is exposed to the discerning eye of his unit 'in his work and when relaxing, in his room, in his relations with the opposite sex, and in his relations with society. In every instance his behaviour must be exemplary. He has no extra privileges in return for the extra duties he has taken upon himself: great responsibility and, in battle, greater risk.'[8] Yitzhak Sadeh's words are as forceful today as when he first addressed them to members of the Palmach. They are especially applicable to an army in which the volunteering spirit is still dormant.

Warfare—and all that is involved in the formation, training and organization of armies in preparation for war—is a science. It is a social phenomenon yet, like other fields of social activity, it is a science, based on accurate observation, which may be studied. Some hold that command is an art, not a science. But the numerous subjects, the principles and the laws of which the commander must have a sound knowledge, clearly imply a science

[8] Yitzhak Sadeh, *Sefer HaPalmach* I, pp. 292–3.

rather than an art. It is nevertheless true that certain spiritual or psychological elements, including that of leadership, occupy an important place in the work of command; there is therefore no better commander than the one who, in addition to his technical knowledge, has a sense of command as an art. The art required by the commander is the art of humanity, the art of contact with other men, of the comprehension of human behaviour—including that of the enemy. The most desirable type of commander is the one who combines within his personality both the technical and the spiritual: the synthesis of craftsman and artist.

Though the commander should be encouraged to study, so that he is the better equipped technically and spiritually to perform his duties, it is questionable whether command should be allowed to become a profession for life. The military life is inevitably one-sided and non-constructive. Technological development is dynamic in the extreme; and the constant need for change and development will necessarily prove an obstacle to most commanders if they are allowed to retain their positions beyond a certain age. As they grow older they tend to rely more on past experience; their minds become gradually less receptive to the new ideas and possibilities emanating from technological and sociological developments. The constant introduction of new blood and the continual transference of responsibility from one generation to the next are essential in military service.

There are many officers and commanders—in the armaments and armoured corps, in the air force and the navy, for example—whose services are vital, or whose technical knowledge is indispensable, and who should be encouraged by all means to remain at their posts for longer than the usual span. As a general rule, however, a maximum period of service must be laid down, just as a certain minimum service is demanded of those who are to hold vital positions. This need not be wasteful since all those who are released from the regular army automatically take their place in the reserves, where they are assigned to tasks in keeping with their knowledge and ability.

Along with their military education it is desirable that most command personnel be given the opportunity to study civilian trades or professions; thus when they complete their military service they will be able to take their place smoothly and naturally in the civilian community. Some there must always be who are called upon to remain in military service for many years. They should be allowed to take time off at intervals—either for the purpose of maintaining contact with their civilian field of work or in order to pursue non-military studies. In this way they will not become divorced from the life of the society in which they live, and they will be given the opportunity to broaden their interests and retain a sense of proportion. The aim must be constantly to avert the danger of a 'Prussian'-style officer class, a danger ever-present in all armies.

Command, then, is a complex amalgam of theoretical and practical knowledge and the art of leadership. Of no lesser importance, however, is the practical experience acquired over a long period of time in the daily work of organization and education and the planning and execution of military operations. Here it is to be emphasized that the experience of every officer must include a considerable period in the ranks, and an extended period of training and practice as the leader of a section (corporal or sergeant). Without this experience, the officer will be lacking in one of the most important fields of knowledge which as a commander he should possess. No matter how brilliantly strategy may be conceived and applied, its success depends in the final analysis on the last and lowest of the ranks. The commander must therefore be able to sense every mood, every thought of his men; he must know the limits of their ability, and give due consideration to their limitations. This he clearly cannot do if he himself has never served in the ranks.

Furthermore: the soldier is a compound forged and tempered by every stage of his military training and battle experience. This process is the foundation upon which his whole military personality is built, a foundation essential to every commander at every level up to and including the highest staff officers. Some time ago a system was introduced in China whereby every officer, having served a lengthy period in command, has to return for a time to the ranks—so that he may know, once again, what it is to be a common soldier, and not have to rely solely on his intellectual appreciation of the men's experience and attitudes. In the Palmach such a system was unnecessary because officers and men shared most activities and enjoyed the same standard of life: in camp, at meals, in entertainment, work and play, and in training.

Of all the levels of command the position of the section leader (the corporal or lance-corporal) is probably the most unclear. It is a kind of intermediate, undefined position. He is not accepted among the officers as an equal; it is, on the other hand, 'beneath his dignity' to stay among the men longer than his position officially requires since he is after all 'in command'. In fact, the non-commissioned officer performs an indispensable function. The most brilliant plan devised by the most capable general depends for its tactical execution on the section-leaders. Poor section-leaders may ruin the best-laid plans; first-rate section-leaders will often save badly devised plans. This for one simple reason: the section-leader is the *sole* level of command that maintains constant and direct contact with the men who bear the brunt of the actual fighting.

It follows, then, that the section-leader is to be trained as a tactical commander and as an educator of his men. It is not true that only in an army of partisans—which fights under special conditions and often splits up into small, independent units—is the section-leader to be trained as a tactical commander capable of weighing up situations, making decisions and putting them into effect on his own authority. In a modern army equipped with up-to-date weapons—in the Israeli army in particular—section-leaders are trained to command independently in the field in every instance in which they are required to operate alone with their units. In 'regular combat', moreover, when the section-leader acts within the framework of his platoon and under orders from his superior officer, he still requires a high standard of knowledge and an ability to sum up the situation. Modern fire-power and the development of tactical atomic weapons may compel armies to operate in small, dispersed detachments both in attack and defence, while at the same time maintaining a high standard of co-operation and co-ordination between units and sub-units. All levels of command must therefore be trained to think and act independently whenever circumstances demand that they should, and section-leaders are no exception to this rule. Besides, modern weapons which provide small groups of men with greater fire-power and more flexibility of movement, call for a high standard of command at all levels. The section-leader is therefore to be trained technically as an officer, not as a corporal—as was done in the Palmach.

And once again it must be stressed that an officer who serves for a reasonable period as a corporal will gain experience which no military academy can ever give him. The well-known French saying may well be applied to Israel: 'Every section-leader carries in his knapsack a brigadier's baton.' Whatever respect one may have for military colleges and the general and technical training they give, no military college graduate is fit to bear the title and responsibility of 'officer' before he has served for a period as a section-leader.

In some countries the army, or more correctly the senior officers of the army, constitute a threat to democracy or an obstacle to the establishment of a democratic regime. The Israeli army is undoubtedly one of the most democratic armed forces in the world, both from the standpoint of its internal organization—though this leaves much to be desired—and from that of its loyalty to the state's parliamentary democracy. It is nevertheless no aspersion on it to suggest that even here there lurks the danger of weariness of democracy, and the desire for a more 'efficient', authoritarian system instead of the present 'cumbersome' democratic one.

The officers of the Israeli army are granted an opportunity which no other section of the community is afforded on the same scale or with the same facilities: all the country's youth, of both sexes, are given into their charge for a period of at least two and a half years. The army has at its disposal powerful instruments of influence, including a broadcasting station, a press, and direct contact with large numbers of individuals. The army's command personnel are therefore in a position to educate the younger generation towards a better democracy. And the present generation of youth, it may be added, needs to be imbued with the democratic idea no less than with the pionering ideal.

Every officer has the right to belong to a political party and ought indeed to be encouraged to do so. As a citizen he has full equality of rights with his fellow citizens, and as a soldier fulfilling a national mission he should be particularly alert to political events and developments. But the Israeli officer occupies a position of general national importance, and as such, more than any other public servant, he must serve his country with scrupulous fairness and objectivity comparable in many ways to that demanded of a high-court judge.

It is to be taken for granted that the selection of officers and their assignment to duty will be absolutely free of any form of discrimination. In the appointment of officers there can be but one criterion: ability, suitability and loyalty to the state. Discrimination in the armed forces is more than an infringement of the law and a violation of democracy; it is fraught with danger to the military capability of a small state such as Israel. Hence the aim must be to preserve the army—in which all the nation serves—as a general, supra-party instrument in the service of the whole nation.

It transpires, then, that the Israeli commander is called upon to undertake many duties which are of a public or 'civilian' nature. There is no contradiction between any of these and his military commitments; nevertheless it must be firmly implanted in his mind that he is entrusted with a special security mission, a mission which marks him out as different from all other 'civil servants'. That mission is to prevent war, and this he does by maintaining a well-trained, efficient army. But his supreme test is on the battlefield, and the nation therefore looks to him to display the same courage and personal example as did his predecessors in the past. The Israeli commander detests war but goes forth willingly to battle. He does not send his men against the enemy, he leads them: 'Follow me' has become the expected cry of the Israeli commander in battle.

To sum up: the best commander is a man endowed to a greater or lesser degree with certain qualities which enable him to undertake the numerous duties and responsibilities with which he is entrusted. He has the qualities of a father and a youth leader, an instructor and an educator, a leader of men and a commander in battle. He must prove himself to be a man who thinks and acts, who plans and organizes, who weighs up all sides of an argument and comes to a firm, clear-cut decision. The impression may be gained that the author is asking too much of the average commander, expecting him indeed to be superhuman, capable of the impossible, perfect. This is not so. For though war is very much an inhuman act and nothing short of a superhuman effort is required to combat it successfully, the commander need not be superhuman. Of course no man will possess *all* the qualities desirable in a commander. Each has his own peculiarities, his strengths and weaknesses. But no commander will be worthy of the name who does not possess outstanding positive attributes, just as no man may command who has outstanding weaknesses.

Nature provides enough young men suited to assume tasks of command. One only has to discover them, to train and educate them, and future generations will carry on the great tradition of Hebrew commanders.

This address was delivered by Major-General Yitzhak Rabin, Chief of Staff of the Israel Defence Forces during the Six Day War, at a ceremony on Mount Scopus[1] in Jerusalem on 28th June, 1967, at which the degree of honorary Doctor of Philosophy was conferred on him by the Hebrew University of Jerusalem in recognition of his services to the nation and those of the whole Army in the recent victory.

General Rabin started his military career as a private in the Palmach rising quickly from rank to rank, distinguishing himself as a Palmach battalion commander during the struggle against the British, and later as a brigade commander and as Chief of Operations in the head-quarters of the Palmach. During the War of Independence he was my Chief of Operations in the Southern Command, in the campaigns which ended with the expulsion of the Egyptians from the Negev. He continued to serve in the permanent army, and was appointed Chief of Staff in 1963. After the Six Day War he became Israel's Ambassador in Washington.

Rabin's simple, moving address at Mount Scopus, delivered less than three weeks after the end of the Six Day War, shows among other things the importance that an Israeli general attaches to the moral and spiritual aspects of a war, to the spirit of fellowship and mutual responsibility of an army, and to a humanity which extends to a concern for the sufferings of the enemy.

———◆———

Address at Mount Scopus

Yitzhak Rabin

Mr President, Mr Prime Minister, Mr President of the Hebrew University, Mr Rector of the Hebrew University, Members of the Board of Governors, Ladies and Gentlemen:

I am filled with reverence as I stand here before the teachers of our generation, in this ancient, magnificent place overlooking

[1] Site of the original Hebrew University, opened in 1925 by Lord Balfour and cut off by the Jordanians in 1948. A new university was subsequently built in Western Jerusalem.

our eternal capital and the sacred sites of our nation's earliest history.

You have chosen to do me the great honour of conferring upon me the degree of Doctor of Philosophy, along with a number of distinguished persons who are doubtless worthy of this honour. May I be allowed to speak the thoughts that are in my heart?

I consider myself to be here solely as the representative of the whole Israel Defence Army: of the thousands of officers and tens of thousands of soldiers who brought the victory of the Six Day War to the State of Israel.

It may well be asked why the University should have been moved to bestow the degree of honorary Doctor of Philosophy upon a soldier in recognition of his war services. What have soldiers to do with the academic world, which stands for the life of civilization and culture? What have those who are professionally occupied with violence to do with spiritual values? The answer, I think, is that in this honour which you have conferred through me upon my fellow soldiers you choose to express your appreciation of the special character of the Israel Defence Army, which is itself an expression of the distinctiveness of the Jewish people as a whole.

The world has recognized that the Israel Army is different from most other armies. Though its first task, that of maintaining security, is indeed military, it also assumes numerous tasks directed to the ends of peace. These are not destructive but constructive, and are undertaken with the object of strengthening the nation's cultural and moral resources. Our work in the field of education is well-known: it received national recognition in 1966 when the Army won the Israel Prize for Education. NAHAL, which already combines military duties with work on the land, also provides teachers for border villages, thus contributing to their social development. These are only a few examples of the special services of the Israel Defence Forces in this sphere.

Today, however, the University is conferring on us an honorary degree not for these things but in recognition of the Army's moral and spiritual force as shown, precisely, in active combat. For we are all here in this place only by virtue of the hard-fought war which, though forced upon us, was transformed into a victory that has astounded the world.

War is intrinsically harsh and cruel, and blood and tears are its companions. But the war we have just fought also brought

forth marvellous examples of a rare courage and heroism, and
the most moving expressions of brotherhood, comradeship and
even spiritual greatness. Anyone who has not seen a tank-crew
continue its attack even though its commander has been killed
and its tank almost destroyed, who has not watched sappers
risking their lives to extricate wounded comrades from a mine-
field, who has not witnessed the concern for a pilot who has
fallen in enemy territory and the unremitting efforts made by the
whole Air Force to rescue him, cannot know the meaning of
devotion among comrades.

The nation was exalted and many wept when they heard of
the capture of the Old City. Our *sabra* youth, and certainly our
soldiers, have no taste for sentimentality and shrink from any
public show of emotion. In this instance, however, the strain
of battle and the anxiety which preceded it joined with the sense
of deliverance, the sense of standing at the very heart of Jewish
history, to break the shell of hardness and diffidence, stirring up
springs of feeling and spiritual discovery. The paratroopers who
conquered the Wall leaned on its stones and wept. It was an
act which in its symbolic meaning can have few parallels in the
history of nations. We in the Army are not in the habit of speaking in high-flown language, but the revelation of that hour at the
Temple Mount, a profound truth manifesting itself as if by
lightning, overpowered customary constraints.

There is more to tell. The elation of victory had seized the
whole nation. Yet among the soldiers themselves a curious
phenomenon is to be observed. They cannot rejoice wholeheartedly. Their triumph is marred by grief and shock, and there
are some who cannot rejoice at all. The men in the front lines
saw with their own eyes not only the glory of victory but also
its cost, their comrades fallen beside them soaked in blood. And
I know that the terrible price the enemy paid also deeply moved
many of our men. Is it because neither their teaching nor their
experience has ever habituated the Jewish people to exult in
conquest and victory that they receive them with such mixed
feelings?

The heroism displayed in the Six Day War generally went far
beyond that of the single, daring assault in which a man hurls
himself forward almost without reflection. In many places there
were long and desperate battles: in Rafah, in El-Arish, in Um
Kataf, in Jerusalem, on the Golan Heights. In these places, and

in many others, our soldiers showed a heroism of the spirit and a courage of endurance which inspired feelings of wonder and exaltation in those who witnessed them. We speak a great deal of the few against the many. In this war, perhaps for the first time since the Arab invasions in the spring of 1948 and the battles of Negba and Degania, units of the Israel Defence Forces in every sector stood few against many. Relatively small units entered long, deep networks of fortifications, surrounded by hundreds and thousands of enemy troops, through which they had to cut and cleave their way for many long hours. They pressed on, even when the exhilarating momentum of the first charge had passed, and all that was left to sustain them was their belief in our strength, in the absence of any alternative, and in the end for which the war was being fought, and the compelling need to summon up every resource of spiritual strength to continue to fight to the end. Thus our armoured forces broke through on all fronts, our paratroopers fought their way into Rafah and Jerusalem, our sappers cleared minefields under enemy fire. The units which penetrated the enemy lines after hours of battle struggled on, refusing to stop, while their comrades fell to the right and to the left of them. These units were carried forward, not by arms or the techniques of war, but by the power of moral and spiritual values.

We have always insisted on having the best of our young people for the Israel Defence Forces. When we said *Hatovim L'Tayis* ('The best for the Air Force'), and this became a standard for the whole Army, we were not referring only to technical skills and abilities. What we meant was that if our air force was to be capable of defeating the forces of four enemy countries in a few short hours, it could do so only if it were sustained by moral and human values. Our airmen who struck the enemies' planes with such accuracy that no one understands how it was done and the world seeks to explain it technologically by reference to secret weapons; our armoured troops who stood their ground and overcame the enemy even when their equipment was inferior to his; our soldiers in all the several branches of the Army who withstood our enemies everywhere despite the superiority of their numbers and fortifications: what they all showed was not only coolness and courage in battle but a passionate faith in the justice of their cause, the certain knowledge that only their personal, individual resistance against the greatest of dangers could save their country and their families, and that the alternative to victory was annihilation.

In every sector our commanders of all ranks proved themselves superior to those of the enemy. Their resourcefulness, their intelligence, their readiness, their power of improvisation, their concern for their troops, and above all their practice of leading their men into battle: these are not matters of technique or equipment. There is no intelligible explanation except one—their profound conviction that the war they were fighting was a just one.

All these things have their origin in the spirit and their end in the spirit. Our soldiers prevailed not by the strength of their weapons but by their sense of mission, by their consciousness of the justice of their cause, by a deep love of their country, and by their understanding of the heavy task laid upon them: to ensure the existence of our people in their homeland, and to affirm, even at the cost of their lives, the right of the Jewish people to live its life in its own state, free, independent, and in peace.

The Army which I had the privilege of commanding through this war came from the people and returns to the people: a people which rises above itself in times of crisis, and prevails over all enemies in the hour of trial by its moral and spiritual strength.

As representative of the Israel Defence Army and in the name of each and every one of its soldiers, I accept your appreciation with pride.

The following three maps illustrate graphically three major campaigns on Israel's Southern Front in 1948–49, 1956, and 1967 respectively. The first campaign begins far north, almost in the centre of the country; it liberated the southern coastal plain, the entire Negev (except for the Gaza Strip which was not taken for political reasons), and northern Sinai. The second and third campaigns were spread over the whole Sinai peninsula, based on the liberated Negev.

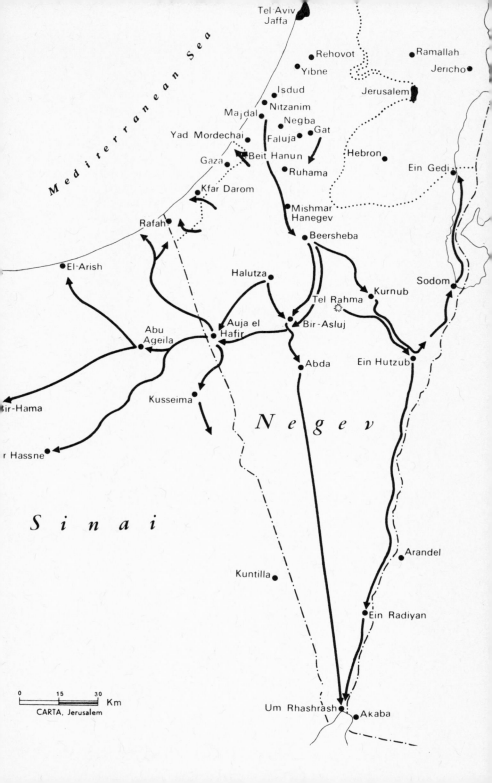

Nablus

Tel Aviv
-Jaffa

Jerusalem

Mediterranean Sea

Hebron

Gaza

Khan Yunis

GAZA STRIP

Port Said   Port Fuad

Rafah

Beersheba

El-Arish

Romani

Bir Lahfan

I S R A E L

Kantara
(west)   (east)

CANAL

Abu Ageila

Um
Kataf

Nizzana

Jebel Libni

DAIKA PASS

Ismailia

Bir Hama

Bir Rod Salim

Kusseima

SUEZ

Bir Gafgafa

Bir Hassne

J O R D A N

GIDDI PASS

Bir Themade

MITLA PASS

Kuntilla

Suez   Port Tewfik

Nakhal

Ras Suder

Et-Tamad

Ras en-Nakeb

Eilat
Akaba

S i n a i

Ein el Furtage

Gulf of Eilat

Abu Zeneima

✕ Um Bugma

Nueiba

S A U D I

Ras Abu Rudeis

Firan

A R A B I A

JEBEL MUSA ▲

St. Catherine's
Monastery

Dahab

*E
G
Y
P
T*

*G
u
l
f
o
f
S
u
e
z*

Et-Tur

Nabek

Ras Nasrani

Sharm-al-
Sheikh

STRAIT OF TIRAN

TIRAN

Gulf of Eilat

Red Sea

0   25   50
Km

CARTA, Jerusalem

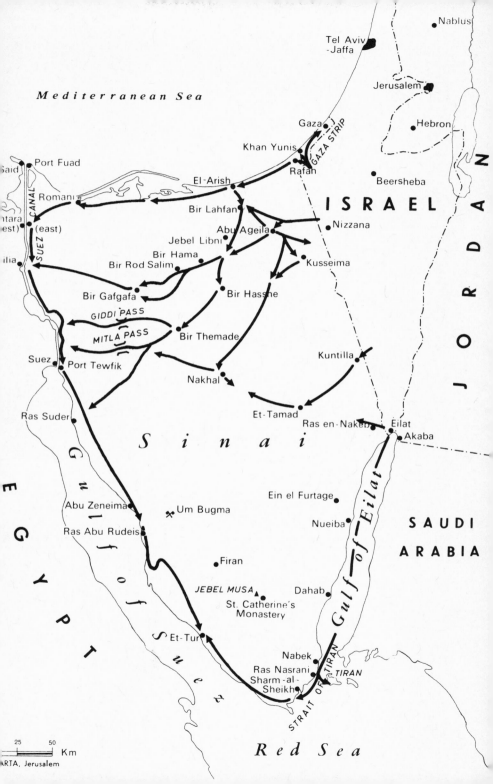

Mediterranean Sea

Nablus

Tel Aviv
-Jaffa

Jerusalem

Hebron

Port Fuad

Port Said

Gaza
GAZA STRIP

Khan Yunis

Rafah

Beersheba

Romani

(east)

(east)

Qantara
(west)

El-Arish

Bir Lahfan

I S R A E L

SUEZ CANAL

Ismailia

Abu Ageila

Nizzana

Jebel Libni

Bir Hama

Bir Rod Salim

Kusseima

Bir Gafgafa

Bir Hassne

GIDDI PASS

MITLA PASS

Bir Themade

Kuntilla

Suez

Port Tewfik

Nakhal

Et-Tamad

Ras en-Nakeb

Eilat

Akaba

Ras Suder

S i n a i

J O R D A N

Ein el Furtage

Gulf of Suez

Abu Zeneima

✕ Um Bugma

Nueiba

S A U D I

Ras Abu Rudeis

Firan

A R A B I A

JEBEL MUSA ▲
St. Catherine's
Monastery

Dahab

Gulf of Eilat

Et-Tur

Nabek

Ras Nasrani
Sharm -al-
Sheikh

TIRAN

STRAIT OF TIRAN

E G Y P T

25   50

Km

ᴀRTA, Jerusalem

Red Sea